For the Sake of the World

For the Sake of the World

The Spirit of Buddhist and Christian Monasticism

Patrick G. Henry
Donald K. Swearer

FORTRESS PRESS
Minneapolis, Minnesota

THE LITURGICAL PRESS
Collegeville, Minnesota

to

The Monks of Wat Suanmokh
Chaiya, Thailand

The Monks of Wat Haripunjaya
Lamphun, Thailand

The Nuns of Saint Benedict's Convent
Saint Joseph, Minnesota

The Monks of Saint John's Abbey
Collegeville, Minnesota

Library of Congress Cataloging-in-Publication Data
Henry, Patrick G. (Patrick Gillespie)
  For the sake of the world.

  Bibliography: p.
  Includes index.
  1. Monasticism and religious orders. 2. Monasticism
and religious orders, Buddhist. I. Swearer, Donald K.,
1934–   . II. Title.
BL630.H46 1988   255   88–45240
ISBN 0-8006-2310-X
ISBN 0-8146-1588-0 (The Liturgical Press)

Printed in the United States of America   1–2310

Contents

Acknowledgments

Grateful acknowledgment is made to the following for the use of copyrighted material:

Basil Blackwell, for quotations from Derwas J. Chitty, *The Desert a City*, 1966.

Beacon Press, for quotations from Thich Nhat Hanh, *The Miracle of Mindfulness: A Manual on Meditation*, 1976.

Bear and Company, for quotations from Matthew Fox, ed., *Hildegard of Bingen's Book of Divine Works with Letters and Songs*, 1987.

The Catholic University of America Press, for quotations from Odo John Zimmerman, O.S.B., *Saint Gregory the Great: Dialogues* (Fathers of the Church 39), 1959.

Commonweal, for quotation from Thomas Merton, "Is the World a Problem?" 84/11 (1966), reprinted in Merton, *Contemplation in a World of Action* (Doubleday Image Books, 1973).

Doubleday, for quotations from Thich Nhat Hanh, *Zen Keys*, 1974.

Excerpts from *Thoughts in Solitude* by Thomas Merton. Copyright © 1956, 1958 by the Abbey of Our Lady of Gethsemani. Reprinted by permission of Farrar, Straus and Giroux, Inc.

Excerpts from *The Sign of Jonas* by Thomas Merton, copyright © 1953 by The Abbey of Our Lady of Gethsemani; renewed 1981 by The Trustees of the Merton Legacy Trust, reprinted by permission of Harcourt Brace Jovanovich, Inc.

Franciscan Herald Press, for quotations from Thomas of Celano, *The First Life of Saint Francis*, trans. Placid Hermann, O.F.M., 1963.

Henry Holt and Company, Inc., for quotation of "The Secret Sits" from Edward Connery Lathem, ed., *The Poetry of Robert Frost*, 1967.

The Liturgical Press, for quotations from Alfred Deutsch, O.S.B., *Bruised Reeds and Other Stories*, copyright © 1971 by The Order of Saint Benedict, Inc. Published by Saint John's University Press. Used with permission.

The Liturgical Press, for quotations from Timothy Fry, O.S.B., ed., *RB1980: The Rule of St. Benedict in Latin and English with Notes*, copyright © 1981 by The Order of Saint Benedict, Inc. Published by The Liturgical Press,

9

Preface

More than forty years ago Arnold J. Toynbee predicted that when historians in the twenty-first century write about our own they will be more interested in the interaction between Buddhism and Christianity than in the conflict between communist and democratic systems. Whether Toynbee's prediction proves true or not, there can be no doubt that in the past three decades many Western Christians have found the history, teaching, and practice of Buddhism to be of compelling interest.

For the Sake of the World: The Spirit of Buddhist and Christian Monasticism explores, through the lens of monasticism, the two religious traditions whose interrelationship Toynbee believed to be of such current and historic moment. Christianity and Buddhism are distinct, to be sure, but they share much in their visions of the deepest meaning of human existence, visions that have inspired the monastic ideals in both traditions. Monasticism is not unique to Buddhism and Christianity, but in these religious traditions the monastic manner of life has been longest and most thoroughly developed. Studying Buddhist and Christian monasticism side-by-side highlights the distinctiveness of each tradition while, simultaneously, yielding deeper insight into what characterizes a religious or spiritual perspective on the world and human life.

Although the book will be of interest to specialists in Buddhism and Christianity and to teachers and students in comparative religion, we intend also to capture the attention of anyone who wants to understand religious perspectives of relevance for our age. It may seem curious to claim that monasticism has something significant and compelling to say to the late twentieth century. We seriously and urgently make that claim.

We approach the subject matter as students and teachers of Buddhism and Christianity with a special interest in their monastic traditions. We have sought to bring to this study both empathy and scholarly responsibility. The chapters were forged in the classroom, at professional conferences, and in interreligious dialogue meetings. We are particularly grateful to our students at Swarthmore College; to Professor David Chappell and other leaders of the East-West Religions Project at the University of Hawaii, where a version of chapter 1 was presented in 1980; to Professors Robert Thurman and David Wills for inviting us to try out our ideas on them and other participants at a conference on Buddhist and Christian monasticism at Amherst College in 1983; and to Nancy C. Swearer, who prepared the Index. Acknowledgment is also made to the National Endowment for the Humanities and to Swarthmore College for support of Patrick Henry's research leave in 1979–80.

It has been our good fortune to meet many persons who have chosen the monastic life. Along with other research, this book draws on our own experience. One of us (Swearer) has spent several extended periods in close association with Thai monks and monasteries, especially those of Haripunjaya in Lamphun, Phan Dong in Chiangmai, and Suanmokh in Chaiya. The other (Henry) currently works at the Institute for Ecumenical and Cultural Research, which was founded by the monks of Saint John's Abbey in Collegeville, Minnesota. He has had close association with those monks for many years, and also with the nuns of Saint Benedict's Convent in Saint Joseph, Minnesota. In ways probably deeper than either of us knows, our understanding of monasticism has been shaped by our friendships with persons who have added their own stamp to the traditions and communities that have shaped them.

Patrick G. Henry
Institute for Ecumenical and Cultural Research
Collegeville, Minnesota

Donald K. Swearer
Swarthmore College
Swarthmore, Pennsylvania

Introduction

You might expect a book about the spirit of monasticism to be called *Forsaking the World*. Haven't monks and nuns turned their backs on the world, opted out of society, for the sake of some personal and otherworldly spiritual goal? But the title is *For the Sake of the World*, and it is not a typographical error.

The apparent withdrawal of persons who inhabit monasteries is a way of closer engagement with the life of the larger community. Nuns and monks make the choices they make, live the way they do, work and pray and chant and meditate, ''for the sake of the world.''

Father Zossima, in Dostoevsky's *The Brothers Karamazov*, says that monks are not a special sort of person, but only what all persons ought to be.[1] Such a claim was a challenge to nineteenth-century Russia, but Dostoevsky's first readers could at least understand the terms in which Father Zossima spoke, even if they rejected what he said. In our time the assertion that a monk or nun is what every person ought to be falls on the ear not as a challenge but as an utterance in an unknown foreign tongue.

Monasticism is so tangential to our culture, so remote from the slightest acquaintance of most of us, that we quite honestly do not know what Father Zossima is talking about. We suspect that his claim is preposterous at best or pernicious at worst, but mainly we do not consider it of much significance one way or another.

BETWIXT AND BETWEEN

This book intends to make sense of Father Zossima's claim. Two convictions underlie the choice of subject and the shape of the book:

(1) the religious life is a way of being "in the world but not of it," and (2) monasticism is a distinctive and instructive expression of the "betwixt-and-between" nature of the religious life.[2] Father Zossima's claim is not a tribute to monasticism; it is an insight into the nature of human life itself.

The book is not a comparison of Buddhist and Christian monasticism as such. It explores monasticism as a distinctive vision of the religious life. To be sure, throughout the volume there are comparisons, both implicit and explicit, between Christian and Buddhist forms of the monastic life, but our intention is to understand monasticism in terms of the traditions of Buddhism and Christianity rather than to compile a catalogue of similarities and differences. The comparisons we do make are to illuminate the general betwixt-and-between monastic/ascetic vision of the religious life.

Our students' fresh and frank curiosity about monasticism confirms our conviction that the monastic vision offers an important challenge and hope for today's world. At the beginning of the semester we asked them to express their impressions of monasticism. One wrote:

> How do monks and nuns really feel? Are they the happy, mystical saints we read about in children's books, or are they suppressed, blighted beings hiding their wicked desires beneath the monastic mask? Do they hold their opposite gender in contempt, or can they see beyond our mere outer selves and love us for what we are regardless of race, creed, or gender? How do they view those who are not monastics? Is it true that they wear hairshirts and mortify themselves? How do they spend their days? On what do they depend for their livelihood? What and how much do they eat? How do they like being who and what they are? What do nuns think of monks and vice versa?
>
> There will always be monastics, for there is, though it may be unrecognized, a monastic in everyone. In the minds of many, there exists a paradox. It seems a blissful, blighted life of difficult ease. A monastic wavers and doubts faith as much as any other person does. This should be obvious, but it seems not to be. What will be found when one talks to a person who is a monastic? I don't know, for I have scarcely met any.[3]

This book is an invitation and an opportunity to meet some.

THE PLAN OF THE BOOK

Chapter 1, "Contemplation and Action," states the fundamental paradox of monastic life—withdrawal for the sake of engagement, giving up all things in order to have all things, renouncing individualism for the sake of individuality—and illustrates the power of the paradox in the lives of two twentieth-century monks: a Christian, Thomas Merton, and a Buddhist, Thich Nhat Hanh. The remainder of the book helps to explain how—through ideals, history, rules, training, and the challenge of modernity—exemplary characters such as Thomas Merton and Thich Nhat Hanh have come to be who they are.

Chapter 2, "The Ascetic Ideal," discusses the fundamental theory that underlies monastic life. The main monastic traditions in both Buddhism and Christianity have opted for a moderate asceticism (the "Middle Way" of the Buddha, the "nothing burdensome" of St. Benedict), but both traditions insist that a degree of renunciation beyond what most people undertake is necessary to achieve the highest religious goal. In our student's fine phrase, it is a life of "difficult ease."

Chapter 3, "The Historical Road," elaborates the ascetic ideal through an account of the historical origins of monasticism in the two traditions. We concentrate on the early centuries of both Buddhism and Christianity not out of a particular antiquarian interest, but because the fundamental issues that have exercised monastic development and debate throughout history almost all came quickly to the surface in the initial stages of the movements.

Chapter 4, "The Rule of Life," examines the nature of the monastic life as lived in distinctive communities governed by explicit rules. The regulation of monastic life is perhaps its most curious feature in our time. We value freedom so highly that we cannot imagine submitting ourselves to a rule. Both the Buddhist and Christian monastic traditions suggest strongly that discipline is the precondition for spontaneity and true self-direction.

Chapter 5, "Transformers and Transmitters," places the monastery in a broader context, with special attention to its role as a center of learning and to the monk's/nun's function of teaching as a moral-spiritual exemplar.

Chapter 6, "Monasticism and Modernity," explores a wide range of issues Christian and Buddhist monasticism face in the contemporary world. The question of the viability and survival of monasticism is serious, though it is instructive to reflect on how many previous modern worlds that can now be reconstructed only by historians have themselves thought they were writing the obituaries of monasticism.

Chapter 7, "Habits of the Monastic Heart," gathers the insights and observations of the previous chapters into a statement of what the Buddhist and Christian monastic traditions have to offer by way of challenge and hope to our distracted and frightened world.

A NOTE ON TERMINOLOGY

A book twice the length of this one could be written simply sorting out the problems of monastic terminology. In order not to get bogged down in technicalities—which are important, but do not all have to be settled in order to say what we want to say in this book—we use common terms without trying to specify their exact frame of reference too closely.

There were *monks* before there was *monasticism*—that is, people were identified as monks, and then the life they lived came to be called monasticism (or, sometimes, *monachism*). From the beginning, both Buddhist and Christian monasticism have been characterized by two quite distinct ways of living: the *eremitic* (same root as the word hermit), which means living alone, and *coenobitic*, which means living in community.

The term *monk* in the Christian context originally could refer to either a man or a woman, but for many centuries *monk* has denoted only male monastics. There is a trend now among some female monastics to recover use of the term *monk* for themselves, but the exclusively male usage is so familiar in our culture that we have chosen to use the term *nun* in referring to women who are living the monastic life. The term *nun* itself has a complex history, which involves technical distinctions in Catholic church law, but many monastic women who until recently were technically sisters now are recovering the use of the term *nun*, and are comfortable being so designated.

The term *abbot* is almost universally used for the leader of a male monastic community; some female leaders are called abbess, but we have chosen to use the more common term, *prioress*.

While we are using different terms for male and female monastics, we have chosen to use the term *monastery* to refer to the homes of both monks and nuns. It is common today for new women's monastic foundations to call themselves monasteries rather than convents.

The term *religious* (used as a noun, e.g., "she is a religious") is much broader in Catholic usage than *monastic*; it refers to persons in all sorts of orders, including monastic orders. Some of the best-known nonmonastic religious orders are the Jesuits (men), Franciscans (men and women), Dominicans (men and women), Paulists (men), Ursulines (women), but there are hundreds of others. A book simply listing Roman Catholic religious orders is more than five hundred pages long.[4] The term *religious* will occasionally be used in this book to designate monks and nuns, usually when the decrees of the Second Vatican Council are being referred to.

The development of Buddhist monasticism in various historical and cultural contexts resulted in sectarian or school distinctions. Three broad streams of tradition eventually emerged: *Theravada, Mahayana,* and *Tantrayana.* The term *Hinayana,* historically applied to Theravada schools in India, is no longer current. All the streams have their sources in India, include numerous distinctive subtraditions, and have both similarities and differences in text, doctrine, and practice. These three streams are sometimes associated with distinct regions of Asia: Theravada linked to Southeast Asia, Mahayana to East Asia, Tantrayana to Central Asia. These regional differentiations have merit and are useful, but if pressed too far they blur the complex historical development of Buddhism.

Our use of the term *monk* as translation for the Pali term *bhikkhu*[5] runs the risk of blurring some distinctions, but the usage is so common in the literature and, indeed, within Buddhist communities themselves, that the risk of confusion seems minimal. On the other hand, we usually employ the Pali term *sangha*, untranslated, when referring to the Buddhist monastic Order. *Sangha* can designate a particular community in one place, or the entire Buddhist population of a given area, or the collection of monastic communities within a country. We try to be clear how the term is being used in various contexts in the book, but part of the power of such a term is that its boundaries are not always precise.

Occasional reference is made to the *bhikkhuni*, the Buddhist female monastic. As we indicate later, there was a female part of the Order early in the history of Buddhism, but in many parts of Asia it died out, and has only very recently begun a revival. Hence, our characteristic use of monk/nun in discussing Christian monasticism but not in most of our discussion of Buddhism: women's monasticism has always been a significant part of Christian monastic tradition (though historians have seldom paid it much heed, and church officials, who have paid it heed, have done so mainly when telling the nuns what to do).

The transliteration of proper names and place names follows widely used convention or a specific reference/source.

To reiterate: it would be misleading, as well as dauntingly difficult, to give comprehensive definitions of *monk, nun, monastery, monasticism*, before beginning to tell the story of this form of life and the persons who live it. The meaning depends on the story, not the other way round.

1

The Monastic Vision: Contemplation and Action

Solitary contemplation and active involvement in the world: these are the poles around which the monastic vision has been shaped from its earliest beginnings. Indeed, the "in the world but not of it" or "betwixt-and-between" nature of the monastic ideal, past and present, rests on this seeming paradox. The monastery is created by the urge toward transcendence, our desire to express the highest aspirations of the spirit in a wide range of human creations: ideas and art, prayer and literature, philosophy and theology, ethics and social action.

While monks and nuns may have specialized in disciplines aimed at radical personal transformation or become administrators of complex monastic institutions, many, such as Antony and Hildegard, Bodhidharma and Sanghamitta, have stood out as moral and spiritual exemplars, not only for other monastic persons but also for laity. Our study of the spirit of monasticism begins with an examination of two exemplary monastic figures of our own time, Thomas Merton, an American Trappist, and Thich Nhat Hanh, a Vietnamese Zen monk. Their lives and teachings embody a monasticism "for the sake of the world," a vision shaped by contemplation and action.

THOMAS MERTON

Thomas Merton, born in 1915, spent most of his youth in Europe and England. He graduated from Columbia University in 1938. In 1947 he took solemn vows committing himself to the life of a monk at Our Lady of Gethsemani Trappist monastery in Kentucky, and two years later was ordained a priest. In 1951 he became Master of Scholastics at Gethsemani; four years later he was Master of Novices, a position he held until 1965. He died in 1968 in Bangkok, where he was attending a conference of Asian Christian monastic leaders.

Merton left a detailed record of his life in autobiography (e.g., *The Seven Storey Mountain*), journals (e.g., *The Asian Diary*), and thousands of letters, a legacy greatly enhancing his exemplary influence. Indeed, the Merton written corpus has provided a rich mine for theses, dissertations, and biographies.[1]

Merton wrote more than memoirs, however. His sixty books, completed over a period of twenty years, include not only autobiography, but poetry, mythic narrative, prose essays, translations, theological and philosophical treatises. As a consequence, he became the best-known Christian monastic figure in the world, an unrivaled spokesperson for a religious life of active contemplation. His influence in the Christian world, both Roman Catholic and Protestant, can hardly be exaggerated. Nor was his inspiration confined to the Christian world. He was in contact with such non-Christian religious spokespersons as the Dalai Lama and D.T. Suzuki, the foremost interpreter of Zen Buddhism to the West.

Merton's life and thought are paradoxical. He joined one of the most withdrawn Roman Catholic monastic orders (*Trappist* is the colloquial name for Cistercians of Strict Observance) but was an outspoken advocate of social and political justice. He took a vow of silence, but volumes of prose and poetry flowed from his pen. He was dedicated to Christ but felt a deeper spiritual kinship with many of the Buddhist monks he met on his Asian travels than with some of his coreligionists. Because of these seeming paradoxes some have interpreted Merton as a man torn with deep conflicts and inner tensions. Such an interpretation fails to recognize Merton's spiritual genius, his betwixt-and-between synthesis of solitary spiritual quest and desire to contribute to the creation of a just and peaceful world.

"In the Belly of a Paradox"

Of himself Merton said, cryptically, "I find myself travelling toward my destiny in the belly of a paradox."[2] Elaborating upon this statement more fully in his preface to Thomas McDonnell's collection of his writing, Merton wrote:

> I have had to accept the fact that my life is almost totally paradoxical. I have also had to learn gradually to get along without apologizing for the fact, even to myself. . . . It is in the paradox itself, the paradox which was and still is a source of insecurity, that I have come to find the greatest security. I have become convinced that the very contradictions in my life are in some ways signs of God's mercy to me: if only because someone so complicated and so prone to confusion and self-defeat could hardly survive for long without special mercy. And since this in no way depends on the approval of others, the awareness is a kind of liberation.[3]

Merton embraced paradox because not to do so would be to reject life in its totality. The inner quest for personal transformation is incomplete without active concern for the welfare of others, just as the struggle for social, political, and economic justice leads to violence and the breakdown of community when not rooted in the depth of one's spiritual quest.

Life is a paradox but not a contradiction. When the personal quest for insight, transformation, and perfection excludes active concern for others, life becomes imbalanced and disharmonious. An aggressive self-assertion of one's rights devoid of interior vision rejects the deepest sources of life for confrontation with death.

> When society is made up of men who know no interior solitude it can no longer be held together by love: and consequently it is held together by a violent and abusive authority. But when men are violently deprived of solitude and freedom which are their due, the society in which they live becomes putrid, it festers with servility, resentment and hate.[4]

While for Merton monks relinquish the cares, desires, and ambitions of other people in order to seek God,[5] they do not, thereby, give up their concern for the world. Merton sought to challenge and change the image of the monk as one who had resigned from the world. Granting that his best-selling autobiography, *The Seven Storey Mountain*, might have been partially responsible for helping to create the image of a contemplative as one "who had spurned New York, spat on Chicago, and tromped on Louisville, heading for the woods with Thoreau in one pocket, John of the Cross in another, and holding the Bible open at the Apocalypse,"[6] he argued forcefully that monks are necessarily and inextricably part of the world, and that the world should not be understood as a physical place "out there," but a "complex of responsibilities and options made out of the loves, the hates, the fears, the joys, the hopes, the greed, the cruelty, the kindness, the faith, the trust, the suspicion of all."[7] No more than anyone else can the monk escape Pogo's dictum: "I have met the enemy and it is me." Or, as Merton put it, "If there is war because nobody trusts anybody, this is in part because I myself am defensive, suspicious, untrusting, and intent on making other people conform themselves to my particular brand of death wish."[8]

Merton sees monastic life, ultimately, as one of "final integration" with society: the monk/nun is one who, more than others, assumes a vocation where he or she is "poured out into the world." While an incarnational theology justifies the Christian monk's commitment to the world, Merton contends that the monastic life everywhere depends on such a premise—that the openness, emptiness, and poverty of the Rhenish mystics or St. John of the Cross also characterize the Sufis, Taoist masters, and Zen Buddhist monks. Monks, moreover, not only inevitably play a part in the world, they have a special role in it—to bear witness to the deepest human capacities they discover in the contemplative experience. In the face of rampant secularism and materialism, the monastic contribution to personal and social well-being has become increasingly important, if not imperative. To misconstrue the monastic life as world-denying has even more serious consequences for the health of the world today than in times past.

PILGRIM: INTERIOR AND EXTERIOR

Merton's sense of the monastic vision of human nature and life in community inspired him to be both pilgrim and poet, one whose life and literary output exemplified the ineffable truth of mystical experience, the mutual interpenetration of the divine and the whole of humankind. His pilgrim quest moved symbolically, metaphorically, and literally between the desert and the city, America and Asia, Marx and Chuang Tzu, Christianity and Buddhism. In his circular letter of September 1968, he wrote, "Our real journey in life is *interior*: it is a matter of growth, deepening, and of an ever greater surrender to the creative action of love and grace in our hearts."[9] But he also took an *exterior* journey, traveling to Asia to meet with monks and religious leaders from different traditions. In a paper to have been delivered in Calcutta he said,

> I have left my monastery to come here not just as a research scholar or even as an author . . . [but] as a pilgrim who is anxious to obtain not just information, not just "facts" about other monastic traditions, but to drink from ancient sources of monastic vision and experience.[10]

Merton's intention was fulfilled when he met the Tibetan Buddhist monk, Chatral Rimpoche, in northern India. They spoke for several hours about Buddhist meditation and points of comparison between Buddhist and Christian doctrine, confessing to one another that they had not attained to "perfect emptiness" even after thirty years of practice. Merton felt such a kinship with Chatral Rimpoche that he wrote in his diary entry of November 16, 1968:

> The unspoken or half-spoken message of the talk was our complete understanding of each other as people who were somehow *on the edge* of great realization and knew it and were trying, somehow or other, to go out and get lost in it—and that it was a grace for us to meet one another.[11]

Rimpoche apparently felt the same way, referring to Father Merton as a "natural Buddha."

The sources of monastic vision and experience, particularly the Christian desert fathers, had a special fascination for Merton, not because of their asceticism or their renunciation but for the clarity and simplicity of their insight. He said of them: "These fathers distilled for themselves a very practical and unassuming wisdom that is at once primitive and timeless, and which enables us to reopen the sources"[12] which flow directly from experience. This simple and concrete way of appealing to experience, uncharted and freely chosen, hints at the notion of Zen nonattachment. Merton's description of these desert sages could, in fact, be as aptly applied to a Zen master:

> Their flight to the arid horizons of the desert meant also a refusal to be content with arguments, concepts and technical verbiage. . . . [They lamented] the madness of attachment to unreal values. . . . Rest, then, was a kind of simple no-whereness and no-mindedness that had lost all preoccupation with a false or limited "self." At peace in the possession of a sublime "Nothing" the spirit laid hold, in secret, upon the "All,"—without trying to know what it possessed.[13]

The similarity between the desert fathers and the Zen masters prompted Merton to send a copy of his book, *Wisdom of the Desert*, to D.T. Suzuki, initiating a dialogue published in a sensitive and insightful collection of Merton's essays, *Zen and the Birds of Appetite*.

Merton's pilgrimage to Zen was to the Zen experience of personal transformation cutting through the false, misleading, artificial, and unreal. He contended that Buddhism and Christianity have ultimately the same aim: personal transformation through direct experience.[14] The Word of the Cross demands a radical transformation of consciousness, not a discourse by the rational intellect. The experience of dying and rising with Christ is likened by Merton to the Zen notion of the Great Death experience associated with *satori* or enlightenment.

Zen, for Merton, symbolizes that in religion which plunges us toward "the quest for direct and pure experience on a metaphysical level, liberated from verbal formulas and linguistic preconceptions."[15] Merton believed that Christian dialogue with Zen would help focus the Christian life on the personal, experiential basis of the Christian message rather than on discourses about it. Both the church and the world need to be reminded that the most profound dimensions of community cannot be legislated or even verbalized.

Merton's pilgrimage to Asian religions, especially Zen Buddhism and Taoism, was not in the first instance an attempt to find affinities between these traditions and Christianity, but to point to two other directions: to help Christians recover the true meaning of the Christian faith, and to discover a common ground of religious experience. Merton's writings bear clear testimony to some of the directions in which his encounter with Taoism and Zen influenced his thinking. Although the early Merton of *The Seven Storey Mountain* is moved by the conception of God as "pure being" (*aseitas*), he is equally preoccupied with the polarity of good and evil, natural and supernatural, heaven and hell: "Man's nature, by itself, can do little or nothing. . . . If we follow our own level of ethics, we will end in hell."[16] By 1966 Merton's earlier sharp distinctions between good and evil had become, "He who grasps the central pivot of Tao, is able to watch the 'Yes' and the 'No' pursue their alternating course around the circumference."[17]

Furthermore, the sometimes authoritarian God who rewards and punishes becomes the limitless, self-emptying ground, the God who gives without self-conscious afterthought. In this God all persons find themselves truly reborn when they have emptied all contents of their ego consciousness "to become a void in which . . . the full radiation of the infinite reality . . . [is] manifested."[18]

Merton's personal pilgrimage, which took him first to Gethsemani and later to Asia to experience directly the religious traditions he had only studied secondhand, led to a transformation of his consciousness, not a consciousness "of" any thing but an intuition of what Merton called a *"ground of openness, . . .* an infinite generosity which communicates itself to everything that is."[19] This kind of openness cannot be acquired by a mere act of the will. It is a radical gift that has been lost and must be recovered through an inner journey which may, as in Merton's case, take an unusual outer form. The journey has no stipulated goal as such but leads to an awareness of that ground which underlies the experience of being an individual self.

THE JOURNEY BACK TO THE CITY

But what of moral responsibility toward society, acting on behalf of peace, justice, and the human rights of all peoples? We have explored Merton's quest for personal self-transformation, his pilgrimage to the desert, as it were. But what of his journey back to the city? This part of his pilgrimage literally began seven years after he had entered the monastery, when he reencountered the outside world for the first time. He describes his return in these words:

We drove into town with Senator Dawson, a neighbor of the monastery, and all the while I wondered how I would react at meeting once again, face to face, the wicked world. I met the world and I found it no longer so wicked after all. Perhaps the things I had resented about the world when I left it were defects of my own that I had projected upon it. Now, on the contrary, I found that everything stirred me with a deep and mute sense of compassion. . . . I went through the city, realizing for the first time in my life how good are all the people in the world and how much value they have in the sight of God.[20]

He speaks in even more moving and graphic terms of the absolutely necessary interconnection between the two poles of the pilgrimage: "For if our emotions really die in the desert, our humanity dies with them. We must return from the desert like Jesus or St. John, with our capacity for feeling expanded and deepened. . . ."[21] In short, for Merton, solitude and withdrawal are necessarily linked to relating to others in the fullness of their humanity, to being truly concerned for their well-being, and to creating community.

The pilgrim returns from the desert experience to the city not only to affirm his/her love and compassion for humankind, but, like the prophet, to speak out against those powers working to prevent individuals from realizing their deepest nature, against those powers that undermine the building of true community. Merton's spiritual journey, which took him to the monastery, returned him to the world as a critic of racism, Nazism, war, injustice, and intolerance. In a letter written a few months before his death he affirmed:

I am against war, against violence, against violent revolution, for the peaceful settlement of differences, for nonviolent but nevertheless radical changes. Change is needed, and violence will not really change anything: at most it will only transfer power from one set of bullheaded authorities to another. If I say these things, it is not because I am more interested in politics than in the Gospel. I am not. But today more than ever the Gospel commitment has political implications, because you cannot claim to be "for Christ" and espouse a political cause that implies callous indifference to the needs of millions of human beings and even cooperate in their destruction.[22]

Merton's concern for the poor and needy, the exploited and dispossessed; his demands for social, economic, and political justice;

and his criticism of the exploiters, warmongers, and well-meaning but misguided liberal do-gooders, led him to a dialogue with Marx. Merton saw real convergences between Christianity and Marxism as well as important divergences:

> Where Marx spoke of the alienation of labor, Merton speaks of the alienation of our hearts. Where Marx argued that capitalism robbed people of both the meaning and the benefits of their work, Merton argues that modern life robs us of our hearts. . . . What does it mean to be robbed of our hearts? For one thing, it means that our ability to feel connected with others, implicated in their lives, has been stolen from us, for it is through our hearts that we feel solidarity with our brothers and sisters. . . . The conditions of modern life have calloused so many hearts. We seem unable to feel, unable to have our hearts broken by the fact of children who are starving and parents who are unable to provide. Our individualized way of life makes us feel alone and unrelated; our competitive way of life makes us feel that our gains must come at the expense of others. . . . We don't have the possession of our hearts. They have been seized by concerns for self-preservation and self-enhancement, and by the maintenance of institutions which serve these ends. If we are to give our hearts we must get them back. . . . This is the first task of the spiritual life.[23]

In short, while Marx argued that alienation was rooted in economic and class struggle, Merton saw alienation as isolation from the Ground of Being underlying all forms of distinction and identity. True community, therefore, depends on a recovery of the spiritual depth of existence, a journey in which monks and nuns play a crucial exemplary role.

To walk the pilgrim's path between the desert and the city is to experience life, as Merton put it, in the belly of a paradox. How does the pilgrim express this paradox? Sometimes, like Merton, by becoming a monk in a literal sense. Merton, however, often seems to speak of the monastic life almost metaphorically as a symbol of the most fully integrated life. Merton, then, might be said to exemplify not only the betwixt-and-between nature of the ascetic/monastic ideal, but the paradoxical nature of the religious life in its most genuine and profound form, a paradox he embodied in his concerns and actions, and in his writing.

Merton wrote in a variety of genres. He spoke in moving autobiographical prose of his personal conversion and monastic experience. Yet, like others who have experienced that "ground of openness" beyond the ordinary, the accepted, the conventional, Merton sought to express himself in terms other than ordinary and conventional prose forms. He bore witness to the ineffable depths of selfhood in such poems as "Night-Flowering Cactus":

I know my time, which is obscure, silent and brief
For I am present without warning one night only.
When sun rises on the brass valleys I become serpent.

Though I show my true self only in the dark and to no man
(For I appear by day as serpent)
I belong neither to night nor day.

Sun and city never see my deep white bell
Or know my timeless moment of void:
There is no reply to my munificence.

When I come I lift my sudden Eucharist
Out of the earth's unfathomable joy
Clean and total I obey the world's body
I am intricate and whole, not art but wrought passion
Excellent deep pleasure of essential waters
Holiness of form and mineral mirth:

I am the extreme purity of virginal thirst.

I neither show my truth nor conceal it
My innocence is descried dimly
Only by divine gift
As a white cavern without explanation.

He who sees my purity
Dares not speak of it.
When I open once for all my impeccable bell
No one questions my silence:
The all-knowing bird of night flies out of my mouth.

Have you seen it? Then though my mirth has quickly ended
You live forever in its echo:
You will never be the same again.[24]

In an even more powerful poem, "The Fall," Merton contrasts

this nameless ground of personal identity with the false and artificial social identities imposed by context and environment:

There is no where in you a paradise that is no place and there
You do not enter except without a story.

To enter there is to become unnameable.

Whoever is there is homeless for he has no door and
no identity with which to go out and to come in.

Whoever is nowhere is nobody, and therefore cannot exist
except as unborn:
No disguise will avail him anything.

Such a one is neither lost nor found.

But he who has an address is lost.

They fall, they fall into apartments and are securely
established!

They find themselves in streets. They are licensed
To proceed from place to place
They now know their own names
They can name several friends and know
Their own telephones must some time ring.

If all telephones ring at once, if all names are shouted
at once and all cars crash at one crossing:
If all cities explode and fly away in dust
Yet identities refuse to be lost. There is a name and
number for everyone.

There is a definite place for bodies, there are pigeon
holes for ashes:
Such security can business buy!

Who would dare to go nameless in so secure a universe?
Yet, to tell the truth, only the nameless are at home in it.

They bear with them in the center of nowhere the unborn
flower of nothing:
This is the paradise tree. It must remain unseen until
words end and arguments are silent.[25]

Merton's poetry, as we might expect, expressed not only his experience of the ineffable ground of existence, but his love and concern for the well-being of all peoples, especially those deprived and dispossessed, those exploited by the wealthy and the powerful:

> And the children of Birmingham
> Walked into the story
> Of Grandma's pointed teeth
> ("Better to love you with")
> Reasonable citizens
> Rose to exhort them all:
> "Return at once to schools of friendship.
> Buy in stores of love and law."
>
> (And tales were told
> Of man's best friend, the Law.)
>
> ***
>
> But what the children did that time
> Gave their town
> A name to be remembered![26]

And we remember Thomas Merton, monk, who looked for the "night-flowering cactus" and "the unborn flower of nothing" not only in a Trappist monastery or on a pilgrimage to sources of Asian spirituality, but also in the black struggle for liberation in Birmingham, in Gandhi's nonviolent movement for India's right to self-determination, in the voices crying out against the insanity of nuclear war, and in Thich Nhat Hanh's attempts to create a peaceful and just solution to violence and bloodshed in Vietnam.

THICH NHAT HANH

Thomas Merton had many friends and acquaintances all over the world. One of them was the Vietnamese monk, Thich Nhat Hanh, for whose book, *Vietnam: The Lotus in a Sea of Fire*, Merton wrote the foreword.[27] Nhat Hanh and Merton had much in common: both were monks, poets, and deeply concerned about social, political, and economic injustice in the world. Nhat Hanh was also a university professor, founder of the School of Youth for Social Service in Vietnam, headed the Vietnamese Peace Delegation in Paris during the Vietnam war, and has served as vice chairperson of the Fellowship of Reconciliation. In addition to his book describing the political situation in Vietnam in the late 1960s and proposing a constructive alternative to either communist or capitalist domination of his country, Nhat Hanh has published several books in English, including *Zen Poems, Zen Keys, The Miracle of Mindfulness: A Manual on Meditation, The Cry of Vietnam, Being Peace,* and *The Raft Is Not the Shore,* coauthored with Daniel Berrigan. These writings represent his deep indebtedness to his own religious tradition and training, his vision of a more just and humane world, and his commitment to the necessity of integrating social and political activism with interior disciplines such as meditation. Since the end of the Vietnam war, Nhat Hanh has divided his time between a retreat-meditation center in France and an active pursuit of solutions to conflict, violence, injustice, and war. He embodies in both his style of life and his writings a ''caring for the world'' through contemplation and action.

RAIN FALLING ON FIRE

A story about Nhat Hanh during the Vietnam War exemplifies these betwixt-and-between sides of the ascetic/monastic ideal, a vision he then develops in his book, *Zen Keys.* James Forest of the Catholic Peace Fellowship tells the story. It dramatically illustrates the connection between the depth of Nhat Hanh's spiritual quest and the breadth of his political and social concerns.[28]

In 1968 Nhat Hanh was on a speaking tour in the United States, trying to help Americans understand the horrors of the Vietnam war through the eyes of peasants laboring in the rice paddies and raising their children in villages. After a lecture in the auditorium of a large Christian church in a St. Louis suburb a man stood up and asked with a scorn-filled voice: ''If you care so much about your people, Mr. Hanh, why are you here? If you care so much for the people who are wounded, why don't you spend your time with them?'' When he had finished, Forest looked at Nhat Hanh with apprehension. What would he say? The spirit of the war itself had suddenly filled the room, and it seemed hard to breathe. There was a deafening silence.

Then Nhat Hanh began to speak—quietly, with deep calm and a sense of personal caring for the man who had just attacked him.

The words seemed like rain falling on fire: "If you want the tree to grow," he said, "it won't help to water the leaves. You have to water the roots. Many of the roots of the war are here, in your country. To help the people who are to be bombed, to try to protect them from this suffering, I have to come here." After this response, Nhat Hanh whispered something to the chairperson and walked quickly from the room.

Sensing something was wrong, Forest followed him out. It was a cool clear night. Nhat Hanh stood on the sidewalk struggling for air. Finally he was able to explain to his friend that the man's comments had been terribly upsetting. He had wanted to respond with anger so he made himself breathe deeply and slowly in order to find a way to respond calmly and with understanding. But the breathing had been too slow and too deep, and he had to excuse himself in order to restore normal respiration. For the first time Forest realized there is a connection between the way one breathes and the way one responds to the world.

The dramatic nature of the story should not obscure its simplicity: a monk embodying the Zen ideal not in some retreat far away from the hustle and bustle of the world, but in a midwestern auditorium in front of a hostile audience. It seems like a contemporary form of the lesson of the Zen Ox Herding Pictures, which make the point that the search for and mastery of the self does not mean negating the world,[29] or the threefold dialectical saying about mountains and rivers being nothing but mountains and rivers, which makes the point that the ultimate or absolute is not to be distinguished from the relative (*samsara* is *nirvana*),[30] or the profound lesson in such spare and simple Zen fables as the one about Chao-Chou that Nhat Hanh retells in *Zen Keys*:

One day a monk asked Master Chao-Chou to speak to him about Zen. Chao-Chou asked: "Have you finished your breakfast?" "Yes, Master, I have eaten my breakfast." "Then go and wash the bowl." "Go and wash the bowl." This is also, "Go and live with Zen." Instead of giving the questioner explanations about Zen, the Master opened the door and invited him to enter directly into the world of the reality of Zen. "Go and wash the bowl." These words contain no secret meaning to explore and explain; it is a very simple, direct, and clear declaration. There is no enigma here, nor is this a symbol, either. It refers to a very concrete fact.[31]

Nhat Hanh, responding with compassion and understanding to anger and hostility, was living Zen; he was embodying the ascetic/ monastic ideal of contemplation and action, not theorizing about it.

WASHING THE DISHES

Nhat Hanh brings this same simplicity and directness to his book on meditation, originally subtitled ''A Manual of Meditation for the Use of Young Activists.'' There he recreates the story of Master Chao-Chou's advice to go and wash the bowl.[32] One winter evening Nhat Hanh's friend, Jim Forest, was visiting his apartment. After the evening meal and before sitting down for tea, Jim asked if he might not wash the dishes in Nhat Hanh's stead. ''Go ahead,'' Nhat Hanh replied, ''but if you wash the dishes you must know the way to wash them. There are two ways to wash the dishes. The first is to wash them in order to have clean dishes and the second is to wash the dishes in order to wash the dishes.'' If while washing dishes, we think only of the cup of tea awaiting us and hurry to get the dishes out of the way as if it were a nuisance, then we are not ''washing the dishes to wash the dishes''; we are not alive during the time we are washing the dishes; in fact, we are completely incapable of realizing the miracle of life while standing at the sink. If we cannot wash the dishes, the chances are that we will not be able to drink our tea, be attentive to our studies, do our job, love our neighbors, or act on their behalf.

The story of Nhat Hanh's response to the angry listener in the St. Louis church auditorium demonstrates, as James Forest observed, the connection between the spiritual discipline of meditation and the way one acts in the world. Nhat Hanh's writings promote the same essential interrelationship between the realization of one's deepest, spiritual self and active involvement on behalf of the well-being of others. Or, in more Buddhist terms, the monk exemplifies the wisdom (*prajna*) of self(less)-realization and the compassion (*karuna*) that flows from such understanding. The two are so essentially intertwined that they presuppose one another. One does not practice the disciplines leading to wisdom *and then* act compassionately, or practice mind*ful*ness during meditation and then act mind*less*ly the rest of the day. Mindful awareness should be cultivated at all times and places, not just in the monastery or in a quiet retreat:

> Active, concerned people don't have time to spend leisurely, walking along paths of green grass and sitting beneath trees. One must prepare projects, consult with the neighbors, try to resolve a million difficulties; there is hard work to do. One must deal with every kind of hardship, every moment keeping one's attention focused on the work, alert, ready to handle the situation ably and intelligently. . . .
>
> Mindfulness is the miracle by which we master and restore ourselves. Consider, for example: a magician who cuts his body into many parts and places each part in a different region—hands in the south, arms in the east, legs in the north, and then by some miraculous power lets forth a cry which reassembles whole every part of his body. Mindfulness is like that—it is the miracle which can call back in a flash our dispersed mind and restore it to wholeness so that we can live each minute of life.[33]

Nhat Hanh structures his book, *Zen Keys,* to illustrate the essential interrelationship between contemplation and action. On one level Nhat Hanh tells the reader about Zen Buddhism: stories of the Zen masters, the meaning of such popularly known Zen sayings as, ''If you meet the Buddha, kill him!'' the basic philosophical principle of nonduality, the method of the school of consciousness only (*Vijnanavada*), and so forth. Yet on a deeper level Nhat Hanh's entire discussion of Zen teaching and practice is really about awareness and awakening: one comes to the truth through the development of the awareness of things-as-they-are:

> To reach truth is not to accumulate knowledge, but to awaken to the *heart of reality.* Reality reveals itself complete and whole at the moment of awakening. In the light of this awakening, nothing is added and nothing is lost. . . .
>
> The moment of awakening is marked by an outburst of laughter. But this is not the laughter of someone who suddenly acquires a great fortune; neither is it the laughter of one who has won a victory. It is, rather, the laughter of one who, after having painfully searched for something for a long time, finds it one morning in the pocket of his coat.[34]

A NEW CULTURE

Nhat Hanh's discussion of Zen encompasses a description of Zen practice; the development of the tradition in India and China; the three gates of liberation—emptiness (the absence of permanent identity of things), no-sign (the nonconceptuality of the true nature of things), nonpursuit (not running after enlightenment as a goal); the negative dialectic of Nagarjuna's Madhyamika philosophy; and various relatively abstruse ideas basic to Yogacara thought. Nhat Hanh is both a practitioner and a scholar. He does not shy away from difficult philosophical concepts, but they are to be understood at the proper time and in the proper context—after presenting Zen as a practice leading to awareness and liberation and depicting Zen through lives of the Zen masters. In short, Nhat Hanh does not reject the place of ideas and concepts, but they make sense only after one has lived the truth to which the concepts point through personal practice and sitting at the feet of the saints.

As with the Chao-Chou story, having "eaten breakfast" one then goes out into the world to "wash the bowl." Nhat Hanh concludes *Zen Keys* with a discussion entitled "The Zen Person and the World Today," in which he offers a critique of the problems of the modern world and how they can be addressed. He speaks of the problems of overpopulation, famine, political repression, nuclear war, and the threat to the entire ecosystem by industrialization and technology. Nhat Hanh argues that the basic solution to the massive problems we all face is in the development of a new culture in which we can discover our true selves. It must be a culture in which we do not allow ourselves "to be invaded by material goods," a civilization where community life is possible, unlike the impersonal urban megalopolis of today. What Zen has to offer is a vision of universal harmony, to be sure, but more important, it is a practical teaching, exemplified by the likes of Thich Nhat Hanh, that points us to a place in the world encompassing the transmundane and the mundane, the yes and the no, contemplation and action.

Nhat Hanh, like Thomas Merton, is a poet as well as a pilgrim. His poetry likewise expresses a balance between solitude and involvement from that limitless ground beyond words in which all existence finds its deepest meaning:

Recommendation

Promise me this day,
promise me now
while the sun is overhead
exactly at the zenith,
promise me.

Even as they
strike you down
with a mountain of hate and violence,
even as they
step on your life and crush it
like a worm,
even as they dismember you, disembowel you,
remember, brother,
remember
man is not our enemy.

Just your pity,
just your hate
are invincible, limitless, unconditional.

Hatred will never let you face
the beast in man.

And one day
when you face this beast alone,
your courage intact, your eyes kind,
untroubled
(even as no one sees them),
out of your smile
will bloom a flower
and those who love you
will behold you
across ten thousand worlds of birth and dying.

Alone again
I'll go on with head bent
but knowing the immortality of love.
And on the long, rough road
both sun and moon will shine, lightening my steps.[35]

A GIFT TO BE SHARED

Both Nhat Hanh and Thomas Merton propose a transformation of our awareness through solitude, meditation, pilgrimage. Both espouse a transformation that reveals the hidden meanings of life, the sources of its becoming, its fundamental wholeness. Both describe a transformation so miraculous as to be considered a gift attributed to grace or enlightenment. By its very nature such a gift is to be shared, and the sharing radiates the power of the transformation. As Nhat Hanh sees it:

> In a family, if there is one person who practices mindfulness, the entire family will be more mindful. Because of the presence of one member who lives in mindfulness, the entire family is reminded to live in mindfulness. If in one class, one student lives in mindfulness, the entire class is influenced. In . . . communities we must follow the same principle.[36]

Thomas Merton and Nhat Hanh have the idealistic and politically naive conviction that true community develops from transformed persons rather than from political ideologies and manipulation of political structures. Idealistic, to be sure. However, the vision of Buddhist and Christian monks like Nhat Hanh and Merton may not be as naive as it seems. We have arrived at the most serious crisis point the world has ever known. We are threatened by overpopulation and malnutrition, the possibility of worldwide chemical contamination, the prospect of nuclear holocaust, international political confrontation, and the dissolution of traditional social structures and values. Some of us reel in confusion, some are numb, others react with mindless violence, while still others, anticipating the apocalypse, retreat to a self-sufficient existence cut off from a world apparently gone insane. Nhat Hanh put it in these terms: "The East, like the West, is witness to the spiritual bankruptcy of man. The complete destruction of the human race can only be avoided by finding a new cultural direction in which the spiritual element will play its role of guide."[37]

Thomas Merton and Nhat Hanh challenge us to see the world not as something "out there," but within each of us: "Since the world is in us, we are responsible for the world; and the shape the world takes depends on how we live our lives."[38] In contemplation we recover our true self, and, thereby, our capability of living "for the sake of the world."

2

The Ascetic Ideal

The great historic religions—Hinduism, Buddhism, Judaism, Christianity, Islam—are rooted in the distinctive vocation of the religious person. Religious persons live in varying degrees of tension with their secular environment. To the degree that their environment threatens their vocation they seek to cast off, minimize, or transform that threat. Asceticism can be broadly characterized as one of the means religious persons use to defend and express their vocation. Hence, asceticism can be seen to embody the highest ideals of the historic religions and the paradoxes that characterize these ideals as exemplified in the lives of Christians and Buddhists.

Asceticism appears to nonreligious persons to be a joyless naysaying, a taking away from, a denial of full humanity. The term calls up images of hairshirts, lying on beds of nails, eating little and sleeping seldom—in short, asceticism is perceived as masochism dressed up to look like virtue. But the religious person perceives asceticism as a fundamental expression or fulfillment of the religious life. Asceticism protects against the threat of nonreligious or perilous powers and is instrumental in the realization of the highest good, whether that highest good be symbolized as entrance into Nirvana or the Kingdom of God. To the nonreligious person, therefore, an ascetical view of life seems to sit squarely in the midst of a paradox of negation and affirmation. Is asceticism such a paradox? Or are the various forms of asceticism different ways religious persons perceive what is needed for self-identity and self-fulfillment?

The forms of religious asceticism, to be sure, vary greatly from tradition to tradition, culture to culture, person to person. Some types of asceticism might be characterized as inner-worldly and others as other-worldly, depending on the nature of their world view and religious practice.[1] Such distinctions, however, miss a basic similarity between the various forms of asceticism and of monastic vocation often associated with it. For religious persons seeking their own highest fulfillment, asceticism is a quest to overcome limitations of the mundane world, in order either to actualize another kind of being or reality, or to transform the mundane so that it properly reflects its transmundane ground.

Does this mean that the ascetical perspectives found within the historic religions are necessarily dualistic, dependent on a radical distinction between this world and another world, flesh and spirit, as some scholars have suggested?[2] There is certainly much evidence of sharply dualistic thinking in Buddhist and Christian asceticism. But Buddhist and Christian expressions of asceticism characteristically reflect a subtler appreciation of the requirements of life betwixt and between the mundane and the transcendent. The basic question the ascetic asks is not, How can I make the ideal real? but How should I live in this kind of world?

Genuine asceticism, far from being a clear symptom of a two-tiered world view associated (sometimes erroneously) with the historic religions, is a challenge to that view from within those religious traditions. The ascetic is proposing a way of getting the broken-apart world back together again. Only in terms of such an understanding of asceticism do the ringing world affirmations of a Thich Nhat Hanh and a Thomas Merton make consistent and coherent sense.

The twentieth-century tendency to seek psychological explanations for seemingly extreme or world-denying behavior has been applied to the origins of both Christian and Buddhist monasticism. Recent studies of early Christianity have had to fight against this tendency by insisting that Late Antiquity in the Mediterranean world was not a particularly gloomy time, that the culture was not over-burdened with anxiety. We see people doing strange things—or at least things we would not do, such as choosing an ascetic style of life—and we reach for the comfortable and comforting conclusion that they had a major psychological problem (e.g., they simply could not cope with life as it was presented to them). Asceticism does not mesh with our culture's popular conception of mental health. Yet, a psychological trauma explanation leaves unintelligible the fact that in the Roman Empire "without exception, the most effective politicians and organizers of the fourth century [C.E.] were either men of ascetic taste or leaders of ascetic movements."[3]

BUDDHISM

It may be that the beginnings of Buddhist monasticism owed more to the charismatic appeal of a leader called the Buddha (the Enlightened One) than to a "psychological malaise" brought on by social, economic, and political change.[4] At the very least, if we concluded that a psychological malaise was what the Buddha took as the starting point of his analysis of the human condition, we would be imposing modern categories on unfamiliar ancient experiences.

THE BUDDHA AND THE ASCETIC IDEAL

A noted nineteenth-century scholar of Indian Buddhism began his discussion of the Buddhist monastic Order (*sangha*) as follows:

> In many countries and at various times there were men who, dissatisfied with the condition of society around them or disappointed in their dearest expectation, fled the bustle, troubles, deceptive pleasures and wickedness of the world in order to seek in solitude or in the company of sympathizers quietude and peace of mind. Nowhere the conditions are so favorable for the development of the anachoret [anchorite] and monastic life as in India. Climate, institutions, the contemplative bent of the national mind, all tended to facilitate the growth of a persuasion that the highest aims of human life and real felicity cannot be obtained but by seclusion from the busy world, by undisturbed pious exercises, and by a certain amount of mortification.[5]

This broad generalization about the coincidence of factors leading to the rise of monasticism in India can be debated, but there is no doubt that Buddhism developed in an ethos favorable to ascetic ideals.

The Buddha (traditional dates: 563–483 B.C.E.) taught in the kingdoms of northern India known then as Magadha and Kosala, located roughly in the area bordered by the modern Benares, Patna, and Gaya in the states of Uttara Pradesh and Bihar. It was an area in which ascetic movements competed for adherents. The Buddha himself is reported to have studied with a teacher of Yoga, to have mortified his body to the point of starvation in his quest for truth, and, after gaining a following of his own, to have distinguished his path from that of more extreme ascetical groups such as the Jains and Ajivakas.[6]

The relationship between a religious movement and the era in which it is born is always complex, but we can say at a minimum that early Buddhism was part of an exuberant flowering of religious groups, many of which were ascetic and monastic in character. Several factors contributed to the emergence in Northern India of new religious ideals and communities embodying those ideals: traditional tribal identity was challenged by new monarchical states; population increased with improvements in agriculture; towns grew, the economy became more diversified with the use of money, leisure time expanded; Brahmanical and non-Brahmanical indigenous traditions increasingly interacted. In short, the Buddha lived in a betwixt-and-between time, when one world view and its ethos were breaking down and another was emerging.

The historical beginnings of Indian Buddhist monasticism will be treated in chapter 3. There we shall see Buddhism as one of several ascetic movements sharing the same milieu. Our present task is to see how the early Buddhist ascetic ideal is exemplified in the founder of the tradition (the Buddha), rationalized by his teachings (the *dharma*), and instituted by his early followers (the *sangha*).

"Tying the air into knots"

Not everyone today would agree that the Buddha personifies an ascetic ideal, nor did everyone in his own time. The legends recounting the Buddha's six-year quest for an understanding of the nature of reality emphasize his rejection of extreme austerities and his adoption of a more moderate set of practices:

> The future Buddha, thinking "I will carry austerity to the uttermost," tried various plans, such as living on one sesamum seed or on one grain of rice a day, and even ceased taking nourishment altogether. . . . By this lack of nourishment his body became emaciated to the last degree, and lost its golden color, and became black, and his thirty-two physical characteristics as a Great Being became obscured. . . . Now the six years which the Great Being thus spent in austerities were like time spent in endeavoring to tie the air into knots. And coming to the decision, "These austerities are not the way to enlightenment," he went begging through villages and market-towns for ordinary material food, and lived upon it. And his thirty-two physical characteristics as a Great Being again appeared, and the color of his body became like unto gold.[7]

Trying to tie the air into knots is clearly a pointless activity. The Buddha's way specifically rejects the exercise of extreme austerities because they undermine bodily health without producing enlightenment. Compared with the life of the ordinary person in the world, however, the Buddha's path is ascetic. One becomes a mendicant or "homeless truth-seeker" cut off from dependence upon the support and reward provided by the world. An early Buddhist text contrasts the way of the mendicant with the life of the householder:

> Full of hindrances is household life, a path for the dust of passion. Free as the air is the life of him who has renounced all worldly things. How difficult it is for the man who dwells at home to live the higher life in all its fullness, in all its purity, in all its bright perfection! Let me then cut off my hair and beard, let me clothe myself in the orange-colored robes, and let me go forth from the household life into the homeless state.
>
> When he has thus become a recluse he lives self-restrained by that restraint that should be binding on a recluse. Uprightness is his delight, and he sees danger in the least of those things he should avoid. He adopts, and trains himself in the precepts. He encompasses himself with good deeds in act and word. Pure are his means of livelihood, good is his conduct, guarded the door of his senses. Mindful and self-possessed he is altogether happy.[8]

The Buddha fashioned just such a mendicant path for himself. The legends describe the pleasant luxury of a princely upbringing, protected from all experience of life's pain and suffering by a royal father who lavished the world's rewards on his only son. The gods, well aware of the promised fate of the future Buddha, fashioned for the young prince Siddhartha a dramatic encounter with the fleeting nature of the world's pleasures. One day while driving through his private gardens Siddhartha happens upon Four Sights: a decrepit old person, one who was diseased, a corpse, and a mendicant truth-seeker.

Shocked into awareness that life in the world—even a prince's life "on top of the world"—is characterized by old age, sickness, and death, he decides to dedicate himself to a quest for a goal not limited by sensory perceptions about the nature of the world. After six years of searching he achieves this end, characterized in the Pali texts of Theravada Buddhism by the following formula: "Thus set free, there arises the knowledge of his emancipation, and he knows, 'Rebirth has been destroyed. The higher life has been fulfilled. What had to be done has been accomplished. After this present life there will be no beyond!'"

The goal was not easily won. The search concluded only after a final battle with the pleasures and rewards of the mundane world of the senses personified in the forces of the god Mara, the Buddhist equivalent of Satan. As Joseph Campbell points out, the rite of passage narrated in this legend is a classical example of the hero myth, in which a hero like Prometheus or the Buddha passes from the ordinary to the extraordinary after winning a decisive victory and then returns from this conquest with the power to bestow boons on others.[9]

The Middle Way

The Buddha's own life history outlines such a heroic, religious vocation, an exemplification of the ascetic ideal. He embodies the truth (*dharma*), for he has been victorious in achieving it and the power it represents. His moderate asceticism—if we may call it that—does not create the power represented by the *dharma*, but is the medium through which that power is realized in his own life. In Buddhism, the ascetic ideal and the new conception of religious self-identity coincide. As we shall see, there is no such clear coincidence in Christianity. The realization of a new truth (*dharma*) and the adoption of a Middle Way for its realization are synthesized in the same person—the Buddha. The Buddha, therefore, does nothing less than present a new conception of the religious person.

This new conception certainly did not spring out of or into a void. The Buddha's model of religious self-identity is indebted especially to Indian ascetic traditions, though mostly by way of contrast to them.[10] The Buddha counters an ascetic tradition characterized by extreme austerities and the belief that these austerities produce supernatural powers of great value. Tension between the Buddha's new conception of religious vocation and the old ascetic ideals has characterized the entire history of Buddhism. On the one hand, the Buddha is perceived primarily as a teacher of *dharma* or Truth. On the other hand, however, he is venerated as an ascetic who has acquired supernormal mental and physical powers elevating him to a superhuman status, which leads to a cult of Buddha relics and Buddha images.

The Buddha as miraculous wonderworker appears in the following episode. Here he exercises his psychic powers to destroy the psychic power of a serpent in the fire room of a matted-hair ascetic, Kassapa of Uruvela, to whom we shall have occasion to refer at greater length in chapter 3.

Then the Lord, having entered the fire-room, having laid down a grass mat, sat down cross-legged keeping his back erect, having caused mindfulness to be present in front of him. Then that serpent saw that the Lord had entered, and seeing this, pained, afflicted, he blew forth smoke. Then it occurred to the Lord: "What now if I, without destroying this serpent's skin and hide and flesh and ligaments and bones and the marrow of the bones, were to master [his] heat by heat?"

Then the Lord, having worked a work of psychic power, blew forth smoke. Then that serpent, not conquering anger, blazed up. The Lord, having attained the condition of heat, also blazed up. When both were in flames, the fire-room became as though burning, ablaze, in flames. . . .

Then the Lord at the end of that night, without having destroyed that serpent's skin and hide and flesh and ligaments and bones and the marrow of the bones, having mastered [his] heat by heat, having placed him in his bowl, showed him to the matted-hair ascetic, Uruvela Kassapa.[11]

The Buddha is perceived here as an ascetic who through his magical power is able to counter the power represented by the serpent. The references to mindfulness and anger suggest an interpretation more consistent with the model of the Buddha as a teacher of the *dharma*. This story illustrates the resistance of the old ascetic ideals to the more moderate religious life proposed by the Buddha, and the eventual success of the latter. After additional miraculous wonders, Kassapa and his followers are converted to the Buddha's path.

The Buddha set forth a new religious model that in effect transformed an earlier and more extreme form of asceticism into a Middle Way, which for two and one-half millennia has appealed to the minds and hearts of millions of people in Asia and throughout the world. Buddhism has evolved into many different forms, accompanied by differing conceptions of the Buddha. Yet at the core of the tradition stands the vision of an Enlightened One who defined a special religious vocation that promised an extraordinary way-of-being-in-the-world.

THE DHARMA AS THE RATIONALIZATION OF THE IDEAL

Dharma is the teaching of the Buddha. On another level, however, *dharma* is the truth this teaching seeks to represent. The Buddha is the personification of *dharma* as the truth, and *dharma* as the Buddha's teaching is the rationalization of that truth. The ascetic ideal is thoroughly consistent with the Buddhist conception of the world, humankind's place in that world, and the ultimate, salvific goal—all of which are rationalized in the teachings of the Buddha, namely, his *dharma*.

The essence of the Buddha's teaching is said to have been presented in the First Discourse delivered after his enlightenment to five of his former disciples in the Deer Park outside of Benares. These disciples had deserted Siddhartha when he had given up the practice of extreme austerities, but upon hearing the First Discourse they acknowledged his Buddhahood. Their initial ambivalence toward their teacher suggests again the tension between the moderate ascetic way proposed by the Buddha and the more extreme forms of asceticism advocated by certain Yogic and Jain teachers.

In the Discourse the Buddha first spells out the Middle Path between the two extremes of the "habitual practice . . . of those things whose attraction depends upon the passions . . . and the habitual practice of self-mortification which is painful, unworthy, and unprofitable."[12]

The four noble truths

The Buddha then sets forth the fundamental world view of Buddhism, which even today informs most of its major schools from Sri Lanka to Tibet and on to Japan, in terms of four categories (the Four Noble Truths):

> Now this, monks, is the noble truth of *suffering*: birth is suffering, old age is suffering, sickness is suffering, death is suffering, sorrow, lamentation, dejection, and despair are suffering. Contact with unpleasant things is suffering, not getting what one wishes is suffering. In short the five groups of grasping [human existence comprising these five components] are suffering.
>
> Now this, monks, is the noble truth of the *cause of suffering*: the craving which tends to rebirth, combined with pleasure and lust, finding pleasure here and there; namely, the craving for passions, the craving for existence, the craving for non-existence.
>
> Now this, monks, is the noble truth of the *cessation of suffering*, the cessation without a remainder of craving, the abandonment, forsaking, release, and non-attachment.
>
> Now this, monks, is the noble truth of the *way that leads to the cessation of suffering*: this is the Eightfold Way; namely, right views, right intention, right speech, right action, right livelihood, right effort, right mindfulness, right concentration.[13]

This summation of *dharma* or the Buddha's truth assesses the human situation as *dukkha*, a term most often translated as *suffering* or *pain*. *Dukkha*, however, means much more than either simply physical pain or mental suffering. It denotes the fundamentally unsatisfactory nature of sensory experience, of life in the mundane world.[14] Life is suffering because our ordinary worldly expectations are bound to end in disappointment. Youth becomes old age, pleasure turns into pain, happiness into sorrow, life leads to death, and so on. The root cause of our disappointment is desire or craving, which blinds us to the true nature of the world. The apparent world seems stable, so we base our expectations of the world on its presumed stability. This tendency inevitably leads to dissatisfaction since, in the biblical phrase, "the grass withers, the flower fades." In short, the world we perceive as permanence is impermanence.

Children's wanting what they are told they cannot have, or the nearly universal conviction that the grass is greener on the other side of the fence, when interpreted from the Buddhist perspective become the frantic desire to grasp an illusory permanence which, like a mirage, dissolves before our very eyes. Our inability to secure ultimate happiness within the everyday world enhances our desire for the unattainable until we are consumed by our own desire:

> Monks, everything is burning. And what, monks, is everything that is burning? The eye, . . . material shapes, . . . consciousness through the eye, . . . impingement on the eye—all are burning. With what is it burning? I say it is burning with the fire of passion, the fire of hatred, with the fire of stupidity; it is burning because of birth, aging, dying, because of grief, sorrow, suffering, lamentation and despair. [And so it is with the ear, the nose, the tongue, the body and the mind.][15]

The wheel of becoming

In the Buddhist analysis of the world, then, the individual is blinded to the true nature of things and is being consumed by a set of misconstrued and destructive drives—ambition, hatred, and lust. Suffering in this sense affects humankind's very being. We move like blind and wounded animals, worsening our situation by frantic and aimless thrashing. This condition has been symbolized most graphically in the Buddhist tradition by a wheel in whose hub three animals are depicted, representing greed, aversion, and delusion. These forces perpetuate the endless motion of the wheel—sensory experience dominated by ignorance, grasping, and attachment to objects of the senses, leading to a never-ending cycle of death and rebirth.

The Wheel of Rebirth or Wheel of Becoming, as it is called, in-corporates the teaching of the Four Noble Truths.[16] It vividly illus-trates humankind's bondage to the mundane or the realm of rebirth, a condition created by our ignorance of the true nature of the world. We live a conditioned existence. We are qualified by our body, sen-sations, perceptions, consciousness, and will (the five components of human existence). In particular we are limited by the composite of what we have become through our several existences, a compos-ite known in Buddhism as *karma*. The fourth noble truth points the way out of this Wheel of Becoming, a way in which the effects of attachment to the world of apparent realities created by our lack of awareness can be transcended.

The fourth noble truth, customarily called the Eightfold Path, summarizes the Buddha's way of moderate asceticism. It is struc-tured in terms of moral virtue, the practice of constant attentive-ness, and transcendent wisdom. It leads to the vision of things as they really are rather than as they appear to be, and, in turn, brings about the cessation of grasping. The final stage of the path cul-minates in a total reorientation from the bondage of ignorance and the continuous cycle of birth and death to a state of perfect free-dom. The fully realized person achieves an unconditioned state of being termed Nirvana. One early Buddhist view interprets Nirvana as Emptiness, a state beyond qualification, of infinite possibility, the end of the path leading from the conditioned to the unconditioned, the beginning of a new mode of life.

The Buddha's *dharma*, summarized above, sets forth an under-standing of human experience in the world, and charts a path to the attainment of a higher truth thoroughly consistent with the as-cetic ideal personified by the Buddha. The teachings rationalize or justify—indeed, make mandatory—an ascetic relationship with the world of ordinary sense experience. One may change living condi-tions with relative ease, but to bring about a fundamental change of being demands an arresting of all former habits and the structur-ing of new perspectives. It is no less than a con-version, the dra-matic shift from the princely Siddhartha to the mendicant Sakyamuni (sage of the Sakya clan). Such a change is described in the following similes:

Just . . . as if a man were bound in a prison house, and after a time
he should be set free from his bonds, safe and sound, and without
any confiscation of his goods. . . .

Just . . . as if a man were a slave, not his own master, subject
to another, unable to go whither he would; and after a time he should
be emancipated from that slavery, become his own master, not subject to others, a free man, free to go whither he would. . . .

Just as if a man, rich and prosperous, were to find himself on a
long road, in a desert, where no food was, but much danger; and
after a time were to find himself out of the desert, arrived safe, on
the borders of his village, in security and peace. . . .[17]

THE MONASTIC LIFE AS THE INSTITUTIONALIZATION OF THE IDEAL

The life and teachings of the Buddha offer precedent for two institu-
tionalizations of the ascetic ideal: eremitic, the homeless monk wandering alone in uninhabited or sparsely inhabited regions; and
coenobitic, a community of monks living simply and in obedience
to the instruction and rule of the founder. The Buddha himself
sought the path of the lonely wanderer during most of his pre-
enlightenment period. Yet, much as the first act of Jesus after his
forty days in the wilderness was to call his disciples, the first act
of the Buddha was to attract followers both through his presence
and through his teachings. The legends surrounding the Buddha's
enlightenment recount his own inner struggle over the decision
whether to share his newly found wisdom with others or merely
to keep it for his own self-realization. The sharing of his message
or teaching becomes one of the principal functions of the community that gathers about the founder.

Ordination into the community of monks in Thailand serves to
illustrate the way in which the monastic life institutionalizes the
ascetic ideal personified in the life of the Buddha and rationalized
by his teachings. The ordination ceremony dramatizes the movement from ordinary mundane existence to the betwixt-and-between
state of the religious vocation.

First, the ordinand's hair and eyebrows are shaved. He is then
bathed and clothed in white robes. In giving up the distinguishing
marks of the male householder's life, he enters a neutral or transi-
tional state.[18] Proceeding into the ordination hall he is tested by the

assembled monks before being dressed in the traditional saffron-colored robes and given the begging bowl as a sign of his new status.

The new monk is called a *bhikkhu*, a beggar or almsman, because he has given up a conventional mode of life and its ordinary means of support. He has entered into a community whose ideal purpose is the pursuit of the same enlightenment realized by the Buddha. He has enacted the Buddha's own going-forth even to the point of casting aside his sexual identity and the customary productive mode of livelihood associated with being a male householder. He has taken on a new vocation, a new identity symbolized by the assumption of a new monastic name. He is now like all who have given up the signs of their former existence and adopted the ascetic ideal of the Buddha.

"Fare lonely as rhinoceros"

This ideal is acted out in its eremitic form by those monks who choose to spend most of their time living by themselves or in small groups outside monastic compounds. The praises of eremiticism are sung in the *Sutta Nipata*, one of the oldest portions of the Pali canon of Theravada Buddhism.

> Put by the rod for all that lives,
> Nor harm thou anyone thereof;
> Long not for son—how then for friend?
> Fare lonely as rhinoceros.

> Love cometh from companionship;
> In wake of love upsurges ill;
> Seeing the bane that comes of love,
> Fare lonely as rhinoceros.

> In ruth for all his bosom friends,
> A man, heart-chained, neglects the goal;
> Seeing this fear in fellowship,
> Fare lonely as rhinoceros.

> The deer untethered roams the wild
> Whithersoe'er it lists for food:
> Seeing the liberty, wise man,
> Fare lonely as rhinoceros.

> Casting aside the household gear,
> As sheds the coral-tree its leaves,

With home-ties cut and vigorous,
Fare lonely as rhinoceros.

Crave not for tastes, but free of greed,
Moving with measured step from house
To house support of none, none's thrall,
Fare lonely as rhinoceros.

Free everywhere, at odds with none,
And well content with this and that:
Enduring dangers and undismayed,
Fare lonely as rhinoceros.[19]

The eremitic ideal symbolized by the rhinoceros must have approximated the actual situation in the early days of the Buddha's teaching. As we shall see in chapter 3, the growth of the monastic Order (*sangha*) eventually led to the development of communal, long-term dwelling places. While communal life is the norm of Buddhist practice throughout Asia, a small minority of monks still follow the rhinoceros way of austerities. In the Theravada tradition of Southeast Asia these austerities number thirteen: (1) wearing robes made from refuse heaps, (2) having only three robes, (3) eating only food collected from almsrounds, (4) going from house to house and not choosing only the homes of relatives or wealthy persons, (5) eating only one meal a day, (6) eating only from the begging bowl and not a plate, (7) not eating more food than sufficient even when it is given by laypersons, (8) living in a secluded place away from towns and villages, (9 and 10) living under a tree without the shelter of a roof, (11) living in or near a graveyard or cremation ground, (12) being willing to sleep anywhere, (13) living in the three postures of standing, sitting, and walking, without lying down to sleep.[20]

As this list indicates, even the "austere practices" do not entail extreme forms of physical and mental self-mortification. Nevertheless, eremitic monks have attracted the admiration of Buddhist laypersons, who perceive them as leading lives more closely approximating the ascetic ideal. It has been observed that in recent years there has even been an increase in eremitical, strict ascetical monastic practice in parts of Buddhist South and Southeast Asia. There may be a correlation between this type of monastic life and highly stratified societies. The monk, from this point of view, gains a remarkable social status through his very rejection of the rigidity of the customary social and economic structures, as in the case of modern Sri Lanka, for example.[21] Similar observations have been made about medieval Europe, a stratified society with elaborate ascetical orders.

Although the sociological context for the development of the ascetic ideal should be taken into account, the inherent appeal of this ideal should not be minimized. So far as we know, ascetical groups in the age of the Buddha did not arise within highly stratified societies. Indeed, an opposing argument has been made for the rise of monastic life in India in the sixth century B.C.E., namely, that it was a response to the breakdown of traditional political and social structures.[22]

Furthermore, in Thailand, a more loosely structured society than that of Sri Lanka, the eremitic monk is accorded a very high degree of veneration by the populace. For example, popular respect for the former abbot of a monastery (Wat Phra Bat Dak Pha) in Lamphun province, northern Thailand, was fairly typical of the attitude of laypersons toward monks thought to be exceptionally holy. Laity from all over the country came to bring gifts or simply to pay him their respects. His status as a holy man did not depend on his being abbot of a monastery, but rather on his many years as an eremitic monk who rigorously practiced the teachings of the Buddha. As abbot he continued to practice meditation regularly, and despite the rapid development of his monastery he resided in a simple hut at the edge of the monastery compound. In short, he sought to infuse his role as the head of a thriving monastery with the ideals of the ascetic path more nearly represented by the wandering mendicant.

The sangha

The norm of monastic life throughout Buddhist Asia is now collective. Even during the lifetime of the Buddha himself, coenobiticism was on the rise; and according to the Buddhist tradition, rules of communal conduct were set forth by the Buddha. These rules, while less rigorous than eremitic practice, nevertheless prescribe an ascetical way quite distinct from the style of life of the Buddhist layperson. For example, while the laity are enjoined to observe five fundamental moral precepts (no taking of life, no illicit sex, no lying, no stealing, no drinking of intoxicants), the monk vows to uphold more than two hundred rules of monastic conduct regulating his relationships with laypersons and the other ordained brethren, his use of money, the possessions he can acquire, the way in which he adorns his body, and so on. Thus, the coenobitic monk in countries like Burma and Thailand is accorded an equally high degree of respect. While this respect comes with the *office* of the monk, its degree is calculated in terms of the personal integrity of the particular individual. Thus, while the monastic Order as a collective body ideally represents the ascetic ideal personified by the Buddha, everyone recognizes that in practice some monks approximate the ideal more nearly than do others.

The monastic Order is a body of monks and sometimes nuns who have chosen a distinctive style of life modeled on the Buddha and his teachings. Yet in Buddhism the *sangha* in its broadest sense includes laymen and laywomen as well. This concept of *sangha* is known as the Sangha of the Four Quarters and includes monks, nuns, laymen, and laywomen. In the ideal sense, all segments are to lead lives dedicated to the pursuit of the teachings of the Buddha. In the midst of the universal *sangha* the monk has the particular role or obligation to be a living presence of the ascetic ideal represented by the founder.

As Buddhism grew and developed throughout the ages and in different cultures, its institutional form necessarily changed, becoming more complex and varied, responding to new currents of thought and competing traditions. Buddhist monks and institutions became inextricably involved in social, economic, and political structures and contexts. Monks became advisers to kings and, in the case of Tibet, rulers of the country. In some sectarian traditions the ascetic ideal embedded in the disciplinary rules and practices became obscured. Monks married, monasteries became sizable landholders, and in highly esoteric forms of meditation sexio-yogic practices were appropriated. Still, it might be argued that all of these developments were but counterpoints to the ascetic ideal embodied in the life of the Buddha and the structure of the early monastic Order. This ideal has provided an uncompromising vision of life, challenging subservience to the limited goals of the getting-and-spending world, and has functioned throughout the history of Buddhism to integrate the tradition around a common core at the heart of its wide-ranging diversity.

CHRISTIANITY

After the Buddha achieved enlightenment, he responded to those who asked what had happened, "I am awake." Jesus instructed his followers, "Keep awake, then; for you do not know on what day your Lord is to come."[23] Both Buddhism and Christianity use the metaphor of wakefulness, but the two traditions mean something different by it.

Buddhist wakefulness is the individual's own resolution of suffering and tension. Christian wakefulness heightens tension, anticipating a resolution promised for the future. This resolution, which may include intensified suffering, depends not on individual achievement but on renewed divine intervention. Both the Buddhist and the Christian have awakened from delusion. The Buddhist now realizes that the flux of events does not conceal an ultimate being or reality. The Christian now realizes that the sequence of events is not a flux but is God's story moving toward its preordained climax.

The awakened Buddhist and the wakeful Christian may both establish for themselves ascetic styles of life, but they have their own reasons for doing so. The two asceticisms are embedded in distinctly different patterns of religious thought and values.

As we have seen, not all Buddhists agree on just what the ascetic ideal means in practical terms. All would agree, however, that the Buddhist conception of the world requires some renunciation of material accumulation and some detachment from secular affairs. To be a Buddhist is to acknowledge that the ascetic life as the Buddha embodied it is the ideal life.

For a very long time—almost fifteen hundred years—the same could have been said of the relation of Christianity to the ascetic ideal.

JESUS AND PAUL

In the earliest Christian generations the ideal of detachment was grounded in the conviction that Christ would soon return. As the apostle Paul puts it, you should be unencumbered with worldly attachments so you will be ready. But the return of Christ at some point in the future is not all that renders attachments unwise. Paul adds that even now the very form of this world is passing away.[24] Attachment is no security if what you are attached to is dissolving. Despite Paul's critical assessment, the world remains for him the good creation of a good God, though there is the ever-present danger that human beings will succumb to the illusion that the world belongs to them. In Paul's judgment, asceticism is a remedy not for ignorance but for pride. Our problem is not that we think more highly of the world than we ought to think, but that we think too highly of ourselves.

The traditions about Jesus include a number of sayings that appear to rest on an ascetic ideal. He praises those who have renounced family ties to follow him, declares taking up one's cross to be the sign of discipleship, puts forth the challenging paradox of losing one's life in order to find it. He instructs his followers to consider not Solomon in all his glory, but the birds of the air and the lilies of the field. He tells of a man who dies just when his barns are bursting with grain—what then does he have? The disciples, when called to follow Jesus, simply drop everything, instantly. Challenged at his trial to say whether he is a king, Jesus replies enigmatically that his kingship is not of this world.[25]

However, there were contemporaries who thought Jesus insufficiently ascetic to be a worthy religious leader:

> Now [John the Baptist's] disciples and the Pharisees were fasting; and people came and said to [Jesus]: "Why do John's disciples and the disciples of the Pharisees fast, but your disciples do not fast?"

We might have expected an answer similar to the Buddha's justification for moderate asceticism, especially from one who is reported to have said that the Sabbath was made for human beings, not the other way round. But what we find is a distinction between present and future proper behavior:

And Jesus said to them, "Can the wedding guests fast while the bridegroom is with them? As long as they have the bridegroom with them, they cannot fast. The days will come, when the bridegroom is taken away from them, and then they will fast in that day."[26]

This remark of Jesus illustrates a basic difference between Buddhism and Christianity, one with profound consequences for the two monastic traditions. The historical Buddha makes no claim to divine status; the truth is not absolutized in a particular historical person. So whatever is the ideal for the Buddha in his time is the ideal for everyone always. Christ (the title means Messiah, or Anointed One) has significance because of who he is—the bridegroom, not someone who awakened from the sleep of delusion into enlightenment—and the ideal is established in relation to him and his career. "When the time had fully come, God sent forth God's Son."[27] The ideal does not exist independently of him and of the history of salvation of which he is the culmination. What follows from this is ironical. The historical Buddha, who is simply a human being, is the embodiment of the ideal and the model for subsequent practice, while Jesus, who is believed to be God incarnate, has a reputation for being a glutton and a drunkard[28] and says that subsequent generations of his followers will have to live by a different standard.

To a degree remarkable enough to confirm the irony, Christian monastic tradition does not characteristically refer to Jesus as the ideal type of the monk.[29] Because Jesus and the Buddha relate in fundamentally different ways to the ascetic ideal, an analysis of that ideal in Christianity necessarily covers a wider range of history. The Buddha was a monk, so Buddhists must decide how they will relate to asceticism. Jesus was not a monk, so Christians must first decide how much asceticism there is in Christianity to relate to. With Jesus' resurrection and inauguration of a new community for a new age, the question becomes not, How ascetic was Jesus? but rather, What is the proper character of life in this new age? Christian tradition has given a bewildering variety of answers to this question—some ascetic, some not.

The "imitation of Christ" motif is not totally lacking in Christian asceticism, of course. Paul points to the humility of Christ as the standard for Christian behavior:

> Do nothing from selfishness or conceit, but in humility count others better than yourselves. Let each of you look not only to [your] own interests, but also to the interests of others. Have this mind among yourselves, which you have in Christ Jesus, who, though he was in the form of God, did not count equality with God a thing to be grasped, but emptied himself, taking the form of a servant, being born in the likeness of human beings. And being found in human form he humbled himself and became obedient unto death, even death on a cross.[30]

This theological point concerning the condescension of one who was "in the form of God" acquires a more immediate ethical bearing in the story of Satan's temptation of Jesus in the wilderness. There, after fasting forty days, the Son of God rejects three forms of power—miracle (he refuses to turn stones into bread), mystery (he will not leap from the pinnacle of the temple in order to provoke a dramatic angelic rescue), and authority (he turns down the devil's offer of rule over all the kingdoms of the world).[31] The implication of the story is unmistakable. If Christ himself, who has every right to these powers, refuses them, how much more ought his followers to practice renunciation. Paul's admonition, "Be imitators of me as I am of Christ,"[32] sounds rather arrogant on first hearing, but if he had the temptation story, or something like it, in mind, the remark becomes a shorthand expression for the ascetic ideal in Christianity.

Not everybody thought Paul a champion of asceticism. His doctrine of justification by faith, with its insistence that we can do nothing to gain extra credit with God, was apparently thought by some to entail lawlessness: "Are we to continue in sin that grace may abound?"[33] Paul's conviction that obedience is the only proper response to grace was grounded, more than he realized, in his upbringing in the Jewish legal and ritual tradition, and what seemed self-evident to him was strange logic to many of his gentile converts.

World Denunciation and World Renunciation

The tensions already evident in Paul's lifetime increased in subsequent generations. The high-pitched expectation of Christ's return abated. Other motives moved to the center of Christian attitudes. The most significant challenge came from persons who presented themselves as true interpreters of Paul but who had in fact shifted the whole argument onto different ground.

Paul held that the world was in rebellion against its Creator, and salvation was a process of restoration or renovation. The world was infested with spiritual hosts of wickedness—demons whose characteristics would be elaborately charted in the experience of Christian monks in later centuries—but they were clearly invaders in a territory that belonged to the true God.

Mortician or midwife?

In the second century there were many groups, known to modern scholars as Gnostics, who held that the creator was in rebellion against the true God. In the gnostic view, the cosmic spectacle is a pitched battle between spiritual persons on the one side, in league with the true God, and the created order on the other side. Paul's distinctions between Law and Gospel, Old Adam and New Adam, spiritual infants and spiritual adults, were all cut loose from his fundamental theology, and Paul was set forth as the founder of an asceticism that was world-renouncing in the most blatant, uncompromising sense.

According to the gnostic Gospel of Thomas, "Jesus said: He who has known the world has found a corpse, and he who has found a corpse, the world is not worthy of him." Paul had written, "We know that the whole creation has been groaning in travail together until now."[34] From the gnostic perspective, Paul had described the symptoms but had made a faulty diagnosis: he mistook death throes for birth pangs. If Paul's understanding had been complete, he would have recognized that the Christian's true spiritual vocation is to be to the world not a midwife but a mortician.

The sources for the gnostic contempt of the created order are probably as many as they are certainly obscure. For an analysis of the ascetic ideal and its role in the development of Christianity, it is particularly instructive to note traces of Greek philosophy in Gnosticism.

To an extent hard for us today to imagine, philosophy in the ancient world was expected really to influence the way people lived. Religion was thought to be a superficial matter of outward observances. Philosophy converted people, led them to reorient their whole selves. Virtually every Greek philosophical school held up a moderately ascetic ideal. The key concept was *sophrosyne*— moderation, evenness, avoidance of extremes.[35] The world is not a corpse, but it is a vale of shadows, and the wise person will tread warily.

The Gnostics treat Greek philosophy as they treat Paul: certain distinctions are pressed far beyond the qualified, nuanced limits in which they were originally proposed. Plato's distinction between reality and illusion becomes total alienation. Plato talked about the participation of sensible (and inferior) reality in ideal reality. For the Gnostics, this world is not the reflection of anything good, true, and beautiful. The terms they use are separation, distance, ignorance. The Neoplatonists filled the void between God and the world with ranks of spiritual beings to show that God and the world are connected, while the Gnostics kept inserting more and more beings in order to spread God and the world further apart.

Greek philosophy, especially the Platonic tradition, flowed into Christianity through many channels and shaped the ascetic ideal in a variety of ways. Gnosticism isolated the philosophical dualism from the finely balanced context in which Plato had put it, and transformed it into a religiously charged contempt for the world. In the social dislocations and political upheavals of the late Roman Empire the gnostic message of salvation by a hitherto alien God had great appeal. To many observers Christian doctrine appeared to be world-denouncing, not just world-renouncing.

Manichaeism

Gnosticism carried certain features of Platonism and early Christian asceticism to an extreme, and in so doing helped prepare the ground for a movement that was to have a deep and persistent influence on Christian attitudes toward the world. Manichaeism used to be thought a full expression of ancient Persian religion, a quite foreign importation into the Roman religious ferment. But a recently discovered biography of Mani, who lived in the late third century C.E., makes it clear that he was born into a Christian gnostic sect.[36] Mani's accomplishment was to correlate his gnostic heritage with traditional Persian dualism. The cosmic drama is heightened as two equally substantial realms, one of Evil and one of Good, eternally struggle with each other.

One of the institutional expressions of Manichaeism was monasticism; Manichaean monasteries were flourishing in China in the Middle Ages.[37] And one of the most influential Christian ascetics of all time spent nine years as a Manichee. Augustine (354–430 C.E.), bishop of Hippo Regius in North Africa (397–430), who took the momentous step of organizing his cathedral clergy into a quasi-monastic community, spent the early part of his adult life persuaded that Mani had made sense of the world.

Plato himself rescued Augustine from the Gnostic/Manichaean distortion of the Platonic tradition. In Plato Augustine discovered a way of thinking and feeling that allowed primacy to the Good and accounted for Evil as a defection from Good. It became possible once again to understand asceticism as a response to the fallen condition of the world, not as a rejection of the world itself.[38] The Christian midwife ousted the Gnostic mortician.

Augustine saw that Manichaeism was finally static, and that it fed the human desire to evade responsibility. Spiritual growth was at best a theoretical abstraction in the world of Mani. Augustine, like Paul, located the human problem in the will, not in the material world. Asceticism was a preparation for struggle, not an antidote against defilement.

It took more than the authority of an Augustine to counter the attractiveness of the Manichaean motive for world-renunciation. And so ecclesiastical law through the centuries has set itself against any asceticism grounded in contempt. A piece of legislation that dates from about Augustine's time puts the issue in the most straightforward terms:

> If any bishop, priest, or deacon, or any one of the sacerdotal list, abstains from marriage, or meat, or wine, not by way of religious restraint, but as abhorring them, forgetting that God made all things very good, and that God made human beings male and female, and

blaspheming the work of creation, let him be corrected, or else be deposed, and cast out of the church. In like manner a layman.[39]

In parallel with the Buddhist Middle Way, abhorrence was forbidden but "religious restraint" was encouraged, and throughout Christian history most authoritative voices, especially bishops and councils, have avoided the Manichaean pitfall while making it perfectly clear that the ascetic life is the calling of a fully committed Christian. Athanasius, Bishop of Alexandria (328–373 C.E.), insisted that the married state is no sin, and that it brings forth fruit thirtyfold. Continence, however, brings forth fruit a hundredfold. "For there are two ways of life, as touching these matters. The one the more moderate and ordinary, I mean marriage; the other angelic and unsurpassed, namely virginity." And twelve hundred years later the Council of Trent anathematized anyone who either affirms that "the married state is superior to the virgin or celibate state," or denies that "it is better and more blessed to remain in virginity or celibacy than to be joined in marriage."[40]

FORMS OF THE IDEAL: THE HERMITAGE AND THE COENOBIUM

The life of religious restraint can be lived in a variety of ways. In Christianity, as in Buddhism, the two classic options are the isolated, hermit (eremitic) life and life in community (coenobitic). As we shall see in the next chapter when discussing the historical origins of Christian monasticism, the two patterns were established almost simultaneously. Monastic tradition offers many attempts to work out a theoretical compromise between the eremitic and coenobitic forms, the most common being the reservation of the hermit life for those who have spent a long time in training in a community. This resolution implies, however, that the individual life is spiritually superior to life together.

"We need one another"

One major monastic legislator, St. Basil of Caesarea in Asia Minor (c. 330–379 C.E.), rules out any claim that the hermit life is the advanced course for spiritual adepts. He gives several reasons: (1) "None of us is self-sufficient even as regards bodily needs, . . . so in the solitary life both what we have becomes useless and what we lack becomes unprocurable, since God the Creator ordained that we need one another." (2) Living separately, a person "will not even recognize his/her defects readily, not having anyone to reprove him/her and to set him/her right with kindness and compassion." (3) There are many divine commandments, and a group can perform them, while an individual, by doing one commandment, is hindered from another; "for example, when we visit a sick person we cannot receive a stranger; when we bestow and distribute the necessaries of life—especially when these ministrations have to be performed at a distance—we neglect work; so that the greatest commandment of all and that which conduces to salvation is neglected, and neither is the hungry fed nor the naked clothed." (4) "Wherewith shall a person show humility, if he/she has no one in comparison with whom to show himself/herself humble?"[41] Basil has understood that Christian virtues are by their nature communal, and he sees the practical implications of Paul's image of the church as a body[42]—what one member does is as if done by the other members as well. For Basil, the primary aim of ascetic renunciation is to enhance the effectiveness of the church, not to purify the soul or mortify the flesh.

Despite Basil's vigorous argument for the superiority of communal life, Eastern Orthodox Christianity has never been able to divest itself of special admiration for ascetics who are on their own. But if coenobitic monks dream of the eremitic life, hermits, for their part, usually have a hard time maintaining their isolation, since their very reputation for holiness attracts disciples. There is gentle humor in the story of Saint Antony, the first Christian monk, who keeps moving farther and farther into the desert, trying—unsuccessfully—to evade the crowds flocking around him.

Christianity is too complex in its origins and subsequent developments for there to be any neat conclusion to the question, Which expression of asceticism is the authentic one? The motives of service to others on the one hand and the conquest of self on the other hand are not easy to balance, and it may be that Basil's argument needs to be stretched so that the hermits themselves appear as serving one of the functions of the body of Christ. There is a certain implausibility in using the same term *monk* to refer to fifth-century saints sitting atop pillars for decades at a time, exposed to the scorching sun of the Syrian desert, and to twentieth-century university presidents in Minnesota, but they are linked spirits, both drawing on the rich and highly differentiated tradition of Christian renunciation. That they strike us as so different is a reminder that our definition of the ascetic ideal must be flexible. That they would insist on their common identity is a reminder that there is, in fact, a Christian ascetic ideal.

ASCETICISM CHALLENGED: THE REFORMATION

> Speaking now in behalf of the church's liberty and the glory of baptism, I feel myself in duty bound to set forth publicly the counsel I have learned under the Spirit's guidance. I therefore counsel those in high places in the churches . . . to abolish all those vows and religious orders, or at least not to approve and extol them. If they will not do this, then I counsel all who would be assured of their salvation to abstain from all vows, above all from the major and lifelong vows. I give this counsel especially to teenagers and young people.[43]

Martin Luther (1483–1548 C.E.) was one of those the Council of Trent had in mind as denying the spiritual superiority of the celibate state. Indeed, Luther declared explicitly that the celibate state might be spiritually inferior:

> I advise no one to enter any religious order or the priesthood, indeed, I advise everyone against it—unless he . . . understands that the works of monks and priests, however holy and arduous they may be, do not differ one whit in the sight of God from the works of the rustic laborer in the field or the woman going about her household tasks, but that all works are measured before God by faith alone. . . . Indeed, the menial housework of a manservant or maidservant is often more acceptable to God than all the fastings and other works of a monk or priest, because the monk or priest lacks faith. Since, therefore, vows nowadays seem to tend only to the glorification of works and to pride, it is to be feared that there is nowhere less of faith and of the church than among the priests, monks, and bishops.[44]

There is no small irony in Luther's being the one to challenge the ascetic ideal. He was an Augustinian monk, and his religious revolution grew out of his study of Paul. In other words, his deepest affinities were with two of Christianity's strongest advocates of the ascetic ideal.

Luther became suspicious of asceticism on two grounds. First, it seemed inextricably linked to a more-or-less Manichaean denial of the goodness of the created world. Luther was by training and employment a professor of Old Testament, and the ancient Israelite love of the world had worked its way into the marrow of his thinking and feeling. God had instituted marriage and procreation as a blessing, and the world of everyday occurrences—the world of crafts, of commerce, of eating and drinking, of sex—was the arena in which human beings were expected to work out their salvation with fear and trembling. If someone wanted to live a life of separation and contemplation, Luther would not object:

> I am indeed far from forbidding or discouraging anyone who may desire to vow something privately and of his own free choice; for I would not altogether despise and condemn vows. But I would most strongly advise against setting up and sanctioning the making of vows as a public mode of life. It is enough that every one should have the private right to take a vow at his own peril; but to commend the vowing of vows as a public mode of life—this I hold to be most pernicious to the church and to simple souls.[45]

The *vowed* life: this is the key to Luther's other major objection to the ascetic ideal. In the long stretch of centuries since Augustine's time the church had elaborated a penitential system which eventually became a kind of bartering with God. In Luther's view, ascetic practices carried out in fulfillment of vows had become especially odious instances of the human attempt to buy salvation. Athanasius had said that the celibate life would bring forth three and one-third times the spiritual fruit of the married life (a hundredfold as against thirtyfold). By Luther's time it was commonly assumed that those fruits could be exchanged in the divine marketplace for that much more credit with God. Paul had advised asceticism as a hedge against pride. Luther saw it having become a prime vehicle for the ultimate in human pride, the confidence that we can earn our way back into God's favor.

John Calvin (1509–64 C.E.) adopted Luther's fundamental principles, but being a man of much more austere temperament, he portrayed an ideal of life which, without vows, included strict discipline and severe self-control. In the Old Testament, where Luther had found a robust affirmation of the goodness of the world, Calvin found the model for a meticulously organized community in which priests had extraordinary civil as well as religious authority. Calvin intensified Luther's declaration that all sorts of vocations are divinely sanctioned, and insisted that one's calling itself required many renunciations.

The development of the Calvinist tradition is a complex story, but even in Calvin himself there are already the elements of what Max Weber, in *The Protestant Ethic and the Spirit of Capitalism*, would call "inner-worldly asceticism." The delay of present satisfactions in the interest of future profit, and, more generally, the rationally calculated adaptation of means to ends, is seen by Weber as a secularizing of what had been for a millennium and more the Christian ideal of spiritual asceticism.[46]

The Protestant Reformers insisted that there is no spiritual elite group. With God's sovereign grace governing the whole scheme of doctrine, there was in theory no style of life with more claim than any other to divine sanction. In practice, elites did emerge. In the Calvinist tradition the respectable and successful entrepreneur, the pillar of the community, became the ideal type, while in Lutheranism the pastor and his family became the model of Christian living. The businessman and the clergyman were expected to be frugal and unostentatious, but in no major way was their life one of more renunciation than that of most of their fellows. Whatever remained in Protestantism of the traditional ascetic ideal, it was certainly not invested in the monk or nun committed to poverty, chastity, and obedience.

The Reformation was of course far more than Luther and Calvin, and some expressions of the reforming impulse gave rise to asceticisms as rigorous as any to be found in previous ages of Christianity. With such groups as the Hutterites (sixteenth century) and Shakers (eighteenth century), intense expectation of Christ's imminent return, or near-Manichaean contempt for the world, had effects similar to the ones they had had earlier.

Still, there can be no doubt that the Protestant Reformation makes an account of the ascetic ideal in Christianity more problematical than it would otherwise be. Prior to the sixteenth century there was certainly no unanimity on the details of the ascetic ideal, but there was hardly any significant exception to the rule that everybody acknowledged some kind of superiority in a life that had renounced wealth, marriage, and individual autonomy. Not everybody aspired to be a monk or nun, but everybody knew that those who did were the best Christians. Luther and Calvin thought that those who thus aspired were at best harmless and at worst serious threats to the integrity of Christian doctrine and the health of the Christian community.

AGAINST THE GRAIN: THE ASCETIC IDEAL TODAY

As we have seen, the initial Roman Catholic response to the Reformation attack was to reassert the spiritual superiority of traditional asceticism. In the centuries since the Council of Trent, Catholic monasticism has been subjected to severe stresses and even near extinction, as nationalism and Enlightenment rationalism, and indeed the whole collection of forces we call the modern world, have had their effect on the church as on all other institutions and values.

At the beginning of the nineteenth century a prediction that Christian monasticism, and with it the Christian ascetic ideal, would soon disappear from the earth would have seemed a sober judgment. By the century's end Marx's classification of religion as opium for the people, Nietzsche's savage assault on all Christian values, and the suspicion cast by Freud over the motives underlying most of the ideals traditionally espoused by Western civilization were fostering a climate in which asceticism appeared outmoded and perverse. What Luther had criticized as being at odds with the Gospel was denounced by the cultural arbiters of three and four generations ago as being at odds with genuine humanity. Like Father Zossima, they would have said that "a monk is not a special sort of person"; but where he went on to say, "a monk is simply what every person ought to be," they would have said, "a monk is just a particularly striking illustration of what is wrong with most people."

The ascetic ideal has not died, however. Despite all the celebrations of the secular meaning of the Gospel, despite all the declarations that Christianity has come of age and is fully compatible with both the affirmations and denials of the modern world, despite the consumerist spirituality that promises worldly success as the fruit of the Christian faith, there remains in many Christians a suspicion that some degree of renunciation is an ineradicable part of genuine Christianity.

There are many reasons for this. The Bible contains too much about renunciation for the principle to be put out of mind entirely. The modern world itself has notoriously failed to live up to the advance billing provided by some of its early prophets. The stark realities of economic contraction and limited natural resources are making some form of asceticism appear not an optional exercise for spiritual virtuosos, but a prescription for individual and community survival.

Underlying all these reasons is a shift in the perception of how Christianity and culture are related. From the time of the Reformation, especially in the Calvinist tradition and particularly in the United States, there has been a deeply felt concern to make society "Christian" in one or other specifiable sense. Confronted with the tidal forces of secularization—forces the Reformation itself helped unleash—many Christians concluded that the secularization forces themselves must be the agent by which God is acting in the world. The hope of Christianizing society has been maintained, though inverted, by the claim that the world is humanizing and refining Christianity. To admit that Christianity and the world march to very different drummers would be to abandon the long-held hope for a synchronization of Christianity and culture.

Indeed, to oppose everything would be to slip back into gnostic or Manichaean contempt. The pillar saints of Syria may be as much a distortion of the Christian tradition as is the "power of positive thinking," but they at least made clear that there is a Christian alternative to what the world calls reasonable and successful. And it is the perception of Christianity as an alternative, as something other than what any sensible person would rationally calculate to be advantageous, that helps most to explain the current interest in monasticism.

The monasteries which are growing fastest are the strictest ones, and virtually all monasteries today emphasize in their recruitment literature the toughness of their way of life. In such literature there are, to be sure, echoes of recent self-fulfillment fads, but there is also the warning that gratifications will not be instant. The whole portrayal of monasticism is in fundamentally countercultural terms. Until recently many Christians would have thought that was a very archaic way to present any form of Christian life. Now there is a growing conviction that Christianity is most truly itself when it is a minority and appears foolish in the eyes of the world.

To what extent is the ascetic ideal alive and well in Buddhist Asia? Or, are the developed (e.g., Japan) and developing (e.g., Thailand) countries of Asia striving so blindly to emulate the West that the traditions of Buddhist monasticism and asceticism have succumbed to rock music and designer jeans? The question cannot be easily answered.

The region we designate as Buddhist Asia includes many different countries throughout Southeast and East Asia. Marxist revolution in China, Vietnam, Laos, and Cambodia has decisively affected the plight of Buddhist institutions. While the Buddhist monastery will probably never recover the place it once had in these countries, some observers have noted that the disestablishment of Theravada Buddhism in Laos, for example, has enhanced those aspects of the tradition most closely associated with the ascetic ideal. It is also important to note that Buddhist monks and institutions played a crucial role in the early nationalist movements in Sri Lanka and Burma, not only because they represented traditional Lankan and Burman culture, but also because of the ascetic ideals they embodied.

The economic development of Asia both for and by the West has been one of the major features of Asian experience since the colonial period. How has the ascetic ideal of the Buddhist tradition survived that onslaught? Once again the answer is varied.

In Japan, one of the most economically powerful countries in the world, the Zen monastic tradition stands as a constant reminder of a more holistically integrated and authentically human way of life than capitulation to consumerism. In Thailand, informed and concerned Buddhists, both monks and laity, are advocating a Buddhist economics reflective of the ascetical ideals of nonattachment and equanimity. Reformers use these same ideals to criticize monastic support of the political and business establishment.

One of the most typically Buddhist aspects of the ascetic ideal is meditation. In recent years interest in meditation practice on the part of both monks and laity has increased rather dramatically, especially among the urban elites. In America and Europe as well, Buddhist meditation has had a strong appeal. Buddhist meditation centers have been established throughout the United States, and Buddhist meditation techniques have been appropriated into the practice of Christian spirituality in Roman Catholic, Orthodox, and Protestant circles.

How can we account for this interest? The answer takes us back to the beginning of this chapter, to our contention that asceticism is not a nay-saying, a taking-away-from, or a denial of our full humanity. Quite the contrary—to meditate, to expect of our religious life more than conventional churchgoing, to withdraw from the workaday world for a weekend or longer periods, to fast and engage in other ascetical practices, become a way of not being overcome by the world, a way of discovering the depths of our being and the freedom it takes to be authentically human in relationship to others.

Throughout their histories Buddhist and Christian monasteries have regulated, structured, and institutionalized the ascetic ideal. In the following chapters we explore the ways in which these two monastic traditions have attempted to embody and express that ideal.

3

The Historical Road

BUDDHISM

The historical beginnings of monasticism in Buddhism and Christianity are, as noted in chapter 2, quite different. While the Buddha himself is credited with formulating the monastic character of Buddhism, monasticism in the Christian tradition does not emerge as an institution until some three hundred years after the time of Christ. This difference must be taken into account in analyzing both the ascetic ideals and the historical road of monasticism in the two traditions. Put quite simply, in Buddhism the founder both embodies the ascetic ideal and puts his indelible stamp on the form and substance of the institution of Buddhist monasticism.

To be sure, both the ideal the Buddha embodied and the institution he initiated were partially anticipated by earlier religious, social, and political developments. We shall investigate some of these antecedents, explore in more detail the special characteristics of the age of the Buddha that encouraged a monastic style of life, and then turn to the founding of the Buddhist monastic Order, its formative years, and the nature of its later development.

Buddhist Monasticism: Antecedents

Prior to the emergence of Buddhism in the sixth century B.C.E., Indian religion was an amalgam of animistic beliefs and practices that had emerged from the earliest known settlements in the subcontinent in the Indus River valley, and the priestly cultus of the Aryan peoples who had migrated into the area from approximately 2500 B.C.E. The legacy of these two religiocultural traditions lies behind all Indian religions, including Hinduism and Buddhism.

Contrary to much popular opinion, Buddhism did not grow out of Hinduism, although many of the antecedents for the development of Buddhism are to be found in the Brahmanical texts or *Vedas* of the Hindu tradition. These texts vary greatly in nature. Some, such as the *Rig Veda*, are associated with sacrificial rituals conducted by a priestly class known as Brahmans. Others, like the *Upanishads*, depict an extraordinary pursuit of knowledge as the highest religious activity, and uphold the sage or wise man, rather than a ritual officiant, as the exemplary religious figure.

The muni

On the periphery of the *Vedas* lurks a lesser known figure, an ascetic or *muni* who was also part of the religious background to the development of Buddhism. He is depicted as one who:

> . . . with long, loose locks supports Agni [the Vedic god of fire] and moisture, heaven and earth;
> He is all sky to look upon; he with long hair is called this light,
> The Munis, girdled with the wind, wear soiled garments of yellow hue,
> They, following the wind's swift course, go where the gods have gone before.
> Transported with our munihood we have pressed on into the winds;
> You, therefore, mortal men, behold our natural bodies and no more.
> The Muni, made associate with the holy work of every god,
> Looking upon all varied forms, flies through the region of the air.[1]

The *muni*, in many respects, fits the description of a shaman, especially in his characteristics of magical flight, intimate association with gods and heavenly beings, his long hair and disheveled appearance, and his association with the Hindu god Rudra-Siva, in the latter's manifestation as the Great Yogin.[2] We cannot designate with certainty the origins of this strange figure. It is clear, however, that before the appearance of the Buddha the *muni's* presence had become familiar enough to gain recognition in the oral traditions of the Brahmanical priests. A somewhat more eclectic and popular Vedic text, the *Atharva Veda*, corroborates the existence of the shamanlike *muni* of the verses quoted above. Here we find a reference to a "roaming *vratya*," whose wanderings are cosmic in scope and who has the capacity of identifying with a wide spectrum of divine beings. His ascetic practices include the ability to stand erect for one year and advanced respiratory control.[3]

If we accept the *muni* and *vratya* as ascetic, shamanlike figures significant enough to be acknowledged in the priestly literature of pre-Buddhist India, then we assume that sometime after 1000 B.C.E. the structured, formal, and ritualized role of the Brahman priest was challenged by religious figures of a different type. As we shall see, in many respects the Buddhist monastic ideal offers a marked contrast to these mysterious, albeit compelling, figures. At the same time, however, the kinds of supernatural powers attributed to these archaic shamans became a part of the popular perception of the very special nature of the Buddha and his followers.

The Upanishadic sage

A model of the ideal religious life much closer to the example of the Buddha emerges in the Upanishadic literature, roughly contemporaneous with the rise of Buddhism and other non-Brahmanical religious groups such as the Jains. The *Upanishads* see the highest religious calling as the pursuit of a metaphysical knowledge or transcendental wisdom based on an understanding not limited by conventional sense perception or reasoning. One who attains such knowledge becomes a sage (*rishi*) whose role in society is to teach this extraordinary truth about the real nature of things. The Upanishadic sage comes close to the picture of the Buddha and his followers. One of the most famous of these figures is Yajnavalkya.

In his later years, having fulfilled his responsibilities as a householder, Yajnavalkya determines to "renounce the world" in order to seek for that "truth which passes all understanding." Before embarking on this quest he calls his wife Maitreyi to make a settlement:

"Maitreyi!" said Yajnavalkya, "Lo, verily, I am about to go forth from this state. Behold! Let me make a final settlement for you and Katyayani."

Then said Maitreyi: "If now, sir, this whole earth filled with wealth were mine, would I be immortal thereby?"

"No," said Yajnavalkya. "As the life of the rich, even so would your life be. Of immortality, however, there is no hope through wealth."

Then said Maitreyi: "What should I do with that through which I may not be immortal? What you know, sir—that, indeed, tell me!"[4]

The knowledge Yajnavalkya seeks cannot be bought. All material things are perishable while the Truth is imperishable. The sage-to-be sets forth on his quest for knowledge intending to leave his wife a comfortable settlement. Maitreyi, however, recognizing the limited, conditioned nature of material satisfactions, determines to attain the same goal as her husband. As this passage indicates, the quest for truth transcends distinctions of gender. Women as well as men could lead a life of renunciation.

The *Upanishads* have their famous teachers, but also an equally well-known cadre of students. Among the most revered is Svetaketu Aruneya, who returns home after twelve years of Vedic study. Like some of today's college students, he sees himself as vastly more learned than his parents. Uddalaka, his father and a wise sage, counters his intellectual arrogance with the following comments:

Svetaketu, my dear, since now you are conceited, think yourself learned, and are proud, did you also ask for that teaching whereby what has not been heard of becomes heard of, what has not been thought of becomes thought of, what has not been understood becomes understood?[5]

Having taken his son down a notch or two, Uddalaka then uses a series of metaphors to instruct him in the nature of the Real, which cannot be limited by hearing, thinking, and conventional modes of understanding:

Just as, my dear, by one piece of clay everything made of clay may be known—the modification is merely a verbal distinction, a name; the reality is just "clay"—

Just as, my dear, by one copper ornament everything made of copper may be known—the modification is merely a verbal distinction, a name; the reality is just "copper"—.

Svetaketu has to admit the superiority of his father's wisdom over that of his teachers: "Verily, those honored men did not know this; for if they had known it, why would they not have told me? But do you, sir, tell it to me."[6]

A narrative *Upanishad* (the *Katha Upanishad*) relates the story of Naciketa, whose instruction comes at the hands of Yama, the god of death. The story of Yama and Naciketa sets out a symbolic paradigm of the quest for religious knowledge typical of the *Upanishads* and, indeed, of Buddhism. Naciketa's visit to the realm of Yama symbolizes Naciketa's "death" to the things of this world: to attain true wisdom one must transcend the conventional distinctions of pleasure and pain, reward and punishment, self and other, and so on, in order to realize an unqualified wisdom and eternal bliss. The Buddha's own quest is anticipated in Naciketa's journey— renunciation, testing, realization, return—stages found in other tales of mythic heroes.[7]

The Buddha as an exemplary religious figure was anticipated by several developments within the religious culture of northern India sometime around the beginning of the first millennium B.C.E. The Buddhist monastic ideal appears to have been directly influenced by the model of the sage-teacher of the Upanishadic tradition. Unlike the Brahmanical priest, whose place was defined by his ritual role in a formal cult and by his place in the social hierarchy, the sage embodied a religious ideal at odds with social hierarchy, calling for an extraordinary discipline leading to a condition of absolute knowledge. The sage's primary social responsibility was that of teacher. An even less conventional religious figure, the shaman to whom supernatural powers were attributed because of extreme ascetic practices, also influenced the image of the Buddha and those who followed him into the monastic life. The figure of the shaman has always existed in tension with the figure of the sage within the Buddhist tradition.

THE AGE OF THE BUDDHA

The seventh and sixth centuries B.C.E. offered many conditions for the emergence of new religious ideas and institutions. The basis of political and social loyalty in northern India shifted from tribes or clans to larger monarchical states. The two most powerful kingdoms were Kosala, which ruled the area from the Ganges north to the Himalayas with its capital at Savatthi, and Magadha, ranging south of the Ganges to the Vindhya mountains. This shift in political power and organization meant a change from a republican to an absolutistic mode of government with its accompanying social and psychological dislocations. It may be that this challenge to the collective consciousness of the tribe stimulated the growth of communal, salvation-oriented religions, and that caste identification became a substitute for the supremacy the tribal group once had over the individual.[8]

The social setting

One of the new salvation religions was Buddhism. Institutionally it offered an alternative to the moral authority held by the clan chief in an earlier day and to the republican nature of the tribal assembly. In this sense early Buddhist monachism can be seen as essentially conservative, reestablishing a form of communal structure of an earlier day. Several aspects of Buddhist doctrine may reflect the impact of profound social, political, and economic change. For example, the transcendental goal of Nirvana individually pursued might be seen as a reaction to the development of a more authoritarian society.[9]

On the economic level Buddhism emerges along with the beginnings of monetary exchange and an urban merchant class. Significant support of the early Buddhist monastic Order came from these merchants, who were less tied to traditional status and rank than the ruling and priestly elites. On a more pedestrian level, the growth of wealth and a leisured class simply made possible the support of nonproductive religious communities like the Buddhists and Jains.

Changes in the material environment such as these spawned numerous salvation-oriented, communal, or sectarian groups. Collectively they were known as mendicant truth-seekers (*parivrajaka*)—

''professed *religieux*, homeless wanderers without kinship or social bonds.''[10] These groups varied considerably in their teachings and practices. As mentioned in chapter 2, some prized the practice of asceticism and extreme austerities, while the Buddhists adopted a much more moderate form of ascetic renunciation. Early Buddhist texts emphasize the fact that the Buddha specifically rejected extreme forms of asceticism, setting forth a Middle Way. Furthermore, as we have seen, considerable tension appears to have existed between those who sought to acquire supernatural powers through strenuous yogic disciplines, and those who aimed at insight and wisdom through more moderate forms of meditation and self-control.[11] We shall examine this distinction in greater detail.

The *Kassapa-Sihanada Sutta*, part of a collection of texts known as the *Dialogues of the Buddha* (*Digha Nikaya*), distinguishes between an extreme ascetic path and the Middle Way taught by the Buddha. Kassapa, a naked ascetic, delineates a list of practices he considers to be conducive to the highest form of religious life. The Buddha refutes his position as follows:

> If a man, O Kassapa, should go naked, and be of loose habits, and lick his hands clean with his tongue, and do and be all those other things you gave in detail, down to his being addicted to the practice of taking food, according to rule, at regular intervals up to even half a month—if he does all this, and the state of blissful attainment in conduct, in heart, in intellect, have not been practiced by him, . . . then is he far from Samanaship, far from Brahmanaship. But from the time, O Kassapa, when a Bhikkhu [monk] has cultivated the heart of love that knows no anger, that knows no ill will—from the time when, by the destruction of the deadly intoxicants [the lusts of the flesh, the lust after future life, and the defilements of delusion and ignorance], he dwells in that emancipation of heart, that emancipation of mind, that is free from those intoxications, and that he, while yet in this visible world, has come to realize and know—from that time, O Kassapa, is it that the Bhikkhu is called a Samana, is called a Brahmana![12]

The Jains and the Ajivakas

Two communal religious groups contemporaneous with the rise of Buddhism that espoused rigorous ascetic regimes were the Jains and the Ajivakas. Like the Buddha, Vardharana Mahavira, the founder of the Jains, sought to discover a higher truth but, unlike his famed contemporary, he never rejected an ascetic pattern of training. To attain Nirvana or the highest salvific goal one must become a monk, abandon all worldly accouterments, including clothing, and subject the body to long periods of fasting and self-mortification. At his initiation the Jain monk's hair is not shaved, but pulled out by the roots. Like Mahavira himself, the monk subjects himself to many hardships, such as meditating in the full sunlight of a hot summer day or maintaining an uncomfortable posture for several hours a day. He takes the commandment not to take life to an extreme, straining his drinking water, brushing insects from his path with a feather-duster, and wearing a mask over his mouth.

The Ajivakas, founded by Gosala Maskariputra, had a reputation for austerities even more severe than those of the Jains. They are said to be fond of "exerting themselves in a squatting posture, the bat-penance, lying on beds of thorns, and the penance of the five fires"—acts of self-mortification practiced by Indian ascetics of all periods.[13] A lone Ajivaka ascetic is described in the following terms:

> Naked and solitary, he fled like a deer at the sight of men. He ate refuse, small fish, and dung. In order that his austerities should not be disturbed he took up his abode in the depths of the jungle. In winter he would leave his thicket and spend the night exposed to the bitter wind, returning to the shade as soon as the sun rose. By night he was wet with melted snow, and by day with the water dripping from the branches of trees. In summer he reversed the process, and was scorched by the sun all day, while at night the thicket shielded him from the cooling breeze.[14]

The various communal, salvation-oriented religious groups of the sixth century B.C.E. may, in a generic sense, be thought of as mendicant truth-seekers (parivrajaka) who followed a religious practice at odds with the cultic tradition of the Brahman priests. Yet these groups varied significantly from one another in both doctrine and practice. The Buddha clearly saw his own teaching as a Middle Way in contrast to such competing groups as the Jains and Ajivakas. The Buddha's teaching stressed the development of insight through the use of the reason, but more important, the attainment of wisdom through the practice of meditative disciplines.

The early Buddhist community focused around the person of the Buddha as a teacher, and those who followed him were allied by a common acceptance of his Truth (*dharma*) rather than by a particular kind of ascetic practice. Consequently, if we were to juxtapose two types of renunciants—the ascetic and the mendicant—the Buddha represents the latter rather than the former. Yet, that he was endowed with the power customarily associated with the ascetic is evident from numerous episodes in the Buddhist texts (e.g., the conversion of Uruvela Kassapa, recounted in chapter 2), and from popular veneration accorded him after his death. In the following section we shall see how these two models exist in uneasy tension in the founding and early years of the Buddhist monastic Order.

The Founding of the Monastic Order

The *Book of Discipline* (*Vinaya Pitaka*), which prescribes the monastic rules for monks and nuns, includes an opening section (the *Mahavagga*) with an account of the formation of the Buddhist monastic Order (*sangha*). While episodic in nature, the account provides us with clues regarding the constituency of the *sangha* and the nature of its growth.

The earliest followers: friends, merchants, aristocrats, ascetics

The Buddha's first disciples were five of his former followers. During his six year period of training they had chosen to leave him when he gave up extreme ascetic practice and adopted a more moderate discipline. Their conversion becomes the occasion for the Buddha's First Discourse, entitled ''Turning the Wheel of the Law.'' In this text the basic scheme of the Buddha's teaching is presented in terms of two formulas—the Four Noble Truths and the Eightfold Noble Path. The teaching provides a rationale for the inevitable sense of lack of fulfillment and happiness we experience in life, and the way to a more lasting peace known as Nirvana. Throughout the history of Buddhism this synopsis has been the most widely known summary of Buddhist thought.

The story of the Buddha and his first disciples emphasizes the compelling nature of the Blessed One's presence as a consequence of his enlightenment, and provides testimony to the power of his charisma:

> The group of five monks saw the Lord coming in the distance; seeing him, they agreed among themselves, saying: "Your reverences, this recluse Gotama is coming, he lives in abundance, he is wavering in his striving, he has reverted to a life of abundance. He should neither be greeted, nor stood up for, nor should his bowl and robe be received; all the same a seat may be put out, he can sit down if he wants to."
>
> But as the Lord gradually approached this group of five monks, . . . not adhering to their own agreement, having gone towards the Lord, one received his bowl and robe, one made ready a seat, one brought water for washing the feet, a footstool, a footstand. The Lord sat down on the seat made ready, and . . . washed his feet. Further, they addressed the Lord by name and with the epithet of "your reverence."[15]

The conversion of the five who had deserted him highlights the Buddha's conception of the nature of the religious life: One must "go forth" or break away from the normal, conventional structures that define success in the world: One should seek instruction from a proven teacher who commands respect: One should live in a community based on a teaching (*dharma*) to which the members give general consent. Although these principles characterize the founding of the early Buddhist community, they have a timeless significance. The religious life in the most profound sense does not confine its meaning to the commonplace, to conventional goals of success or the logic of the ordinary. The monastic dimension of religion in particular has challenged our understanding of personal and social identity in the past and continues to do so today.

The second group of persons to become ordained were merchants. The first of this group to follow the Buddha was Yasa. In a scene reminiscent of the Buddha's own renunciation, Yasa wakes up to the emptiness of the sensory pleasures with which he had been surrounded. Leaving the luxury of his three mansions behind, he encounters the Buddha, who talks to him about "the peril, the vanity, the depravity of pleasures of the senses, the advantage of renouncing them," and teaches Yasa the Four Noble Truths—the nature of suffering, the cause of suffering, the cessation of suffering, and the way to its cessation.[16] The power and truth of the Buddha's message so convinces the wealthy young merchant that he seeks ordination at the hands of the Enlightened One. Yasa's ordination, furthermore, leads to another development in the tradition, the creation of a Buddhist laity, men and women who acknowledge their status as lay followers by taking refuge in the Three Gems—*Buddha, Dharma, Sangha*. The practice of "taking the refuges" continues to this day at the opening of many Buddhist ceremonies throughout Buddhist Asia as a verbal confession of faith in, or loyalty to, the Buddha, his teaching, and the monastic Order.

Following the ordination of Yasa and fifty-four of his friends, the narrative records a kind of missionary manifesto: "Walk, monks, on tour for the blessing of the many folk, for the happiness of the manyfold, out of compassion for the world, for the welfare, the blessing, the happiness of *devas* [divine beings] and men. Let not two [of you] go by one [way]."[17] This statement reveals that the mendicant character of the Order in its early days was for the purpose of maximizing the teaching function of the monk among the laity rather than elevating the eremitic life to an inherently more holy status. In short, from Buddhism's beginnings, the Buddhist monk has been seen as one who has a primary responsibility to serve the lay community by teaching a more complete vision of what it means to be fully human.

The third group to become followers of the Buddha appears to have come from the ruling class. The episode is an amusing one. Thirty men of high standing are bathing in the nude with their wives in a woodland pond. A courtesan who had been invited for the entertainment of one of the unmarried men sneaks away in the midst of the revelry, gathers up all their clothing, and runs off through the woods. One of the men, seeing the courtesan absconding with the clothing, gets out of the pond—still naked—and runs after her in hot pursuit. While dashing through the forest he is caught up short by the sight of the Buddha meditating under a tree. In that rather incongruous situation the Buddha teaches him the *dharma* and, as a result, all of the men of "high standing" seek admission into the Buddha's community. The humor of the situation should not obscure the symbolic meaning of the episode: that one comes to the Buddha-*dharma*, that is, the Truth, without the "clothing" of pretense or preconception.

To wandering truth-seekers, merchants, and aristocrats is added yet another group of followers. In the longest episode of the series, three groups of ascetics numbering a thousand altogether are finally won over by the Buddha. Unlike the other conversion stories, the focal point of the Buddha's appeal is his supernatural and psychic power rather than his *dharma*. It is only after the Buddha performs fifteen occult acts that Uruvela Kassapa, the leader of the largest group of ascetics, is willing to admit the superior power of the Buddha (see chapter 2). In this contest of wills, the Buddha finally confronts his antagonist with what must be considered the ultimate spiritual insult: "Neither are you, Kassapa, a perfected one nor have you entered on the way to perfection, and that course is not for you by which you either could be a perfected one or could have entered on the way to perfection."[18] Convinced of the superiority of the Buddha's way, Uruvela Kassapa becomes one of the Buddha's disciples.

The narrative of the founding of the Buddhist monastic community includes other conversion episodes, although they do not add substantially to the constituencies who become followers of the Buddha. When King Seniya Bimbisara of Magadha becomes a lay follower of the Enlightened One, the claim is made that Brahmans as well as householders also follow suit. Another episode relates the conversion of Sariputta and Moggallana, who were destined to become two of the most famous of the Buddha's disciples. The two become emblematic of two critical facets of monastic life: meditation and study.

The story of the founding of the Buddhist monastic community verifies both the broad-based appeal of the Buddha's teaching (*dharma*) and the variety of types of individuals who became his followers: the ruling elite, merchants, wandering philosophers, shamanlike ascetics, and even Brahman priests. In most instances the appeal was the Buddha's teaching rather than his occult powers or the type of discipline he proposed. The early Buddhist community, both monk and lay, was a group bound together by a teaching and its teacher. It was, if you will, first a sect and only later an Order governed by a rule.[19]

Early growth

While the Buddhist community might not have grown at the rate indicated by some of the stories from the *Book of Discipline*, evidence supports the contention that during the forty-five year teaching career of the Buddha it became a sizable group. Of course, growth in size entails increasing complexity, so the rules governing the monastic Order became more and more detailed. It is not entirely clear, however, that the Buddhist monastic Order evolved in a linear fashion from a simple eremitic form to increasingly complex coenobitic arrangements. To be sure, evidence in the Theravada texts supports the notion that those who followed in the Buddha's footsteps initially formed a mendicant-type group, and the more austere disciplinary regulations (the four *nissayas*), such as dwelling under trees and wearing robes made of rags, do point to an eremitic type of life:

> At that time . . . the Blessed One had not given permission to the [monks] to use dwelling-houses. And the [monks] dwelt . . . wherever they could—in the forest, at the foot of trees, on the hills, in the valleys, in mountain caves, in cemeteries, in groves of trees, in open spaces, or in heaps of straw. And they would return early in the morning from their various resting-places—from the forests, from the foot of the trees, from the hills . . . or from heaps of straw, winning the minds of men with their advancing and their retiring . . . and having their eyes cast down, and perfect in their deportment.[20]

While the above passage from *The Book of Discipline* supports the contention that those who were ordained into the Buddha's special community lived a mendicant, eremitic-type life, it states further that during the Enlightened One's lifetime he also granted them permission to live in settled communities. Moreover, Buddhist texts contain numerous references to land and dwelling-places being donated to the Buddha and his disciples, places where the Lord could "stay that would be neither too far from a village nor too near, suitable for coming and going, accessible for people whenever they want. . . ."[21]

The position of the Buddhist monastic community betwixt-and-between the village and the jungle seems to be the critical consideration in the founding of the Order. Monks lived lives distinct from the laity, but they personified an attainable ideal. They were not spiritual athletes far removed from the day-to-day life of the common people, living an ascetic style of life or performing feats of magical power beyond the emulation of those who considered themselves to be simple, ordinary folk.

Buddhist monks were representatives of the Middle Way. Like their founder, they sought to understand and to teach the nature of suffering (*dukkha*), its cause, and the way to its cessation. In this capacity they needed to live an exemplary life in close contact with the larger lay community. Thus, while in a physical sense they lived between the village and the jungle, the strictures of civilization and the randomness of nature, the familiar and the unknown, in a symbolic sense they mediated between the karmic world of conventional morality and the state of absolute freedom beyond good and evil, namely, Nirvana.

THE NATURE OF THE EARLY MONASTIC COMMUNITY

What was the nature of the early Buddhist monastic community? What functions did it fulfill? To what ends was it dedicated? Generally speaking, the Buddhist monastic Order had and continues to have a dual purpose: for the *teaching* of the *dharma* and for its *realization*. Many Buddhist texts from both the *Book of Discipline* and the *Dialogues of the Buddha* convey the picture of the monastic community as that body where the Buddha and his disciples taught the *dharma*—the truth about the nature of suffering, its cause, and the way to its cessation. The monastic Order was a teaching/learning arena.

Teaching and learning

Even today one of the major purposes of the monastery in Buddhist Asia is instruction in Buddhist thought and practice. Obviously, to teach—and often scores of people at the same time—demands an accessible place where people can gather. The complex, highly developed Buddhist monasteries and monastic schools of today are obviously vastly different from those in the time of the Buddha. However, if we are to accept the textual depiction of the Buddha as a teacher, then it is incontestable that the major functions of the early monastic community necessarily involved outreach to the larger lay society.

The Buddhist monastic community was also the place where the truth about the nature of things (the *dharma*) was realized. While learning the concepts that express this truth is an important part of this process, the practice of meditation is even more crucial. The central Buddhist discipline aiming at the attainment of Nirvana, the *summum bonum* of the Buddha's Path, does involve a withdrawal from the ordinary pursuits of life. Buddhist meditation texts advise the monk to withdraw to the foot of a tree or a cave, that is, away from the hustle and bustle of conventional life.

Yet even individual practice of meditation involves a moral training embedded in a regard for others. Thus, while meditation (*samadhi*) is essential to the Buddha's Path to enlightenment, its foundation stone is an other-regarding morality (*sila*)—for example, not to take life, not to steal, not to become intoxicated, and so on. In one of the episodes from the *Middle Length Dialogues* (*Bhaddali-Sutta, Bhikkhu-Vagga, Majjhima Nikaya*), the Buddha argues that only the monk who carries out the discipline to the full can benefit by a stay in a remote place. In short, the practice of *samadhi* meditation has its place within the larger context of Buddhist practice, which involves being a moral exemplar for society, helping all who choose the pilgrim's way betwixt and between the commonplace and the extraordinary, success in the world and the realization of Nirvana.

The Buddha's way aims to overcome blind attachment to the fleeting pleasures and satisfactions of the world. The way to an understanding of the deepest truth about life demands a special effort, a "cutting off" likened to a "homeless state." To be sure, the monk's vocation is a practical way of life within the matrix of society, yet it is also a symbol for that highest state of individual attainment called Nirvana—wisdom, equanimity, absolute freedom. The "rhinoceros" monk of the *Sutta Nipata* (see chapter 2) is an ideal, as it were, of the person who walks in the world but leaves no footprint. This ideal was important in the earliest days of the Buddhist tradition, as it is today. While early Buddhist monachism provided the opportunity for the monk to pursue an isolated or "lonely" life, to a more profound and subtle degree this picture symbolizes the individual who has overcome attachment to the world and in that sense is "homeless." The betwixt-and-between state typifies not only the monk who has cut off all ties with society or even the monk living in the midst of a well-ordered and disciplined monastic community, but all religious persons who aspire to ultimate transformation.

Our interpretation of the nature of the Buddhist monastic community challenges the notion of a relatively linear development from a mendicant, eremitic-type Order to settled communities. To be sure, as the monastic fellowship grew the organization became more complex: there was a greater need for monastic dwellings, disciplinary rules, and so on. We do not dispute this obvious point. But we see the monastic form or type of monastic organization dependent primarily on the monastic vocation—namely, that monks and nuns, from the time of the Buddha himself, have sought the realization of the Truth (*dharma*) and its propagation rather than the attainment of supernatural powers; that from the beginning his/her asceticism has been part of a training dedicated to social as well as personal transformation; that the monk/nun has been primarily a moral exemplar and teacher rather than an other-worldly mystic or ascetic. In short, the monk/nun is the model of the religious person par excellence.

The emergence of sects

As Buddhism developed in India into a widespread, popular religion from about the third century B.C.E. onward, its institutional forms naturally evolved and changed in various ways.[22] Buddhist sects emerged, sometimes as a consequence of geographical isolation or disputes over doctrine, at other times as a result of disagreement over the nature of the monastic rule and life. Monastic life changed even more with the establishment of Buddhism in Central Asia and China, Korea, and Japan, a process which took place during the first five to six hundred years of the Common Era. A gradual transformation of Indian forms of Buddhist thought, practice, and institutions occurred as Buddhism became increasingly indigenized in non-Indian cultures. Buddhism was changed not only by non-Buddhist religious traditions ranging from animism to Taoism and Confucianism; social norms and mores also greatly affected the development of monastic forms and practices.

Change in the nature of Buddhist monastic life occurred in part simply because it became a major social, economic, and in some cases political institution in the countries where it flourished.[23] Monasteries, for example, had become major landholders in China by the end of the fifth century C.E., and in Sri Lanka monasteries still own extensive paddy land. The political power of the monasteries on the hills surrounding Nara had become so disruptive by the end of the eighth century that the capital city of Japan was moved to Kyoto. By the middle of the seventeenth century, Tibet had become a monastic theocratic state governed by the Dalai Lama.

Socially, the egalitarian nature of the early monastic community became more rigid and hierarchical, even, as in the cases of Nepal and Sri Lanka, absorbing caste distinctions. In Thailand, a national monastic organization was created in the nineteenth century, paralleling the political structures of a modernizing, bureaucratic state. Furthermore, in Central and East Asia the monastic vocation based on celibacy was complemented by the establishment of a married clergy, and, as in the case of Japanese Pure Land Buddhism, a married clergy became the normative religious vocation. Indeed, Shinran Shonen (1215–89 C.E.), the founder of the True Pure Land sect (Jodo Shin Shu), sounds very much like Martin Luther in his criticism of celibate orders.

By the thirteenth and fourteenth centuries C.E., Buddhist monasticism had evolved into a myriad of different forms. To be sure, individual monasteries as well as some sectarian traditions closely resembled the ascetic betwixt-and-between ideals of the early *sangha*, but in many countries the transformation of the tradition was so striking that the Middle Way vision of the Buddha appears to have been qualified almost beyond recognition. Perhaps this is the fate of every profoundly spiritual vision. And for this reason the vision continually reminds us of how far we have compromised the ideal and challenges us to live lives more nearly approximating it.

CHRISTIANITY

The general portrayal of the Buddha as founder of a monastic movement is hardly open to doubt. But the historical connection between Christian origins and the origins of Christian monasticism is not at all clear. The traditional starting date for Christian monasticism is about two hundred and fifty years after the time of Jesus. That gap of two and one-half centuries was a puzzle and problem for ancient monks as well as for modern scholars.

ANCIENT THEORIES OF ORIGINS

The apostolic community

Where in the Bible could monks find their own life anticipated? Appeal has most often been made to the portrait of the earliest Christian community at the end of the second chapter of the Acts of the Apostles. The argument for the apostolic community as the type and origin of Christian monasticism is classically stated by a late fourth-century Egyptian monk, Abba Piamun:

> The system of the coenobites arose at the time when the apostles were preaching. The crowd of believers in Jerusalem was of this sort, as it is described in the Acts of the Apostles: ''The multitude of believers was of one heart and one soul, neither said any of them that any of the things which they possessed was their own, but they had all things in common. They sold their possessions and property and divided them to all, as any had need.'' And, ''For neither was there any among them that lacked; for as many as possessed fields or houses, sold them and brought the price of the things that they sold and laid them before the apostles' feet: and distribution was made to everyone as they had need.'' The whole church, I assert, lived then as the coenobites live, now so few that it is difficult to find them.[24]

Piamun is clearly engaging in polemic. He is challenging those who oppose monasticism as a recent—hence illegitimate—development in the church. He is also challenging those who, while favoring monasticism, elevate the eremitic life over the coenobitic. The apostles were coenobitic monks, Piamun says, and we few Christians today, more than three hundred years later, who are coenobitic monks are the only authentic bearers of the apostolic tra-

dition. It is not monasticism, then, but all the rest of the church structure and paraphernalia that needs to be justified.

The Therapeutae

About a century earlier than Piamun, Bishop Eusebius of Caesarea
had written the first full-scale history of the church. At the time Eusebius wrote, organized Christian monastic life had hardly begun,
but Eusebius wanted to make sure this new movement would be
seen as one of several legitimate forms of the Christian life. Eusebius does not trace monasticism directly back to Acts, but he does
find an early grounding in a treatise, *On a Contemplative Life*, by Philo
of Alexandria, a Jewish thinker who died about the year 50 C.E.

Philo describes a group of ascetics, the Therapeutae, who "have
been instructed by nature and the sacred laws to serve the living
God."[25] They have gone out into the desert, where they live alone,
except for gatherings once a week. The Therapeutae meditate on
holy books. Theirs is a predominantly scholarly and intellectual
asceticism, not unlike that found in the *Upanishads*. Eusebius picks
out several features of the communal life of the Therapeutae, such
as their fasting and their liturgy, draws some parallels with the Acts
account of the apostolic community, and judges that the Therapeutae "exhibit the characteristics of the ecclesiastical mode of life."
He concludes his account with a ringing declaration: "That Philo,
when he wrote these things, had in view the first heralds of the
Gospel and the customs handed down from the beginning by the
apostles, is clear to everyone."[26]

Chronology itself makes Eusebius's conclusion dubious in the
extreme. Philo was dead before any such highly developed form
of Christian community life could have established itself in Egypt.
Moreover, the motivations and goals of the Therapeutae, as Philo
presents them, are quite different from those of the Christian monks
of the Egyptian desert who first make their appearance in the early
fourth century. Like the Christian Desert Fathers, the Therapeutae
challenge "desire, the most insatiable of all beasts," and they "oppose those feelings which nature has made mistresses of the human
race, namely, hunger and thirst," but in Philo's account they live
a relatively placid life, founded on moderation, in the desert where

they have gone to get away from "people of wholly dissimilar dispositions." Unlike the earliest Christian monks, who go into the desert to do battle with their own mortality, the Therapeutae act as men and women who think their mortal life has already come to an end. They are not struggling against great odds to attain a beatific vision; rather, they are "continually taught to see without interruption." Accounts of what filled the imaginations of the Christian monks reflect spirits far less serene than those of the Therapeutae, who "always retain an imperishable recollection of God, so that not even in their dreams is any other object ever presented to their eyes except the beauty of the divine virtues and of the divine powers."[27]

The philosophic life—Origen

Eusebius makes more than a judgment about the past when he says the Therapeutae were Christians. If they were Christians of the first generation, then Origen, Eusebius's hero and one of the greatest Christian scholars of all time, was no innovator but was only doing what the church had been doing from the beginning.

Origen (ca. 186–ca. 254 C.E.) was famous throughout the Roman Empire in his own day, even among people who were unfamiliar with any of his hundreds of writings. What everybody knew about Origen was how he lived:

> For many years he lived philosophically in this manner, putting away all the incentives of youthful desires. Through the entire day he endured no small amount of discipline; and for the greater part of the night he gave himself to the study of the Divine Scriptures. He restrained himself as much as possible by a most philosophic life; sometimes by the discipline of fasting, again by limited time for sleep. And in his zeal he never lay upon a bed, but upon the ground.
>
> Most of all, he thought that the words of the Savior in the Gospel should be observed, in which he exhorts not to have two coats nor to use shoes, nor to occupy oneself with cares for the future. With a zeal beyond his age he continued in cold and nakedness; and, going to the very extreme of poverty, he greatly astonished those about him. And indeed he grieved many of his friends who desired to share their possessions with him, on account of the wearisome toil which they saw him enduring in the teaching of divine things.

But he did not relax his perseverance. He is said to have walked for a number of years never wearing a shoe, and, for a great many years, to have abstained from the use of wine, and of all other things beyond his necessary food; so that he was in danger of breaking down and destroying his constitution.

By giving such evidences of a philosophic life to those who saw him, he aroused many of his pupils to similar zeal.[28]

Origen himself had argued repeatedly that one of Christianity's notable achievements was its making the ideal of "the philosophic life" accessible to the multitudes. Ever since the time of Socrates (fifth century B.C.E.) at least, it had been widely understood that a life stripped down to essentials, unencumbered with sensual and material luxuries, was a precondition for genuine wisdom. Whatever the prescription—with the Platonists to rise above the storm, or with the Stoics to stand unmoved right in the middle of the storm, or with the Epicureans to realize that you and the storm and your perception of the storm are all part of the same material process— the general point was clear: wisdom is the fruit of ascetic discipline. Origen said the Christian church was the first example of a whole community living the philosophic life.[29]

Origen's portrait of the church is idealized, but it makes clear that by the middle of the third century the traditional "philosophic life" had woven itself into the texture of ideals that many Christians considered integral to the faith. Eusebius could welcome the burgeoning monastic movement as a further extension of insights and practices already exhibited in the activity of Origen. The point of claiming that the Therapeutae were truly Christians is to demonstrate that Origen was truly apostolic.

Athanasius's radical solution

As Luther knew, it is hard to extract an ascetic tradition from the Hebrew Scriptures, but notable ascetic figures can be found there, and one of them particularly plays a crucial role in Christian monastic self-understanding from the beginning. Elijah provides, in fact, the most radical of the ancient theories of monastic origins.

Bishop Athanasius of Alexandria, writing in the middle of the fourth century, says of the recently deceased monk, Antony, that "he used to say to himself that the life led by the great Elijah should serve the ascetic as a mirror in which always to study his own life.''[30] What would the ascetic see in that mirror?

Elijah is not bound by ties of family or position; indeed, he had a reputation for disappearing and appearing almost at will.[31] In the midst of Ahab's reign, viewed in retrospect as the darkest valley through which God's people had been led, here was "a hairy man, with a leather apron about his waist," who was speaking directly with the Lord, bringing a young boy back to life, reenacting the experience of Moses at Mount Horeb (Sinai), prompting the wicked Ahab to repentance, and parting the waters of the River Jordan with a wave of his cloak. When everyone else had forsaken the Lord, Elijah alone was still left.

His stature was great simply on the basis of these reports. When it was further believed that he had returned in the person of John the Baptist to herald the coming of the Messiah, and that he had been present, along with Moses, at the Transfiguration of Christ, it was apparent that Elijah was in the forefront of divinely authorized persons. If anyone asked what a man of God should do, one answer would be that he should wear very little, be able to move about freely, and spend a good deal of time in the desert.

For Athanasius, Antony's appeal to Elijah solved at a stroke the problem of accounting for the origins of Christian monasticism. By implying that one of the archetypal prophets of ancient Israel is the model for the monk, Antony evaded the question a skeptic might raise, But Jesus was not a monk, was he? by making monasticism a fulfillment of prophecy—one of those things Jesus came not to destroy but to fulfill. Jesus was not a priest, either, but Christians had early on become persuaded that Jesus had opened the way to the full meaning of priesthood. Just as Elijah was present at the Transfiguration, so monks dwell within the New Israel, the church—as it was *predicted* they would.

Elijah had a few disciples, but he functioned best alone. He hardly provided a model for a monastic community. Later Christian monastic legislators, therefore, apprehensive of the chaos if too many monks saw Elijah in the mirror, would direct attention to other parts of the Bible. Had they known about it, they might have pointed also to the Qumran community, the Jewish monastic group that lived on the shores of the Dead Sea from about 135 B.C.E. to the time of the First Jewish Revolt (66–70 C.E.). The community has come to modern notice with the discovery of the Dead Sea Scrolls.[32]

In terms of structure and regimen, the Qumran community corresponded more closely than the Therapeutae to what we usually think of as a typical Christian monastery. Though there have been efforts to link John the Baptist, and even Jesus, with Qumran, no traceable historical connection existed, and no early Christian proposed any. Qumran does serve, however, to demonstrate conclusively that a rigorously ascetic, highly organized, socially isolated form of community life could grow on Jewish soil and could find its rationale in the Hebrew Scriptures.

The Qumran community's expectation of the imminent end of the world was at least as intense as that of the Christians, and their disaffection from the religious establishment went deeper. They considered the whole history of Israel since the time of Moses to be one giant apostasy, and when they set about to live the way Moses had legislated, a monastery is what they devised. Qumran does not show where Christian monasticism came from, but it does show that Jewish tradition and monasticism were not entirely incompatible.

THE COLONIZING OF THE DESERT

The *Life of Antony* by Athanasius has traditionally been treated as the charter of Christian monasticism. Athanasius presents the *Life* as a regulating as well as narrative text: in the Prologue he writes, "For monks the life of Antony is an ideal pattern of the ascetical life." The Epilogue begins, "Now, then, read this to the other brethren, that they may learn what the life of monks should be like."[33]

Antony

The way was opened to the Buddha's enlightenment by his sight of the misery and suffering from which his upbringing had shielded him. But Antony's conversion was one step removed from this kind of immediate confrontation with suffering. He grew up in the home of a moderately wealthy Egyptian farmer who was an active Christian. Thus from infancy Antony was introduced to the traditions about Jesus.

Upon his parents' death he was left alone with an only sister who was very young. He was about eighteen or twenty years old at the time and took care of the house and his sister. Less than six months had passed since his parents' death when, as usual, he chanced to be on his way to church. As he was walking along, he collected his thoughts and reflected how the apostles left everything and followed the Savior; also how the people in Acts sold what they had and laid it at the feet of the apostles for distribution among the needy; and what great hope is laid up in heaven for such as these. With these thoughts in his mind he entered the church. And it so happened that the Gospel was being read at that moment and he heard the passage in which the Lord says to the rich man: ''If thou wilt be perfect, go sell all that thou hast, and give it to the poor; and come, follow me and thou shalt have treasure in heaven.'' As though God had put him in mind of the saints and as though the reading had been directed especially to him, Antony immediately left the church and gave to the townspeople the property he had from his forebears—three hundred *arurae*, very fertile and beautiful to see. He did not want it to encumber himself or his sister in any way whatever. He sold all the rest, the chattels they had, and gave the tidy sum he received to the poor, keeping back only a little for his sister.

But once again as he entered the church, he heard the Lord saying in the Gospel: ''Be not solicitous for the morrow.'' He could not bear to wait longer, but went out and distributed those things also to the poor. His sister he placed with known and trusted virgins, giving her to the nuns to be brought up. Then he himself devoted all his time to ascetic living, intent on himself and living a life of self-denial, near his own house. For there were not yet so many monasteries in Egypt, and no monk even knew of the faraway desert. Whoever wished to concern himself with his own destiny practiced asceticism by himself not far from his own village.[34]

Athanasius does not claim that his hero was venturing initially into uncharted territory. For the first several years of his renunciation Antony made the rounds of local holy men, beginning ''in the next village [with] an old man who had lived the ascetic life in solitude from his youth.'' Antony started living in places outside his own village, doing manual labor to support himself and to have something to give to the poor, and whenever he heard of a good man somewhere he would go to see him:

He observed the graciousness of one, the earnestness of prayer in another; studied the even temper of one and the kindheartedness of another; fixed his attention on the vigils kept by one and on the studies pursued by another; admired one for his patient endurance, another for his fasting and sleeping on the ground; watched closely this man's meekness and the forbearance shown by another; and in one and all alike he marked especially devotion to Christ and the love they had for one another.

Having thus taken his fill, he would return to his own place of asceticism. Then he assimilated in himself what he had obtained from each and devoted all his energies to realizing in himself the virtues of all.[35]

Athanasius suggests, in short, that Antony went beyond the ascetic specializations of his predecessors to become the first ascetic generalist. Unlike the Buddha, who tries the most extreme forms of ascetic discipline in vogue among his contemporaries and finally establishes his own moderate ascetic program in conscious opposition to the extreme, Antony simply demonstrates how a variety of discrete ascetic practices and goals can be blended into a coherent life. According to Athanasius, Antony did warn against the dangers of ascetic extremism. It may be demons, he said, who try to persuade us that we should not eat at all, or should pray during the time allotted for sleep; they do this "to represent the ascetical life as worthless, and to make men disgusted with the solitary life as something coarse and all too burdensome."[36] But this warning lacks biographical reinforcement. Because the original Christian monk did not try out bizarre austerities and then reject them, the way is left open for others to say that Antony had fallen short of the full ascetic ideal, and some Christian monastic lives make Antony's appear in contrast positively luxurious.

Geographical movement mirrors ascetic progress in Antony's subsequent career. He first goes to tombs some distance from his village and has himself locked in. At about age thirty-five Antony moves across the Nile and seals himself in an abandoned fort, where he stays nearly twenty years, his only human contact being occasional conversations carried on through the closed door. He eventually emerges, to find great crowds gathered to hear his words of wisdom and to benefit from his healing powers:

When he saw himself beset by many and that he was not permitted to withdraw as he had proposed to himself and wished, and concerned that because of what the Lord was doing through him he might become conceited or another might account him more than was proper, he looked about and set out on a journey to the Upper Thebaid to people among whom he was unknown.

[He received direction from a heavenly voice, and made a journey of] three days and three nights and came to a very high mountain. At the base of the mountain there was water, crystal clear, sweet, and very cold. Spreading out from there was flat land and a few scraggy date-palms.

Antony, as though inspired by God, fell in love with the place, . . . [and] for the future he regarded this place as though he had found his own home.[37]

He lived "in his own home," the "Inner Mountain," for approximately forty years, and died there in 356 C.E., at the age of one hundred five.

The structure of the story itself carries much of Athanasius's meaning, for Antony's retreat into more and more remote parts of Egypt is counterpointed by anecdotes of his repeated involvements in the larger life of the Christian community.

Almost one-third of the *Life* is devoted to a long speech on the monastic life which Athanasius says Antony delivered some time after he emerged from his twenty years of solitude in the fort. Antony's speech itself is presented in a way strikingly similar to the Buddha's First Discourse. Just as the Buddha, after his experience of enlightenment won through many years of discipline, makes the moral judgment that he should not pass over into Nirvana but should return to the common world to bring others to enlightenment, so Antony, after decades of struggle and effective victory over demonic forces, decides not to maintain total isolation, but to make available to others the insight he has gained. "I shall perhaps appear foolish; even so the Lord who listens knows that my conscience is clear and that it is not for myself, but out of my love for you and to encourage you that I do so."[38]

If Antony's concern to help his fellow monks, as their senior to share with them his knowledge and experience, reminds us of the Buddha, another facet of his behavior reminds us that Christian monasticism, unlike Buddhist, had to come to terms with an established ecclesiastical structure. There were, of course, elaborate religious institutions in the Buddha's world also, but the sources do not give the impression that the question of how this new teaching might be integrated into the Brahmanic or Shramana systems loomed large. The *sangha* was not under pressure to remain part of something else.

The chapter in which Athanasius describes Antony's devotion to the ordained leaders of the church is the most clearly tendentious in the entire *Life*.

> Renowned man that he was, he yet showed the profoundest respect for the church's ministry and he wanted every cleric to be honored above himself. He was not ashamed to bow his head before bishops and priests; and if ever a deacon came to him for help, he conversed with him on what was helpful; but when it came to prayers, he would ask him to lead, not being ashamed to learn himself.[39]

We cannot know how accurately this passage reflects Antony's attitude or his behavior. Athanasius had either experienced or foreseen the strain between the charismatic spiritual power wielded by ascetics and the routinized official spiritual power in the hands of priests and bishops, and it was critically important to show how Antony, the model of the monastic life, had known and willingly kept his ecclesiastical place.

Not only had Antony been properly deferential; he had also responded to calls for help against heretics.[40] Antony's prestige was at the disposal of the bishop. In this, more than in any other feature of Antony as ideal type of the Christian monk, we see a sharp difference from the Buddha. The Buddha is his own master and teaches others to be their own masters. Athanasius's Antony acknowledges the bishop's authority and by his teaching and example encourages others to do the same.

Another feature of the *Life* takes us even deeper into the social and historical context from which Christian monasticism emerged. More than Antony's willingness to help others or his deference to ecclesiastical officials, his circumspect courting of martyrdom in the year 311 C.E. is a clue to the galvanizing effect the ascetic movement had on Christian society in the fourth century:

When the holy martyrs were taken to Alexandria, he, too, left his cell
and followed, saying: "Let us also go to take part in the contest if
we are called, or to look on the contestants." Now, he had a yearn-
ing to suffer martyrdom, but as he did not wish to give himself up,
he ministered to the confessors in the mines and in the prisons. . . .
[He showed] the eager spirit characteristic of us Christians; for, as
I stated before, he was praying that he, too, might be martyred. Therefore, he also appeared grieved that he did not suffer martyrdom. But
the Lord was guarding him for our own good and for the good of
others, that to many he might be a teacher of the ascetic life which
he himself had learned from the Scriptures.[41]

The situation of Christians in the Roman Empire prior to Constantine's conversion had always been precarious, though the popular picture of unremitting sufferings at the hands of the ever-vigilant
imperial police is the stuff of romantic legend. But the potential for
an outbreak of persecution was ever-present, and there were enough
martyrs to keep vivid in Christian consciousness the sayings of Jesus
that predicted intense sufferings for those who were truly his followers.

Constantine's conversion meant, among many other things, that
the ideology of martyrdom, built up through about ten Christian
generations, suddenly lost its focus, and lines were further blurred
by the new ease with which one could decide to become a Christian. Conversion no longer put one at risk of being a social and political outcast. On the contrary, conversion became a convention,
a means to imperial favor. In this unanticipated, topsy-turvy situation, the monks were seen to embody the old values of strenuous,
uneasy Christianity, and their life was quickly and widely characterized as one of martyrdom:

When the persecution finally ceased and Bishop Peter of blessed memory had suffered martyrdom, [Antony] left and went back to his solitary cell; and there he was a daily martyr to his conscience, ever
fighting the battles of the faith. For he practiced a zealous and more
intense ascetic life.[42]

Since monks were thought to be living martyrs, they became objects of fervent veneration. It is for this reason above all that they
posed a direct threat to ecclesiastical order. A bishop could easily

control the spiritual power of dead martyrs, often by making sure their bones were enshrined beneath the altar of his cathedral. But while the people could gain access to the power of the dead martyr only through the ministrations of their bishop, they could go straight to the monk, the living martyr, expecting him to be of more benefit to them than their bishop because he was on more familiar terms with God. When Athanasius says Antony respected bishops, the message is directed as much to his own congregation in Alexandria as to current and future monks.

The Buddhist monk had to be defined over against the layperson and other mendicant truth-seekers, while the Christian monk had to be distinguished from both the layperson and the priest. The Buddhist example highlights the real possibility that monasticism in the fourth-century Roman Empire might have become an autonomous religious enterprise. A monk who considered himself too good to need to go to communion illustrates the potential for divisiveness.[43] The efforts of Athanasius, Eusebius, Abba Piamun, and others to locate monastic origins in the Christian past can be seen as attempts to rivet into the ecclesiastical system a movement that could have developed entirely apart from, and even in opposition to, the church. It was not a foregone conclusion that Antony's form of renunciation would be universally acknowledged as an—indeed, *the*—appropriate response to Jesus' command, "Come, follow me."

Antony has remained throughout Christian monastic history the classic example of the solitary, eremitical life. As we have seen, he responded to the multitudes who flocked to him by a dual movement—a migration further into the desert and a willingness to come forth repeatedly for the benefit of those multitudes. The monasticism he inspired was for the most part an imitation of his own: the long lonely struggle against temptation, striving to reach the tranquility beyond striving. At least one of his successors reduced the distance of Antony's withdrawal while achieving the same result. Macarius patiently dug a tunnel nearly a kilometer in length from his cell and hollowed out a cave at the end, into which he could escape when he wanted to get away from the crowds that came to learn from him.[44]

The solitary monastic life within the Christian tradition has taken

237/33

all sorts of forms, has appeared in every degree from moderate to extreme. Another Macarius, unlike Antony who sought to equal the specialized ascetic accomplishments of others, "whenever he heard of any asceticism, . . . surpassed it to perfection."[45] Through all the variations of the eremitical life, however, the conviction has persisted that one's salvation must finally be worked out alone. Even if the hermit decides to be of social service to the church, that decision entails a rejection of what is, in the hermit's heart, the more excellent way. Indeed, in terms of the eremitic ideal, a choice of some form of the coenobitic life may be, paradoxically, a further renunciation.

Pachomius

Nearly contemporary with Antony the monastic movement received another impetus, one which gave initial form to the coenobitic ideal. As we saw in chapter 2, Basil of Caesarea in Asia Minor, in the middle of the fourth century C.E., justified this form of monastic life as superior to the eremitic on the grounds that only in community can Christians pursue the way of love, the "more excellent way" prescribed by Paul in 1 Corinthians 13. Prior to Basil's time, and in some quarters ever since his time, the coenobitic life has been justified as a necessary training ground for hermits, a way station for those whose true goal is complete solitude. Basil says, on the contrary, that the hermit ideal and Christian doctrine do not mix.

The way was prepared for Basil by Pachomius. Early in the fourth century he gave organizational shape to the crowds of men and women who, in response to many forces, including the magnetism of Antony's example, were beginning to colonize the desert.

Shortly after Pachomius's death, in 346 C.E., two of his followers paid a visit to Antony, himself now about ninety-five years old.

"I tell you," [Antony said to them] "it was a great ministry [Pachomius] undertook in the assemblage of so many brethren, and he goes the way of the apostles." Zacchaeus protests: "You rather, father, are the light of all this world." But Antony answers: "I persuade you otherwise, Zacchaeus. At the beginning, when I became a monk, there was no coenobium to nourish other souls, but each of the early monks after the persecution used to practice his asceticism alone. And afterwards your father made this good thing from the Lord."[46]

This story is told at the end of an early *Life* of Pachomius, and its author clearly had interests to be served as strong as Athanasius's in the *Life of Antony*. If Antony, the acknowledged master of the isolated hermit life, can be shown to have approved the coenobitic life as superior to his own style, the coenobium will have no rival as an ascetic institute. But whatever its propaganda quotient, the story demonstrates that the early monks themselves believed the isolated life had come first, and that the coenobitic life had begun only slightly later and had grown up beside the isolated life as a self-conscious alternative to it.

At the beginning of the fifth century Palladius went beyond the claim that Pachomius had followed the apostles. According to him, Pachomius had received divine direction. Pachomius was

> a man of the kind who live rightly, so that he was deemed worthy of prophecies and angelic visions. He became extremely kind and brotherly. One time when he was sitting in his cave an angel appeared to him and told him: "So far as you are concerned, you conduct your life perfectly. It is vain for you to continue sitting in your cave. Come now, leave this place and go out and call the young monks together and dwell with them. Rule them by the model which I am now giving you."

There follows an account of the giving of a bronze plaque on which a brief coenobitic rule is outlined.[47] Palladius suggests that far from the coenobium being a preparation for the hermitage, it worked just the other way: Pachomius had achieved in his cave a perfection that qualified him to organize a community. One of the desert fathers, Abba Moses, would perhaps have been surprised at such an outcome of advice he once gave to a monk: "Go and sit in your cell, and your cell will teach you everything."[48]

Pachomius was a pagan soldier before his conversion to Christianity, and it is possible, though not necessary, to see in the general plan of the monastery he established reminiscences of Roman military camps and organization. According to the earliest *Life*, the Pachomian system began not with angelic visitors, but unobtrusively, in much the same way as the Buddha's *sangha*, with three disciples whom Pachomius leads into the ascetic life by way of example as well as teaching. After initial acquaintance with Pachomius they say: "Let us die and live with this man; for he guides us rightly unto God."[49] Thus the coenobium originates from the desire of individuals to learn from a holy person.

What makes Pachomius so important is what he did with and for those who wanted to "die and live with" him. Soon others were joining, and Pachomius began to parcel out the various daily tasks he had initially performed himself by way of service and example to his followers. While it is impossible to derive a precise picture of the earliest Pachomian coenobium from the texts, certain characteristics are clear. There was an enclosing wall, and inside were a gatehouse, guesthouse, assembly hall, refectory, hospital, and houses with separate cells for twenty to forty monks each. Duties would be divided up among the houses, and within each house a chain of command was established. Provisions were made for agricultural activity outside the walls and for commercial interchange with the outside world.[50]

By the early 330s C.E. this system of life was proving so popular that offshoots of Pachomius's original foundation began to be established, and before his death he was ruling over a community of monasteries with a combined population of some seven thousand monks. In the words of the late David Knowles, preeminent historian of Christian monasticism:

> When [Pachomius] died, we might almost say that a perfect monastic order was in existence. Not only was all the material framework there—church, refectory, assembly room, cellar, enclosure wall—not only was the daily life of prayer and work in all its parts arranged, not only was the spiritual discipline of chastity, poverty, and obedience wisely established, but the whole complex was knit together by firm strands of control.[51]

Subsequent developments

Antony had been a hermit who returned periodically to the city. Pachomius had organized men and women who had turned the desert into a city. Within a century after the deaths of Pachomius and Antony monasticism had made explicit many of the tendencies latent in these Egyptian beginnings.

In Asia Minor Basil established the coenobium as something other than an enabling mechanism for persons whose fundamental commitment was to the solitary life. He had visited the monks of Egypt, but was not persuaded of their governing ideal. When asked whether the person who has left common society should live privately or join with others of like mind "who have chosen the object of religion," Basil replied, "I recognize that the life of a number lived in common is more useful in many ways"—more useful, not just more convenient.[52] In a practical departure from the Pachomian system, corresponding to the theoretical distinction, Basil located his monasteries within cities, where the community of monks could readily go beyond the expression of love for one another to the direct, active service of the larger community. Basil's monasteries included hospitals, schools, orphanages. Indeed, they provided social welfare on a scale and with an efficiency the Roman government had never achieved. Basil, who was a bishop as well as a monk, adapted the Pachomian model for purposes quite different from those Pachomius had in mind.

If Basil carries the coenobitic ideal to its logical conclusion, the pillar saints of Syria illustrate the extension of the eremitic ideal to its limit. Symeon Stylites removed himself from social attachments not only by going away, but also by going up. He lived on a platform atop a pillar in the desert for about forty years. Like Antony, Symeon attracted much attention and came to wield enormous power. Emperors consulted him and were careful to let it be known they were acting with his advice. But his contact with people was less direct than Antony's had been. Antony had encountered others face to face; Symeon pronounced from above. Antony's austerities had been for the most part hidden, but they were both geographically and theologically carried out on a human plane, at ground level. Symeon's austerities were spectacularly open to public view, but for just that reason they took on a superhuman cast.[53]

These developments eventually came full circle. In the West, during the Middle Ages, monasteries were situated for the most part in country districts, but they served the social functions Basil had originally designed for the city. And about a century after Symeon's time there were monks living on pillars within the walls of Constantinople itself. The lines of demarcation between desert and city and between coenobitic and eremitic ideals became, in the course of time, harder and harder to locate precisely.

CONTINUITY OR DISCONTINUITY?

Peter Brown, whose interpretations of Late Antiquity have cast fresh light on early Christianity, has recently argued that when the ascetic movement came to prominence in the church, Christianity was thereby effectively cut off from Christian origins. He insists that to understand what it was like to live in the world of Late Antiquity we must take seriously the conviction of people then that they "shared their world with invisible beings, largely more powerful than themselves, to whom they had to relate." Between the second century and the fifth a drastic change occurred in people's "views as to where exactly this 'divine power' was to be found on earth and, consequently, on what terms access to it could be achieved." This shift, toward increasingly explicit focusing of divine power on particular human beings, was culturewide. It was not a Christian specialty, but Christians capitalized on it: "The Christian church was the *impresario* of [this] wider change."[54]

Traditional explanations of the transition to the fourth and fifth centuries have depended on an alleged failure of nerve or similar spiritual/psychic catastrophe, which turned people toward supernatural remedies for unbearable anxiety. Brown calls this whole reading of the evidence into question. He believes that modern historians are "doing the feeling" for ancient persons, and are attributing to those men and women of long ago "holy dread," which is what the historians themselves, with their twentieth-century skepticism, would have to experience to be jolted into an intense regard for the supernatural, but which is not really found in the sources. "If judged simply in terms of religious ferment, Late Antiquity is a singularly sober and serious-minded period in European history."[55] According to Brown, the real battle is not between a paganism no longer capable of providing spiritual security and a Christianity prepared to offer a safe harbor for people drifting on a sea of anxiety. The fundamental debate is over the locus of the holy, the claims of various persons to wield invisible power. Is this or that particular wonderworker a sorcerer or a saint?

The crucial feature of the ascetic program was disengagement, for by cutting the ties of family and other social relationships monks eliminated the suspicion that they were simply applying supernatural sanctions to their natural ambitions. "Prolonged rituals of social disengagement reassured the clientele of the ascetic that his powers were totally acceptable, because they were wielded by a man dead to human motivation and dead to human society." The saint could be trusted because his agenda was not hidden, and he could be admired because his agenda was not set by others. As Athanasius said about Antony, "He had himself completely under control—a man guided by reason and stable in his character."[56]

Brown's analysis directs our attention not so much to the question how the ascetic movement became a force in the Christian church, but how it became a cultural norm for the Roman Empire. Christian monasticism can be seen as part of the church's complex coming to terms with imperial culture, not as a gauntlet thrown in the face of a decadent, hedonistic Rome. Antony appears as a culture hero, not a counterculture one.

Brown's chief interest is in the processes by which people in the Late Antique world came to acknowledge certain of their fellows as authentic bearers of divine power whom they sought out in order to gain access to the source of that divine power. The concurrent question about the rise of Christian monasticism—why did an immense and complex monastic system develop so quickly?—has not received similar attention from Brown, though he has noted that groups that formed around the holy men "cut across the normal tissue of human relations."[57] This is a theme of monasticism that will be sounded repeatedly in succeeding centuries—in putting on the monastic habit, the king and the peasant, the scholar and the shoemaker, are all suddenly equals.

To think about the coenobium is to suspect that Brown has stopped short of considering issues that get fourth-century Christianity back in touch with Christian origins. Brown himself mentions in passing that already in the first century Christians were attributing to the apostles a permanent closeness to divine power, a closeness that had much the same effects as that attributed later to the ascetics.[58]

There is, to be sure, a difference. The apostles can conquer the demons because of the spiritual power Jesus has given them, while Antony achieves his spiritual power because of his long and finally victorious struggle against the demons. But in terms of social dynamics, there is enough similarity between Jesus and the apostles as spiritual fathers and the role of spiritual father among the monks—whether inadvertent, as with Antony, or intentional, as with Pachomius—to make fourth-century monasticism a plausible heir of the apostolic tradition.[59]

One of the few generally acknowledged positive conclusions of the quest for the historical Jesus is that Jesus upset convention by disregarding the social, economic, racial, and religious categories commonly used to distinguish people into acceptable and unacceptable classes. The monastery comes closer than any other Christian institution to expressing in practical terms the implications of Jesus' own disengagement from conventional structures and Paul's insistence that in the new age the old distinctions become inoperative.[60] Indeed, Brown's argument might be turned right around, to say that the ascetic movement of the fourth century succeeded in giving widespread cultural expression to something that, though a central feature of Christian origins, had not been able to develop fully until social conditions throughout the empire were ripe for it.

4

The Rule of Life

BUDDHISM

"**B**lessed Nagasena, you monks say, 'If a layman reach sainthood, there are two courses open to him, and none other: on that day he either retires from the world or else attains Nirvana. . . .' '"[1] While early Indian Buddhism upheld the ideal of a community of four constituencies—laymen, laywomen, monks, and nuns—attention focused on the monastic rather than the social order. In its ideal sense, as the above quotation indicates, the monastic community was one of high spiritual attainment bent on the realization of Nirvana. With the growth of the community, more mundane issues of discipline, daily regime, and monastic routine became increasingly significant. As the followers of the Buddha developed from a sect united by an allegiance to a common *dharma* or teaching to an Order bound by a common discipline, institutional issues became increasingly complex.[2]

The first part of this chapter focuses on Buddhist monastic life primarily but not exclusively in Southeast Asia. The Theravada ("Teaching of the Elders") Buddhism of Southeast Asia—Sri Lanka, Burma, Thailand, Kampuchea, Laos—is strikingly homogeneous relative to the diverse forms of institutional Buddhism through Central and East Asia. To be sure, there are cultural variations among the Buddhisms of the different Southeast Asian nations and even among different geographic divisions of the same country. Nonetheless, the Theravada Buddhist monastic community might be characterized as follows: (1) a community of individuals set apart by a ceremony of initiation or ordination, (2) regulated by a formal rule or code of discipline, (3) informed by the study of Buddhist scripture, doctrine, and traditions, and (4) defined equally by public and monastic ritual roles. Following this working definition, we shall explore the nature of the ceremony of initiation into the monastic community, the regulation of monastic life, and monastic observances, and we will conclude with an analysis of the aims involved in being a monk.

Initiation into the Monastic Community

Life as a monk begins with a ceremony of ordination or initiation. Since, generally speaking, no ritual marks the acceptance of Buddhist laity into their religion, ordination—at least for males— functions in a manner similar to Christian baptism and confirmation or a Jewish bar mitzvah.[3] Traditionally in Theravada cultures, ordination served as a sign of social maturation. Although ordinands might remain monks for the rest of their lives, most returned to lay life after a relatively brief period of training, commonly one to two years. The monastic training included learning how to read and write, and mastering the ritual forms so important to individual life passage observances and occasions of community celebration.

From the point of view of its early historical development, initiation into the Buddhist monastic Order evolved from a simple charge given by the Buddha to a formal ceremony involving a period of instruction and an extensive set of vows. According to *The Book of Discipline*, becoming a monk during the lifetime of the Enlightened One meant responding to his charge: "Come, O Monk, well-preached is the *dharma*. Live a chaste life for the sake of the cessation of suffering."[4]

As the monastic community grew it became increasingly difficult for the Buddha to approve personally of every new ordinand. Consequently, he commissioned his disciples to admit new members into the Order by having them take the vow of the Three Refuges:

> And thus, monks . . . should one ordain: First, having made him have his hair and beard cut off, and having made him put on yellow robes, having made him arrange an upper robe over one shoulder, having made him honour the monks' feet, having made him sit down on his haunches, having made him salute with joined palms, he should be told: "Speak thus, I go to the awakened one for refuge, I go to *dhamma* for refuge, I go to the order for refuge."

A third stage developed later, in which the Order admitted a candidate presented by a preceptor in a formal act of monastic business (*sanghakamma*) consisting of a motion and a resolution proclaimed three times.[5] This method prevails in Theravada countries today, while the form represented by the second stage is used in cases of novitiate ordinations.

Theravada ordination (Southeast Asia)

For an ordination to occur, four conditions must be met, regarding the personal qualities of the ordinand, quorum, place, and announcement. To be ordained as a monk a person must meet such technical requirements as being twenty years of age, having no criminal record or indebtedness, and being physically sound. Admission to the Order also necessitates a quorum, ordinarily ten monks. Ordination must occur in a place consecrated for the purpose of conducting formal monastic business. And the monks within those monastic precincts must give their consent. Ordinarily steps preparatory to initiation will include instruction and examination of the applicant by a preceptor, a special relationship which often continues after the ordination. When everything is in order, a motion to receive the ordinand is repeated three times to the monks assembled for the ceremony. A response of silence on their part indicates their agreement.[6]

In various parts of Southeast Asia, such as Burma, northern Thailand, and Laos, the ceremony of monastic initiation begins as a reenactment of Prince Siddhartha's renunciation of the householder life, an act that initiated his quest for enlightenment. The ordinands dress in princely costumes, mount horses rented for the occasion if family finances permit, and ride through the village to the monastery accompanied by family and friends. In other, somewhat less festively celebrated monastic initiation ceremonies, a candidate for admission to the Order will be clothed in a white robe after having his head and facial hair shaved. Such dress symbolizes the "liminal" stage in the ordination process, between the clearly demarcated life of a layperson and that of the monk. Indeed, the initiation rite in toto marks the passage from one stage of life to another, and in this sense can be considered a rite of transition or a life-crisis ritual. Ritually speaking, initiation into the Order is the quintessential expression of the betwixt-and-between nature of the monastic life— as we noted in chapter 2, a rite thoroughly consistent with the Buddhist ascetic ideal.

Let us assume we are observing a ceremony of full admission or "higher ordination" into the Thai monastic Order (*sangha*). A white-robed twenty-year-old enters the ordination hall carrying a new set of saffron colored robes. He pays respects to his preceptor and requests admission into the Order:

> Venerable Sirs, I take for guidance the Buddha, even though he has long since attained the state of complete extinction (*parinibbana*), together with his teaching (*dharma*), and the monastic Order (*sangha*). Grant me, Venerable Sirs, ordination as a novice and also as a monk in the Blessed One's teaching and discipline.[7]

The young man's preceptor blesses the saffron robes and instructs the candidate in the fundamentals of the Buddhist tradition. Afterward, he is dressed in his new robes, given a monastic name in the Pali language sacred to Theravada, takes refuge in the Triple Gem (*Buddha, Dharma, Sangha*), and subscribes to the Ten Training Rules: abstention from taking life, from stealing, from unchaste acts, from lying, from taking intoxicants, from meals beyond the prescribed time (twelve noon), from entertainments, from bodily adornments, from sleeping on soft beds, and from handling money.

Following this brief novitiate ordination ceremony, the young man is given a begging bowl and again pays respects to his preceptor, asking for his guidance. His teacher asks him a set of formal questions about his qualifications and then presents him to the gathered assembly of monks before whom the ordinand requests admission to the Order: "Venerable Sirs, I desire ordination by the *sangha*. May the *sangha* have compassion on me and lift me up as a monk (*bhikkhu*)." The preceptor then presents his candidate to those gathered for the ceremony, and if there are no objections the young man is considered a fully ordained monk equal to anyone else in the monastic community.

More extensive instruction by the preceptor follows this formal admission. The preceptor's talk may be relatively informal or it may follow a set lesson on the four resources of the monk's life—food, robes, lodging, medication; the four most serious offenses against the discipline—unchaste behavior, stealing, taking life, and claims to superhuman qualities; and the three stages of the path to Nirvana—moral discipline, mental training or meditation, and wisdom. The ceremony concludes with the monk's pouring water from a small jar into a silver bowl, symbolizing the sharing of the meritorious power gained from this sacred event with those deceased. In this manner, all beings, living or dead, benefit from the virtue generated by the ceremony of monastic initiation.

The Buddhist ordination ceremony can be interpreted on various levels. In the first instance, the rite signals entrance into the monastic fellowship. In a broader social sense, it also functions as a rite of passage into adult society. But there are other more symbolic interpretations as well. Thais refer to the candidate for novitiate ordination as a *naga* (water serpent), which may suggest "that a human being in entering the status of ascetic monk leaves behind and renounces the attributes of a *naga*—virility or sexuality, and similar attributes of secular life."[8] From this point of view, the ordination ceremony becomes the passage between the opposing states represented by the serpent, on the one hand, and the monk, on the other.

Another type of symbolic interpretation sees the initiation rite as a representation of an important historical event in the life of the Buddhist Order, the First Council at Rajagraha, which marks the formal beginning of the monastic community. This historical event, moreover, not only initiates the monastic Order, but is also "an event which in some measure started off the cosmic cycle again from the beginning."[9] Because of its nature and varied significations, the ordination ceremony provides a rich resource for understanding the Buddhist monastic life.

Mahayana ordination (Central and East Asia)

Monastic initiation in other parts of Buddhist Asia differs in various respects from the Theravada rite typical of Sri Lanka and Southeast Asia. Generally speaking, monastic ordination in Central and East Asia developed more highly structured and complex forms. In China, for example, a probation period known as "tonsure" preceded ordination. Customarily, the newly tonsured novice trained for ordination for a period of three years, although practically speaking the time may have been considerably shorter.[10]

Traditionally, ordination was divided into three stages symbolizing levels of spiritual progress. In the first stage the ordinand vowed to keep the Five Training Rules—to refrain from taking the life of any living being, from stealing, from sexual misconduct, from lying, and from intoxicants—and to practice the Ten Virtues of action, speech, and will: moral virtue, almsgiving, preservation of life; plain speech, truthtelling, peaceful words, sympathetic speech; abstinence from quarreling, mercy, and acting from good motives.[11] The novice also promised to keep five additional precepts—to abstain from perfume and bodily adornments, from entertainments, from the use of comfortable beds, from taking meals at irregular hours, and from acquiring valuables.

The second stage of the ordination process focused on the acceptance of the 250 rules of the Chinese Mahayana *Vinaya* or monastic code. (In the Theravada tradition higher ordination consists of 227 rules.) The public ceremony in which this occurred would follow about two weeks of additional training, a night of penance, and ritual bathing.

The third stage, completely absent from Theravada practice, was called the *bodhisattva* ordination or the taking of the four *bodhisattva* vows: to lead all beings to salvation, to make an end of all pain and suffering, to study the works of the great teachers, and to attain to perfect Buddhahood. This stage was often initiated by burning twelve incense squares on the newly shaved head of the monk. Such ascetic practice, while difficult to reconcile with the Buddha's Middle

Way, was nevertheless mild in comparison to other forms of self-mutilation that were widespread during the T'ang Dynasty (618–906 C.E.).

Differences in the form of the rite of monastic ordination reflect both doctrinal and cultural influences. For example, the stage of the *bodhisattva* vows points to an important doctrinal distinction between Theravada and Mahayana forms of Buddhism. It has been suggested that the more arduous probationary practices of monastic Buddhism in Central and East Asia may be a result of its more esoteric, mystery-religion character.[12] This ascetic dimension of Buddhist monasticism is embodied in legends of such Buddhist masters as Bodhidharma, who came to China around 520 C.E. to propagate *dhyana* (*Ch'an/Zen*) Buddhism. His most famous student, Hui K'o, was so impressed by Bodhidharma's dedication to meditation practice—nine years staring at a wall—that he cut off his own arm to demonstrate his eagerness to become Bodhidharma's disciple. Similar stories of a more fabulous nature are found in the Tibetan Buddhist monastic traditions.

THE RULES OF MONASTIC DISCIPLINE

Life in a communal, monastic setting must be regulated. In Buddhism the monastic regime became more elaborate as the movement increased in numbers, changing from an informal, mendicant situation to stable groups or communities. A former head of the Thai monastic Order put the need for monastic regulation in this way:

> Men living in society cannot live as individuals without connection to others because men have different dispositions and strengths, the rough and the strong bullying the others so the polite but weak people have no happiness, hence [living like this] society will be disordered. Therefore, the king must establish laws preventing people from doing evil and punishing the guilty. . . . There must also be rules and regulations in the bhikkhu [monk] community in order to prevent wrong behavior and instigate bhikkhus to behave properly. The Master has been established both in the position of the King of the Dharma [Teaching, Truth] whose duty is to govern, and as the Father of the Sangha [monastic Order]. . . . As King of Dharma he has established the rules and laws . . . to prevent wrong behavior. . . . As Father of the Sangha [he] has set up traditions of good conduct . . . urging

bhikkhus to behave properly, just as the revered father of a family who has trained his children to follow the traditions of the family.[13]

The *Book of Discipline* (*Vinaya Pitaka*), which treats the development of the monastic Order and the origin of monastic rules, supports this rather commonsense point of view. The rules and regulations of the Buddhist monastic Order emerge from specific occasions when the Buddha is asked to pass judgment on a particular action or mode of behavior. For example, one of the regulations regarding footwear emerges from the following situation:

> Then the Lord, having dressed in the morning, taking his bowl and robe, entered Rajagraha for almsfood with a certain monk as his attendant. Then that monk went limping along behind the Lord. A certain lay follower, having put on sandals with many linings, saw the Lord coming from afar; seeing him, having taken off his sandals, he approached the Lord; having approached, having greeted that monk, he spoke thus:
>
> "Why, honoured sir, does the master limp?"
>
> "My feet are split, sir."
>
> "See, honoured sir, here are sandals."
>
> "No, sir, sandals with many linings are objected to by the Lord."
>
> "Take these sandals, monk."
>
> Then the Lord in this connection having given reasoned talk, addressed the monks, saying: "I allow you, monks, sandals with many linings that have been cast off. Monks, new sandals with many linings are not to be worn."[14]

By setting the origin of monastic regulations in story or narrative form, the monk-authors of the *Book of Discipline* make the Buddha the authority for the code governing monastic behavior. Furthermore, as the occasion for this particular regulation demonstrates, the justification for the rules of the Buddhist monastic life accords with the principle of the Middle Way. Here we do not find an arbitrary kind of ascetic regimen, but a humane, rather moderate accommodation: not to wear sandals will bring injury to the feet, but a monk should not be attached to expensive, luxurious footwear.

Theravada discipline

The core of the Theravada Buddhist monk's discipline is found in a collection of 227 training rules known as the *patimokkha*, or bond of union. In its earliest form this bond appears to have been simply a common confession of faith:

> The Buddhas call patience the highest penance, longsuffering the highest Nirvana; for he is not a mendicant who strikes others, he is not a Samana [religious] who insults others. This is the Rule of the Buddhas: abstinence from all sins, the institution of virtue, the inducement of a good heart.[15]

From a confessional bond the *patimokkha* became a code of monastic *regula*, although the number of rules appears to have varied. Textual evidence points to an early formulation of 150 training rules, and the Mahayana code consists of 250. In the Theravada tradition, however, the rules became standardized or codified at 227. In contemporary monastic practice in Sri Lanka and Southeast Asia the rules in toto form the substance of a ritual recitation or confessional—a reaffirmation of a shared monastic life—which takes place twice monthly on the occasion of the full and the new moon.

The 227 monastic training rules are arranged in a sequential order according to the seriousness of the offense and ensuing penalty. The first group of four offenses entails expulsion from the Order with no form of expiation: engaging in sexual intercourse, stealing, taking the life of a human being, and making false claims to superhuman attainments.[16] Technically they are known as *parajika*, being "defeated" or no longer a member of the monastic Order.

Other offenses have less severe penalties. Thirteen require a formal meeting of the monastic fellowship to determine the fault and judgment regarding the proper penance and probation. These rules include misconduct in regard to sexual behavior, shelter, and personal actions damaging to the well-being of the monastic community. Thirty relate to the improper acquisition or use of clothing, various kinds of personal possessions, food bowls, and medicines, for which the punishment is forfeiture. The remaining training rules cover more and more minutely detailed kinds of behavior. Ninety-two of them range from slanderous talk to bad manners, and involve some form of expiation to be determined by the abbot or his delegated representative. Four prohibitions concern the kinds of people from whom a monk must not receive food. Such impropriety involves only confession. A large number of training rules (75) cover customs to be observed when entering towns and villages, the manner of accepting almsfood and eating food, and not teaching the *dharma* to disrespectful people. Finally, seven rules cover various kinds of legal or judicial processes within the Order.

Although the canonical disciplinary rules of the Theravada monastic community are quite detailed, they do not cover numerous aspects of daily life within a particular monastery. Consequently, individual monasteries will develop their own rules and operating procedures with a variety of means for enforcement.[17] The key person in the formulation of such rules and the general administration of the monastery is, of course, the abbot.

Individual abbots leave their distinctive stamps on the monasteries over which they have the primary authority. If the abbot promotes meditation as a required part of the monk's daily regimen, he will be sought out by those who strive for Nirvanic attainments. Other abbots gain reputations as strict disciplinarians. Parents may wish to ordain their sons into the novitiate under the guidance of such abbots in the hope of strengthening their moral fiber. On the other hand, some abbots allow monks to dabble in the magical arts—specifically prohibited in the disciplinary code—and provide minimal direction over the life of the monastery. Even the physical surrounding of the monastery will reflect this indifferent leadership, and monks in such monasteries may lose the respect of the laity. Hence, while the status of the monk gives him a place of special veneration within the lay community, respect for an individual monk depends, in part, on the degree to which his behavior appears to embody the monastic ideal.

The daily regimen in a Theravada monastery varies according to the schedule established by the abbot.[18] In a well-administered monastery, the day begins early as all monks and novices arise at 4:30 A.M. to prepare for a communal monastery service of chanting and meditation. From 6:00 to 6:30 they study before going out on their morning food rounds from 6:30 to 7:30. After breakfast the entire community is involved in study and/or the teaching of the Pali language and such subjects as Buddhist history, doctrine, and rituals until the last meal of the day, beginning around 11:00 A.M. Lunch is followed by two to four hours of formal study before the afternoon ends with an hour's required maintenance and cleanup. From 5:30 to 7:00 P.M. the evening communal chanting service and meditation is held in the main temple building. Two hours are then devoted to individual study, followed by an informal meeting in the abbot's rooms for discussion of problems pertaining to monastic study and practice.

The abbot's major responsibility is to oversee and supervise this daily schedule of study, meditation, rest, and communal ritual chanting. The best abbots not only enforce the disciplinary rules; they also have a profound depth of wisdom, compassion, and humor. In most cases the abbot sets the example both for those who are ordained into his particular monastic fellowship and for the laity involved in the life of the community. He may be noted for his spiritual practice, his ability to administer the monastery, and for his skills as teacher and pastor. He is, in short, the exemplar par excellence of a religious life lived in terms of the highest ideals of the Buddhist tradition, or, to put it another way, a life lived betwixt and between the practical necessities of being a leader within a human community and that state of perfect freedom known as Nirvana.

Mahayana discipline

Life in the Buddhist monasteries of Central and East Asia is regulated much as it is in the monasteries of Theravada Southeast Asia. The Mahayana monastic code consists of 250 training rules divided into the same basic categories as those of the Theravada code previously discussed. Furthermore, other operative codes developed, for example, the *Sutra of Brahma's Net,* the *Pure Rules of Pai-chang,*[19] which provided more specific instructions for monastic behavior. With their Theravada counterparts, the Buddhist monks of Central and East Asia ideally embody the virtues of selflessness and compassion. Compassion, in particular, marks the Mahayana monastic ideal as monks seek to dedicate their lives to the *bodhisattva* vow of saving all sentient beings.

Authority for the governance of the Buddhist monasteries of Tibet, China, Korea, and Japan is invested primarily in the abbot. He leads the monks in all of their religious exercises—morning devotions, meals, meditation periods, and sermons—and, in addition, carries out or oversees the administration of the monastery and exercises pastoral care of the lay families in his parish.[20] The founders of monasteries were often considered to be great spiritual masters, embodying the essence of their particular tradition. Stories of their lives exerted a powerful influence on the monastic ethos. What would the Tibetan monastic ethos be without the stories of Padma Sambhava and Milarepa? Or the Ch'an/Zen tradition without the hagiographic legends from the T'ang Dynasty's collection, the *Transmission of the Lamp*? Lists of disciplinary rules lack the exemplary force of such stories as I Hsuan's (Lin Chi) first discussion about the Buddha's *dharma* with abbot Huang Po:

> I Hsuan went to the abbot's room to ask the question, but before he finished it, Huang Po struck him (with a staff). When I Hsuan returned (to the hall), Mu Chou asked Him: "What was the Abbot's reply?" I Hsuan replied: "Before I finished my question, the Venerable Abbot struck me: I really do not understand (why)." Mu Chou urged him: "Go again and ask (the same question)." I Hsuan returned and Huang Po again struck him. Thus thrice he asked and thrice he was beaten by Huang Po. Said he to Mu Chou: "I was urged by the Venerable Sir to ask about the Dharma but was beaten by the Venerable Abbot. I am sorry my own obstructing karma does not allow me to understand the profound doctrine; now I want to go away." Mu Chou said: "If you really leave, you should first bid farewell to the Venerable Abbot." I Hsuan paid obeisance to Mu Chou and withdrew.
>
> (After interviewing I Hsuan), Mu Chou went direct to the abbot's room and said to Huang Po: "In spite of his youth, the questioning monk is very remarkable and if he comes to bid you farewell, will you please receive him helpfully so that he can later become a large tree sheltering men all over the country."
>
> The following day, I Hsuan took leave of Huang Po who said: "There is no need for you to go far; just go down to the river bank at Kao An and call on Ta Yu who will tell you (everything)." When I Hsuan arrived, . . . Ta Yu asked him: "Where do you come from?" I Hsuan replied: "From Huang Po." Ta Yu asked: "What were Huang Po's words and sentences?" I Hsuan replied: "I thrice asked about the deep meaning of the Buddha Dharma and was beaten thrice; I do not know if I was wrong or not." Ta Yu said: "Huang Po had so great a compassionate heart and only wanted to release you from distress, yet you come here to ask whether you were wrong or not!" Upon hearing this I Hsuan was completely enlightened.[21]

MONASTIC OBSERVANCES

Generally speaking, monastic observances can be divided into two different types—the first concerning the life of the monastic community itself, and the second affecting monk-lay activities or the Buddhist community taken as a whole. Too often we perceive the Buddhist monk as a person isolated from the world at large. Although the Buddhist monastery has always provided a retreat from the getting-and-spending syndrome of much lay life, it has, nevertheless, been intimately involved with the life of the broader community. Various types of relationships have developed over the generations between monastic and lay communities, and many monastic activities reflect the fundamental interdependence of monk and lay persons. The laity support the monks materially while the monks, in turn, support the lay community spiritually.

Two of the most sacred monastic observances have been previously discussed: ceremonies of admission into the monastic community, and the fortnightly ritual confession of the monastic code. Other exclusively monastic activities include collective morning and evening chanting ceremonies, special meditation training, and study of Buddhist texts and doctrine. Traditionally, the Theravada monastic regimen has been divided into study and training in meditation (see the discussion of Wat Haripunjaya in chapter 6).

Taking modern Thailand as a case in point, monastic education follows two tracks: a religious curriculum exclusively for monks and novices, and a course of study mandated by the state and leading to a secondary school diploma. The religious curriculum was established in the 1920s by the head of the Thai monastic community as a means of unifying and upgrading monastic education. The course of study includes instruction in the history and doctrine of Buddhism as well as its ceremonials and rituals. In addition to three levels of Buddhist studies, a course of nine levels of Pali instruction enables monks to gain a mastery of the sacred language of the Theravada scriptures. Overall, monks spend a significant amount of time in study, and the sight of novices bent over their books memorizing scripture (Pali: *sutta*; Sanskrit: *sutra*) for various ritual occasions is a familiar one in most monasteries. These chants will be used in collective monastery rites as well as in ceremonies involving the laity.

In addition to academic study and the memorization of special scriptures, monks may devote a significant amount of time to meditation practice. This may be done within one's home monastery if meditation teachers are in residence, or a monk may study for a time with a reputable meditation master living in another part of the country. Often these meditation monasteries will be located in relatively inaccessible forest retreats. While monastic lineages tended to codify certain meditation techniques, particular meditation teachers develop their own unique methods.

Study of texts and doctrine, training the mind through meditation, and adhering to the monastic discipline account for most of a monk's and nun's activities within the context of the religious brotherhood or sisterhood. Monks also devote considerable time and effort to various ceremonial and ritual observances. Some involve only members of the Order, but most ceremonies include the laity in some manner, often as sponsors. These ceremonies may take place at the monastery or in the home of a layperson. Basically, they celebrate the changes in the cycle of the year (e.g., the coming of the rains and the planting of crops), major religious events (e.g., the birth, enlightenment, and death of the Buddha), or transition periods in an individual's life (e.g., marriage, death). In short, Buddhist monks are involved in various ways in the major events, phases, and crises in the life of an individual and of a community. Their training equips them not only to pursue the goal of Nirvana, the highest stage of self-realization, but also to participate in rituals as mundane as dedicating a house or warding off evil spirits, or as historically significant as celebrating the events associated with the founding of Buddhism.

Buddhist Nuns

Very little has been said thus far about nuns or female monks within the Buddhist tradition. While, generally speaking, women have played a much more important role as lay supporters of the male monastic community, there is a tradition of a female Order of monks. According to Buddhist legend the Order was founded with the ordination of the Buddha's aunt and foster mother, Mahapajapati, after the death of Suddhodana, the Buddha's father.[22] The Buddha's widowed stepmother went to him after her husband's death, requesting that women be allowed to leave the world under his doctrine and discipline. The Buddha refused the request three times but Mahapajapati, nonetheless, cut off her hair, put on the yellow robes, and traveled with a group of Sakya women from the capital city to Vesali, where the Blessed One was residing. There, with swollen feet and covered with dust, they met Ananda, one of the Buddha's most beloved disciples. Twice more he took their request to the Buddha, who again refused.

But Ananda was undaunted. Observing that a woman who had gone forth under the doctrine and discipline of the Buddha was capable of enlightenment, Ananda argued that women should be allowed to enter the monastic life. The Buddha finally agreed on the condition that they follow eight strict rules:

> (1) a nun even of a hundred years' standing shall (first) salute a monk and rise up before him, even if he is only just ordained; (2) a nun shall not spend Retreat in a place where there is no monk; (3) twice a month a nun shall ask from the Order of monks the time of Uposatha (fortnightly meeting), and the time when a monk will come to give admonition; (4) after Retreat the final ceremony . . . is to be held by the nuns both in the assembly of the monks and the nuns; (5) certain offences are to be dealt with by both assemblies; (6) a novice who has been trained in the six rules for two years is to ask for ordination from both assemblies; (7) a nun is not to rebuke or abuse a monk on any pretext; (8) from this day forth utterance (i.e., official statement) of nuns to monks is forbidden, of monks to nuns it is not forbidden.[23]

While the fact that an Order of female ascetics was allowed within the early Buddhist tradition evidences a relatively progressive attitude toward women for that time in India, female monks were clearly seen as subservient to their male counterparts. Furthermore, the legend records that the Buddha predicted his religion would flourish for a shorter period of time because of the creation of a female Order of monks.

Although the Buddhist monastic tradition has been more male dominated than monasticism in the Christian West, Buddhism has had its share of female saints and monastic leaders. In the Therava-

da scriptures we find an inspiring collection of poetry attributed to
women who attained sainthood during the lifetime of the Buddha,
and few stories are as touching as Kisa Gotami's entrance into the
monastic life and eventual attainment of enlightenment:

> Her boy died when he was able to run about, and in her distress she
> took him on her hip, and went about asking for medicine. One wise
> man thought that no one but Buddha would know of any, and sent
> her to him. Buddha said, "You have done well to come here for medi-
> cine. Go into the city and get a mustard seed from a house where
> no one has died." She was cheered and went, but soon found that
> Buddha in his compassion had sent her to learn the truth. She went
> to a cemetery, laid her child there, and taking him by the hand said,
> "little son, I thought that death had happened to you alone; but it
> is not to you alone, it is common to all people." There she left him,
> and returned to Buddha, who asked her if she had got the mustard
> seed. "That work is done, Lord," she said, "grant me support."[24]

That Kisa Gotami's entrance into the Order of female monks
serves a didactic purpose—emphasizing the Buddhist teaching of
the impermanence of life—does not detract from the poignancy of
the story or her exemplary role in it. As we have seen, male exemplars within the Buddhist monastic tradition often serve the same
purpose. Indeed, even the Buddha himself may be taken as an exemplification of the Truth (*dharma*) that he discovered. In an ideal
sense, therefore, the monastic vocation in Buddhism should not be
seen as an end in itself, but as the most authentic way of living in
the world. Monks, both male and female, exemplify this ideal by
following the discipline and the teaching, to be sure, but even more
in the nature of their being. To the extent that they inspire the laity,
as well, to embody the ascetic ideal, the values of the monastic life
are extended beyond the confines of the monastery walls into the
world.

CHRISTIANITY

The Buddhist *sangha* has survived for two and a half millennia, Christian monasticism for one and a half. Such institutional longevity is
exceptional in human affairs. Can formal and substantial continuity through all those centuries really have been maintained?

As we have seen, the question of continuity was already an issue at the origins of Christian monasticism: "Is our way of life an innovation or is it the apostolic life?" "What is the connection between Antony in the desert and Basil's coenobium?" By the middle of the sixth century C.E., when St. Benedict wrote the Rule that would eventually become the norm for Western Christian monasticism, there were already ten generations of accumulated monastic lore and experience, reflecting all the regional and social diversity of a Mediterranean world that had itself undergone catastrophic changes since the days of Antony. Like Basil, Benedict made decisive choices among available ideals and practices.

Benedict's Rule is far from being all there is to Western Christian monastic regimen. It was two centuries after Benedict's time that the Rule was officially recognized as binding on most European monasteries. Prior to that time his Rule was simply one among many codes that had precipitated out of monastic tradition. But there can be no doubt that this Rule provides for Western Christianity the historically classic and theologically normative pattern of monastic life. Any consideration of what the life of a Western Christian monk or nun is like must begin with, and keep returning to, the seventy-three brief chapters of "this little rule that we have written for beginners."[25]

INITIATION

When he/she is to be received, he/she comes before the whole community in the oratory and promises stability, fidelity to monastic life, and obedience. This is done in the presence of God and God's saints to impress on the novice that if he/she ever acts otherwise, he/she will surely be condemned by the one he/she mocks. He/She states his/her promise in a document drawn up in the name of the saints whose relics are there, and of the abbot/prioress, who is present. The novice writes out this document himself/herself, or if he/she is illiterate, then he/she asks someone else to write it for him/her, but himself/herself puts his/her mark to it and with his/her own hand lays it on the altar. After he/she has put it there, the novice himself/herself begins the verse, *Receive me, Lord, as you have promised, and I shall live; do not disappoint me in my hope.* The whole community repeats the verse three times, and adds, "Glory be to the Father." Then the novice prostrates himself/herself at the feet of each monk/nun to ask his/her prayers, and from that very day he/she is to be counted as one of the community.[26]

For nearly fifteen hundred years this rite of monastic profession has been the way into the Benedictine monastery. With almost point-by-point fidelity these movements and words are currently the heart of the festival celebration in Benedictine houses throughout the world on July 11, the Feast Day of St. Benedict.

This ceremony is not, however, an initiation in the same sense as the Buddhist rite. Benedict himself specifies a novitiate of twelve months prior to the profession, during which the potential monk/nun lives in the monastery and is "clearly told all the hardships and difficulties that will lead him/her to God":

> If [at the end of twelve months] after due reflection he/she promises to observe everything and to obey every command given him/her, let him/her then be received into the community. But he/she must be well aware that, as the law of the rule establishes, from this day he/she is no longer free to leave the monastery, nor to shake from his/her neck the yoke of the rule which, in the course of so prolonged a period of reflection, he/she was free either to reject or to accept.[27]

Today the probationary period is longer. There is a time of candidacy preceding entrance into the novitiate, and following the year's novitiate there are several years of temporary profession (normally three years, sometimes fewer, sometimes extended through renewals to as much as nine years) before the final, solemn, irrevocable vows. The temporary profession provides an opportunity for testing the monastic vocation, and some monks/nuns leave without proceeding to the final vows.

But there is a fundamental difference from the conventional, socially sanctioned monastic initiation common in Theravada countries like Thailand, in which three months as a monk is regarded as a rite of passage into maturity (although the Roman Catholic bishops of Thailand recommended to the Synod of Bishops at the Vatican in 1977 "that all young Catholics be required—like Buddhists—to take temporary monastic vows of poverty, chastity, and obedience for up to three months before being admitted to the adult Christian community''[28]). There are no temporary Christian monks/nuns in the sense that there are temporary Buddhist monks. Those making the simple profession have already been through a rigorous year of monastic training, and they take on the first vows only because they and the novice master/mistress believe there is a good chance they will want to spend their entire lives this way. The fact that in our society today there are many thousands of former monks and nuns who have left their orders after having made solemn profession does not contradict the basic point that Christian monasticism is presumed to be a lifetime enterprise, and ceasing to be a monk or a nun after full incorporation is a wrenching break of commitments that were not expected to come undone.

Christian monasticism had to find its place within a larger religious institution, one that had established its rituals and rules and authorities before the monastic movement began. By specifying that the written profession of vows is to be laid on the altar, Benedict indirectly acknowledges the authority of the bishop who oversees the eucharistic rite that establishes the altar as the center of a Christian community. But the significance for monasticism of the difference between Buddhist and Christian institutional structure goes even deeper.

The quest for Nirvana and the seeking for God have much more in common than Buddhists and Christians used to think. But Buddhist monks aim at a goal for which their own experience is finally the only test, while Christian monks/nuns at their ceremony of profession state explicitly that what they are doing is done in the presence of God. In theory, at least, it is a personal God who will judge whether the monk/nun has reached the goal. A Christian monk's or nun's vows establish a covenant not only with other members of the monastic community, but also with God. The formal and liturgical affinities of the profession service are chiefly with the rite of marriage, where promises are made for life—for better, for worse. Buddhists may decide that some time spent as a monk would be useful. Christians must decide whether they are up to a lifetime in a particular vowed relationship with God. As the devil reminded Antony, ''The body is weak and time is long.''[29]

THE VOWS

Only one of the promises exacted of the monk/nun by Benedict's
Rule is among the popularly supposed triad of "poverty, chastity,
and obedience." Individual poverty is made explicit in the Rule but
is not actually vowed, and chastity was so widely regarded as an
indispensable element of monastic life that Benedict would simply
presuppose it. But the specific vows, made in the presence of God
and the saints, are *stability*, *fidelity to monastic life*, and *obedience*.

The first of these, stability, is generally regarded as the hallmark
of Benedict's Rule. The monk/nun joins a particular monastery in
a particular place and promises to stay there until death. In so doing Benedict goes beyond Basil, who said the ideal Christian life is
social and must be lived in a community. Benedict believes the community in which the Christian lives should be a genuine family,
where people must learn to live together whether it suits them or
not.

Stability is subject to all sorts of qualifications. Benedict clearly
thought it best for monks/nuns to stay at home, but he did make
provision for journeys away. Just how flexible monks/nuns can be
is, however, a point of some delicacy and controversy. They are frequently called upon to serve the church in ways that require their
prolonged absence from the monastery, and when they say, as some
do, "I am always careful to be back at home on July 11 to renew
my vow of stability," they are revealing both a sense of humor and
an unquiet conscience. Whatever the modifications, however, the
personal commitment to a particular monastery, to calling a set
group of persons your brothers or sisters for life, is essentially
Benedictine.

The second of the specifically monastic vows, fidelity to monastic life, while it lacks the precision of stability and obedience, is really
what gives meaning to the other two. The exact sense of Benedict's
phrase *conversatio morum suorum* is elusive, but scholars are generally agreed that the monk or nun here declares acceptance of the
ideal of life espoused by the Rule and a willingness to be governed
by the Rule in pursuit of that ideal.[30] The vow is to a lifetime process of repentance, of turning, of trying, not to a once-for-all leap
into holiness.

If stability provides the necessary context for amendment of life, obedience is the mechanism. It was a commonplace of Christian theology that the original sin of the human race had been disobedience, rooted in pride. Eve and Adam, thinking to be like God, had disobeyed the one prohibition that had been laid down. The reversal of the tide of original sin had begun with Christ's obedience, and Christians were called to play their part in that reversal.

Benedict's monastery in effect replicates, as far as is possible in the fallen world, the conditions of the Garden of Eden. Monks and nuns, like Adam and Eve before the Fall, have their needs provided for, though in the post-Fall situation they must work to earn the resources from which all in common are supported. Like Adam and Eve before the Fall, they are sexually innocent, though in the post-Fall situation they must do battle with the demon of fornication. And as Eve and Adam had been given a test of obedience that they failed, so monks and nuns are subjected to repeated tests of obedience. Benedict's goal is nothing less than this: that obedience shall become habit. Such a goal entails a program of lifelong learning:

> Therefore we intend to establish a school for the Lord's service. In drawing up its regulations, we hope to set down nothing harsh, nothing burdensome. The good of all concerned, however, may prompt us to a little strictness in order to amend faults and to safeguard love. Do not be daunted immediately by fear and run away from the road that leads to salvation. It is bound to be narrow at the outset. But as we progress in this way of life and in faith, we shall run on the path of God's commandments, our hearts overflowing with the inexpressible delight of love. Never swerving from God's instructions, then, but faithfully observing God's teaching in the monastery until death, we shall through patience share in the sufferings of Christ that we may deserve also to share in Christ's kingdom.[31]

If entrance into Christ's kingdom is the ultimate goal to which obedience is the way, the proximate goal is humility: "The first step of humility is unhesitating obedience."[32] Humility in the Rule is defined operationally rather than abstractly. It is portrayed as a ladder of twelve rungs, like the ladder between heaven and earth in Jacob's vision, which "we descend by exaltation and ascend by humility." The various acts of humility strip away illusion and increase clarity of self-knowledge. "The seventh step of humility is that one not only admits with the tongue but is also convinced in the heart that he/she is inferior to all and of less value."[33] Humility is the antithesis of pride, and it is pride above all that blinds us to our true condition. A century before Benedict Palladius had put it succinctly: "Drinking wine within reason is better by far than drinking water in arrogance." Even more pointed is one of the early "Sayings of the Fathers": "If you see a young man climbing up to heaven by his own will, catch him by the foot and pull him down to earth: it is not good for him."[34] Once the rungs of humility have been climbed, as Benedict says,

> the monk/nun will quickly arrive at that *perfect love* of God which *casts out fear*. Through this love, all that he/she once performed with dread, he/she will now begin to observe without effort, as though naturally, from habit, no longer out of fear of hell, but out of love for Christ, good habit and delight in virtue.[35]

Nearly every rung of the ladder exacts some sort of obedience, and it is clear that for the Benedictine the repeated submission of oneself to the will of another is not a form of slavery but the only means for eventually achieving an ungrudging response to God. Our modern exaltation of the autonomous person, of uninhibited self-expression, of "doing one's own thing," would have struck Benedict as the most dangerous (or perhaps most comical) of self-delusions. Benedict is an exponent of spontaneity, but in his judgment a truly spontaneous act, unfettered by selfishness and manipulation, is the fruit of intense, sustained discipline.

If stability keeps the monks/nuns together and fidelity to monastic life gives purpose to their staying together, obedience is the fundamental ordering principle of their life together. The Rule sets an opportunity for obedience at virtually every turning of the monastic routine. There are reminders of Christ's obedience, and repeated admonitions to obey the Rule itself. Obedience is the texture of the entire community life: "Obedience is a blessing to be shown by all, not only to the abbot/prioress but also to one another as brothers/sisters, since we know that it is by this way of obedience that we go to God."[36] Above all, however, obedience to the abbot/prioress binds the monks/nuns into a family. Benedict places on the shoulders of the abbot/prioress an awesome responsibility for the successful working of the entire monastery, from the setting of times for services to each and every monk's or nun's achievement of Christ's kingdom.

THE ABBOT/PRIORESS

"He/She is believed to hold the place of Christ in the monastery."[37] Undergirding all the specific powers that the Rule grants to the abbot/prioress is this extraordinary declaration. By drawing an analogy with Christ, Benedict at a stroke bestows on the abbot/prioress unlimited authority and simultaneously places him/her under the severest restrictions, for the Christ to whom all authority in heaven and on earth belongs is also the Christ who came not to be served but to serve, who washes the disciples' feet, who did not count equality with God a thing to be grasped but became obedient even unto death.[38]

The second chapter of the Rule details the "qualities of the abbot/prioress." They are such as to cause many a new abbot and prioress to tremble:

> Whatever the number of brothers/sisters he/she has in his/her care, let him/her realize that on judgment day he/she will surely have to submit a reckoning to the Lord for all their souls and indeed for his/her own as well. In this way, while always fearful of the future examination of the shepherd about the sheep entrusted to him/her and careful about the state of others' accounts, he/she becomes concerned also about his/her own, and while helping others to amend by his/her warnings, he/she achieves the amendment of his/her own faults.

The most demanding of all the responsibilities of the abbot/prioress is a corollary of the account he/she must render for each monk/nun committed to him/her. The abbot/prioress must deal with each of those monks/nuns in terms of their own peculiarities and not try to devise a general regime applicable to everybody:

> He/She must know what a difficult and demanding burden he/she has undertaken: directing souls and serving a variety of temperaments, coaxing, reproving and encouraging them as appropriate. He/She must so accommodate and adapt himself/herself to each one's character and intelligence that he/she will not only keep the flock en-

trusted to his/her care from dwindling, but will rejoice in the increase of a good flock.[39]

The analogy between Christ and the abbot/prioress is far from complete. The abbot/prioress is not sent from heaven, but is elected, though Benedict prescribes one of the loosest electoral procedures in the history of politics:

> In choosing an abbot/prioress, the guiding principle should always be that the man/woman placed in office be the one selected either by the whole community acting unanimously in the fear of God, or by some part of the community, no matter how small, which possesses sounder judgment.[40]

The abbot/prioress makes the decisions, but must take counsel:

> As often as anything important is to be done in the monastery, the abbot/prioress shall call the whole community together and himself/herself explain what the business is; and after hearing the advice of the brothers/sisters, let him/her ponder it and follow what he/she judges the wiser course. The reason why we have said all should be called for counsel is that the Lord often reveals what is better to the younger. The brothers/sisters, for their part, are to express their opinions with all humility, and not presume to defend their own views obstinately. The decision is rather the abbot's/prioress's to make, so that when he/she has determined what is more prudent, all may obey. Nevertheless, just as it is proper for disciples to obey their master/mistress, so it is becoming for the master/mistress on his/her part to settle everything with foresight and fairness.[41]

There are, then, some constitutional checks on the power of the abbot/prioress, to reinforce the conceptual check provided by the image of Christ the servant, but in terms of the practical, day-by-day functioning of the monastery the abbot's or prioress's authority is complete. To a greater degree than with any other institution, the history of a monastery can be divided into epochs coextensive with the rule of its successive leaders. Universities, industrial corporations, ecclesiastical dioceses, nations, all gain something of their character from the person in charge, but in none of these institutions is there such scope for imprinting a personal style as there is in the monastery. When the monks/nuns elect a new abbot/prioress they are profoundly determining what they will become.

ORA ET LABORA: PRAYER AND WORK

> On hearing the signal for an hour of the divine office, the monk/nun will immediately set aside what he/she has in hand and go with utmost speed, yet with gravity and without giving occasion for frivolity. Indeed, nothing is to be preferred to the Work of God.[42]

One commonly held image of Benedictines is of black-robed men and women chanting prayers and scriptures in a dimly lit church. Benedictines are popularly regarded as virtuosos of the liturgy. This reputation is a genuine reflection of St. Benedict's original idea: *nothing* shall be put before the Work of God (*opus Dei*, Benedict's technical term for community prayer). Yet Benedict was very far from saying there shall be *nothing but* the Work of God. In the early Middle Ages the Cluniac network of more than a thousand monasteries came close to interpreting the Rule in that extreme way. All the daily services ("offices") had become so elaborate that each one lasted until the next was scheduled to begin, and the activity of the monks was restricted almost exclusively to choral prayer. Monasticism came to be seen not as a complete, differentiated life in itself, but as a particular function within the overall program of the church. The monastery was the part of the church that specialized in prayer.

Benedict's idea was quite different from the Cluniac routine. The *horarium* (daily schedule) in Benedict's monastery included eight communal services (night office, Lauds, Prime, Terce, Sext, None, Vespers, Compline), totaling about four hours; five to seven hours of manual labor; two to four hours for spiritual reading; seven to nine hours of sleep; half an hour for the one meal in winter, an hour for the two in summer.[43] Clearly, the pride of place given to the *opus Dei* is not a preponderance of time but of honor. For some items on the schedule there might be circumstances in which another duty could take priority, but when it is time to be in the oratory praying, there are no excuses.

The Psalms

The prayer life of the monastery revolves around the Psalms. Benedict allows for arrangements other than his own—"Above all else we urge that if anyone finds this distribution of the Psalms unsatisfactory, he/she should arrange whatever he/she judges better"—

but there is a limit to change: ". . . provided that the full comple-
ment of one hundred and fifty psalms is by all means carefully maintained every week." He notes that his own scheme is a drastic
alteration of ancient practice:

> Monks/Nuns who in a week's time say less than the full Psalter with
> the customary canticles betray extreme indolence and lack of devo-
> tion in their service. We read, after all, that our holy Fathers/Mothers,
> energetic as they were, did all this in a single day. Let us hope that
> we, lukewarm as we are, can achieve it in a whole week.[44]

And even today, when ardor has apparently cooled even more and
monks/nuns make sure they complete the Psalter in a month, the
Psalms remain the heart of the Work of God.

The Psalter plays a role like that of the *sutras* in the Buddhist monastery: both provide the texts for communal chanting, both become
the prayer of the monks/nuns themselves. But there is a difference.
The Psalms, which have always had an unrivaled prominence in
Benedictine spirituality, are not the product of monastic
experience—nor were they thought to be, since King David was
credited with composing most of them, and whatever he may have
been, David was certainly not a monk. The *sutras* were composed
by practitioners of the monastic life, so the chief textual reference
points of Buddhist spirituality are themselves products of monastic
experience.

Manual labor and sacred reading

Benedict's schedule includes very little time for individual contemplative prayer. The waking hours apart from choral office are spent
mainly in manual labor and sacred reading. Both activities are treated
in a single chapter of the Rule, "The Daily Manual Labor," and both
are initially justified on the grounds that "idleness is the enemy of
the soul."

The sacred reading, like choral prayer, is treated more practically
than theoretically in the Rule. The time devoted to it is extensive—
four hours on weekdays, and "on Sunday all are to be engaged in
reading except those who have been assigned various duties." The
reading consists of Scripture, with a special regimen of a whole biblical book during Lent. Early Christian writings, with the *Conferences*

and *Institutes* of John Cassian, various lives of saints, and the Rule of St. Basil, are singled out as "nothing less than tools for the cultivation of virtues." And reading is not, in Benedict's view, a matter of choice or mood:

> Above all, one or two seniors must surely be deputed to make the rounds of the monastery while the brothers/sisters are reading. Their duty is to see that no brother/sister is so apathetic as to waste time or engage in idle talk to the neglect of his/her reading, and so not only harm himself/herself but also distract others.[45]

This regimen of sacred reading (*lectio divina*) corresponds to the practice of meditation in the Buddhist monastery. In a sense, the authority spectrum shifts between the two traditions. In the Christian monastery, the words of God (the Bible, especially the Psalter) provide the texts of common prayer, while in the Buddhist monastery it is the *sutras*, often set as the words of the Buddha, that serve this function. For the Christians the writings of the Fathers/Mothers are the focus of meditation, while for the Buddhists meditation leaves the words of others behind and becomes a wholly self-generated and self-sustained activity. Only rarely does Benedictine monasticism undertake such an unsupported self-exploration, and the Rule itself says nothing explicit about it.

Manual labor, the Rule's other remedy against idleness, links Benedictine practice to the earliest forms of Christian monasticism. Antony could not read, but he made a point of supplying his own material needs as far as he could, and he paid with the products of his own hand labor for those he could not produce himself. A story about another of the early Egyptian ascetics makes clear that dependence on alms was exceptional. Abba Arsenius fell ill, "and in his plight needed just one penny. And he could not find one, so he accepted it as alms from someone, and said: 'I thank you, O God, that for your name's sake you have made me worthy to come to this, that I should have to ask for alms.' "[46]

The regular morning begging (*pindapata*) rounds of the Buddhist monk, and the daily manual labor of the Benedictine monk/nun, can both be explained as methods, but very different ones, for reinforcing nonattachment. The Buddhist achieves a degree of nonattachment to the material world at the price of dependence on the larger social world. The Benedictine minimizes social links while being involved several hours a day in material activity and production.

Of course the real situation does not fall into these neat categories. The Benedictines, who on the principle of frugality need very little, but who from the seriousness of their purpose work very hard, produce more than they need, and their surplus becomes part of an economy much larger than that of the monastery itself. In one of the more momentous economic prescriptions in Western history, the Rule orders that "the evil of avarice must have no part in establishing prices, which should, therefore, always be set a little lower than people outside the monastery are able to set, *so that in all things God may be glorified.*"[47] In addition to the glory of God, another consequence of systematically underselling the competition is cornering the market, and it is likely that this principle did as much as gifts and bequests to fuel the stupendous economic engine that monasticism became.

Monks as priests

The world around the monastery has of course undergone drastic changes during fifteen hundred years. Discipline and routines have been periodically adjusted to take account of such changes. The most far-reaching change within the monastery itself happened early, perhaps within two centuries of the time of Benedict. The Rule clearly envisages an institution made up primarily of laypersons. There is a chapter entitled "The Admission of Priests to the Monastery"; Benedict apparently thought it exceptional that they would seek admission, and he states in no uncertain terms that the priest must promise to keep the whole Rule and must not expect to get preferential treatment "out of respect for his priesthood."[48]

For centuries the majority of Benedictine monks have been priests. Not only does this status weave them tightly into the church structure, but it also affects directly the work they do. Monastic work is the office of prayer, but priestly work is the liturgy of the Eucharist, and while it is certainly possible to do both, it is difficult to maintain the sense that the monastic vocation is the primary one. This problem is especially acute for those priest-monks assigned to parish work, often far from the monastery, so that their daily routine is scarcely distinguishable from that of any other priest. And because priests are required by the church to undergo a lengthy and rigorous program of theological study, the intellectual level of Benedictine houses is very different from what Benedict had in mind.

When monks became clerics they were, unwittingly, preparing themselves to be the caretakers and developers of culture through many centuries, but they were at the same time further subordinating the monastic tradition to the values and needs and power arrangements of the larger ecclesiastical institution. As a monk says to his abbot in a story about Vatican efforts to get the monastery's leading scholar to head a theological college in Rome, "From the beginning of this matter I told you that we were possibly fighting a lost battle. An abbot rarely defeats a bishop. Roman politics do not allow it."[49]

Eastern Christianity

Headlines in 1976 announced a relatively rare event: a Benedictine abbot had become an archbishop. Basil Hume, O.S.B., Abbot of Ampleforth Abbey, was named archbishop of Westminster, head of the Roman Catholic Church in England. In the West, abbots are frequently at odds with bishops—they seldom become them. In Eastern Orthodox churches it has been a rule since the sixth century C.E. that only monastic clergy are eligible for the episcopate, so the bishop with whom an abbot contends is himself a monk. In the East, a nonmonastic appointment to a high ecclesiastical dignity would be newsworthy. Orthodoxy permits a married clergy, though not the marriage of the clergy—that is, a married man may be ordained, but a man unmarried when ordained may not subsequently marry— and virtually all parish priests have wives. Bishops, however, must be celibate, and almost without exception unmarried priests have taken monastic vows. The church's leadership, then, necessarily comes from monastic ranks, so in Orthodoxy, even more than in Western Christianity, the institution of monasticism is tightly woven into the fabric of the church.

The monastic influence in the episcopate is only one of the features of Orthodox monasticism unfamiliar to the West. Even more surprising is the absence both of a normative rule, such as Benedict's, and of an organizational structure analogous to the Western orders. Orthodox monasticism is stoutly resistant to tidy categories. To the extent that monasticism in the Orthodox tradition has a classic form, that form was established at the time Benedict was writing his Rule, but in markedly different circumstances and by a different method.

Emperor Justinian I

It was Benedict's Rule, written by a monk and based on his own experience of monastic tradition, that made stability normative for Western Christian monasticism. In the East, stability was mandated by the decree of Emperor Justinian I (527–565 C.E.) that monks should stay in their monastery of profession—a decree motivated more by concern for good order in the state than by a theory of the spiritual life.[50]

Justinian's legislation, which penetrated deep into all ecclesiastical affairs, set the main lines followed by Orthodox monasticism to the present day. There was a great deal of precedent for the emperor to draw on. Early in the fourth century C.E. Constantine repealed traditional Roman legal disabilities against celibates. Subsequent emperors denounced persons who became monks in order to avoid public service, admonished bishops to ordain monks instead of economically productive laymen, regulated the disposition of nuns' personal property, sentenced marauding bands of monks who disrupted dioceses.[51] The Roman state had made unmistakably clear its interest in the monastic life.

Emperor Justinian, like Benedict, had ten generations of monastic lore and experience on which to draw, but unlike Emperor Charlemagne (800–814 C.E.), who ten generations later would regularize monasticism in the West, Justinian did not have access to a comprehensive rule that he could simply declare to be the norm.

Basil of Caesarea

The most widely influential document in the East was the collection of ascetic writings of St. Basil, especially the *Longer* and *Shorter Rules*, but even these texts were not a charter for an institution. They are answers (55 and 313, respectively) to specific questions arising out of mid-fourth-century monastic practice, and they characteristically leave to an individual abbot's or prioress's discretion all sorts of issues that are determined in Benedict's Rule.

Benedict is far more self-conscious than Basil about the function of legislation in organizing and sustaining a community. Basil considers that all the legislation necessary for religious life can already be found in the Bible. All the commandments of God are equally binding, and all are capable of being obeyed. To fail in one is equivalent to disobeying them all.[52] Legislation, then, is collapsed into revelation, and the function of the religious superior becomes in effect the exposition of the meaning of Scripture. The abbot/prioress is not assigned the place of Christ in the monastery. The abbot's or prioress's job is to answer the question, What does the Bible say I should do in this or that circumstance?

As we have seen already in our discussion of the ascetic ideal in chapter 2, Basil develops the most thorough rationale in Christian monastic history for the superiority of the coenobitic life over the eremitic. He outlines the ethical commandments of the Bible and notes that they require a social context for their fulfillment.

He has a ready appreciation for the irony inherent in the effort to show oneself more humble than others. Christ had said his followers should take the lowest seat at table rather than trying to insinuate themselves into the most favored position. Basil sketches a humorous picture of a whole community of monks coming into the refectory and fighting for the lowest seat—which they have good reason to do, since one "who strives to do everything according to the commandment must of necessity not fail to observe this order." But:

> to push contentiously to secure [the lowest seat] is to be reprobated as destructive of good order and the cause of confusion. And to be unwilling to give way to one another and to struggle for this will make us as bad as those who strive for the pre-eminence.

In Basil's view, Christ himself had foreseen this problem "when he said that the ordering of these things pertained to the master of the house." To take the chief seat on order from a superior is a way of achieving "genuine humility by our obedience."[53] The establishing of rules, and especially the vesting of authority in an abbot/prioress, is essential when a whole community is aiming at the Christian goal.

At a deeper level Basil appreciates the irreducibly social nature of our very existence as human beings. The solitary life, which many of his contemporaries thought supernatural, was in Basil's judgment simply unnatural, an evasion of responsibility rather than a strenuous path to perfection. But because, unlike Benedict, he did not sketch in writing a whole institutional embodiment of his ideal, Basil's tradition could not suppress the popular regard for the eremite. Justinian's legislation presupposes that the coenobium is the norm—but the legislation makes specific provision for a limited number of the spiritually advanced to live the solitary life within the coenobium.[54] In other words, the very ideal Basil fought against is established right within the walls of the monastery.

The Great Habit

The class distinction that has bedeviled Western Christian monasticism (besides the second-class status that has de facto been generally accorded women's monasticism) is between priests and lay brothers, but this is a difference grounded in ecclesiastical rank, not ascetic achievement. The monastery to this extent reflects the larger problem of the clericalizing of the Christian community, the according of higher spiritual rank to those who are ordained. The class distinction within Eastern Christian monasticism is specifically monastic—that is, it is rooted in a theory of the ascetic life and its achievements. And it has a striking symbolic expression, called the "Great Habit."

The earliest mention of the Great Habit as distinct from the Little Habit is in the writings of St. Theodore of Studios (759–826 C.E.), abbot of the largest monastery in Constantinople. Theodore was the organizer and codifier that Basil was not, and the influence of the rule he devised for the monastery of Studios comes closer than anything else in the East to matching that of Benedict's Rule in the West. Theodore's fundamental sympathies were attuned to Basil's, and he vigorously denounced the Great Habit/Little Habit distinction.

It is uncertain when and where the custom of a second monastic dress arose, though it appears to be a natural development from

Justinian's homage to the eremitic ideal. The Great Habit is an outward and visible sign of an inward perfection which has propelled the spiritual virtuoso beyond the need for community nurture.

Theodore's polemic against the Great Habit grows out of his whole theory of the place of monasticism in the Christian economy of salvation. How can there be two habits, Theodore asks, if there is only one baptism?[55] For him, entry into the church itself, an entry effected in baptism, is the decisive step from an old existence into a new one, and all Christians share this newness of life. If monastic profession is thought of as a second baptism, it is such only in the sense that the monk/nun is making a commitment to an intensification of baptismal vows.

For Theodore, the task implied in wearing the Little Habit is more than anyone is going to complete in a lifetime. The Little Habit is worn not as a badge of status, but as a constant reminder of the status that has not yet been achieved. As the Russian spiritual leader Bishop Theophan the Recluse (1815–94 C.E.) would later put it: "Progress in our spiritual journey ends with the cessation of our natural breath."[56] Theodore marvels at the way the monastery dissolves all conventional distinctions: the king and the slave are on an equal footing. This is simply radical baptismal Christianity, and Theodore believes it would be a retrograde step to institute new distinctions in place of the old.

Theodore's argument did not prevail. The Great Habit has remained to this day a feature of Orthodox monastic life. In places it has fallen prey to routine, and monks are as a matter of course invested with the Great Habit on their deathbed. But even when the practice is vestigial it testifies to a deep-seated suspicion that the fully coenobitic life is not the school for the Lord's service, as Basil and Benedict and Theodore insist it is, but is rather a school for the eremitic life, which is itself then the true school for the Lord's service.

The staretz

Theodore refused to acknowledge any eremitic aristocracy within the monastic community, but he did recognize an authority inherent in those with highly developed spiritual insight. Charismatic authority independent of ordination, characteristic of Eastern Orthodox Christianity, has been especially powerful in confession and penance.[57] It would not be particularly striking if laypersons confessed to monks who are also priests, in preference to their own priests. The conviction that celibacy is a sign of special holiness is so ancient and so strong that everyone assumes a monk-priest is holier than a married priest.

But in Orthodox history laypersons have not been careful to make sure the monk they are confessing to is a priest. Unordained monks are thought to be just as effective confessors as ordained ones; or rather, the whole question is irrelevant, since effectiveness is a function of demonstrated insight, not of ecclesiastically sanctioned rank. And even within the monastic community itself a monk's spiritual father is not necessarily the abbot. The aristocracy of spiritual insight came to fullest expression in Russian monasticism, where the *staretz*, or spiritual genius, was the true center of authority in the monastery: naming the abbot, having the final say in the admission of novices, usually appointing his own successor in the role of *staretz*.

To read of Russian *startsy* such as Staretz Amvrosy, the model for Dostoevsky's Staretz Zossima, to learn of the way all sorts and conditions of persons hounded them for advice and blessings, to marvel at their capacity to cut straight to the heart of a spiritual or moral dilemma, is to feel oneself back in the atmosphere of original Christian monasticism. There is a degree of artifice in this. The *startsy* were self-consciously living in an earlier age. They insisted that they did nothing original: "I have told you nothing that is an invention of my own. All of what I say comes from the writings of the Fathers."[58] Such disclaimers of originality can be heard repeatedly in Christian monastic history, and while there is always irony in the dogged refusal of innovators to admit any initiative on their part, the Russian *startsy* appear really to have incorporated the spirit of an earlier time into their own being.

Mount Athos

The mystery, the power, the tradition, and the plight of monasticism in Eastern Orthodoxy all come to focus and vivid expression on Mount Athos, the "Holy Mountain." For a millennium this peninsula, extending fifty kilometers into the Aegean Sea near the city of Saloniki in northeastern Greece, has been a unique monastic republic. There are twenty major monasteries, and scores of smaller houses, including individual hermitages. The original impulse was shaped by the coenobitic Rule of Studios, but the entire variety of forms of life that have developed in Orthodox monasticism can be seen side by side on Athos.

In its heyday the Holy Mountain had forty thousand monks (no nuns; the rules of Athos forbid women, and even female animals, to set foot on the territory), and at certain periods it was the center of theological debate and church reform movements. Even as late as the beginning of the twentieth century there were more than seven thousand monks. The communist domination of Eastern Europe has had a devastating effect on Athos, since recruitment of monks for the Slavic monasteries has ceased almost entirely. For many years the Greek monasteries were languishing too. Visitors to the Holy Mountain had a sense of twilight, even nightfall. By the 1960s the numbers were down to little more than a thousand, mostly very old men.

During the past two decades, however, there have been signs of a remarkable revival, a revival that itself highlights two of the perennial issues of the rule of life in monasticism. First, the revival depends on abbots of spiritual insight and administrative ability. Athos is currently blessed with a number of abbots who rank with the great leaders of the past. Second, the revival depends on a return to the coenobitic ideal. Since the fourteenth century C.E. the normative form of life on the Holy Mountain has been "idiorrhythmic," a semi-eremitic arrangement in which monks live in small groups (usually two to six), are allowed to own personal property, and have minimal community life. Each monastery in this system is governed not by an abbot, but by a council of the heads of the small households. In recent decades several of the largest monasteries have opted for a return to coenobitic arrangements (the rules allow a change from idiorrhythmic to coenobitic, but not vice versa), and this move, together with the quality of the abbots, appears to have energized the spiritual life of the monasteries and to have begun attracting new recruits, including some highly educated men.

Nowhere in the Christian world is the continuity of tradition so visible, so palpable, as on Athos. The new vitality is not the fruit of modernization: "It is a strictly traditionalist revival. We may speak of renewal, but certainly not of reform."[59] While Athos is a very special case—an entire region populated and governed exclusively by monks—and therefore not directly a model for monastic communities linked inextricably with the larger society, the influence of the Holy Mountain on Orthodox spirituality in the past has been enormous. A few years ago it would have been a brave prophet who would have even suggested that Athos might once again become a beacon for Orthodoxy—brave but right.

HOSPITALITY

Athos is remote, but welcomes (male) pilgrims. Christian monastic rules, which vary between East and West and within each region, almost all have one prominent feature in common: pride of place given to the virtue of hospitality. We have already seen how Basil of Caesarea's monasteries took in all sorts and conditions of people who were beyond the reach of government concern; that tradition is alive today when monasteries grant sanctuary to persons fleeing persecution, and when nuns and monks organize soup kitchens and take the lead in pastoral care for victims of AIDS. Benedict's Rule assigns only three persons the place of Christ in the monastery: the abbot/prioress, the invalid, and the guest. When guests come to the monastery they are immediately invited to prayer; Benedict says nothing about checking their credentials.[60]

The hospitality of the monastery, characteristic of Orthodox as well as of Western monastic tradition, stands in stark contrast to the defensiveness and turf protection so prevalent in secular society. The welcome offered to everyone by Father Zossima's monastery makes a vivid counterpoint to the plight of a character in another of Dostoevsky's novels, *Crime and Punishment*. Katerina Ivanovna Marmeladov is evicted from her home on the day of her husband's funeral, and she runs frantically "into the street with a vague intention of going at once somewhere to find justice."[61] She does not find it, and she goes mad. The monastery is a place where she could find justice, but she would find more: she would find a welcome, a place where people would not mind that her husband was a scoundrel, her daughter a prostitute, and she herself something of a scatterbrain.

The direct engagement of monks and nuns with the world is a leading fact of contemporary church history. Their effectiveness in the work for justice can be traced to the rule of hospitality, which gives authenticity to their witness. It is simply evident that prior to their advocacy is their hospitality. They accept without doing background checks those whose fight for justice they are supporting and even joining.[62]

5

Transformers and Transmitters

In medieval Europe and in premodern Buddhist Asia the monastery served many functions. It not only provided the context in which devout men and women sought to realize the highest ideals of the religious life. It also became an important and powerful social, economic, and political institution. In various ways the monastery became the center that formed and gave expression to patterns of life that inspired and sustained art, music, and intellectual pursuits. The monastery was architectural achievement, museum, university, landed proprietor, and sociocultural center. Monks were artists, writers, teachers, composers, poets, administrators, and judicial arbiters.

Such activities were not diversions from the monastic path and goal, but were legitimate and natural expressions of the monastic life within human society and culture. To be sure, monks and monasteries have not always successfully maintained the balance betwixt and between the demands of the world, on the one hand, and the pursuit of spiritual transformation, on the other. The monastic life can easily become an escape from the world or, perhaps even more readily, a self-justifying end in itself rather than a context for the re-formation of individuals and society. Yet, at its best, the monastery has always been a visible mediator between the world and the highest calling of the religious life. Indeed, this tension has provided the inspiration behind the finest monastic expressions of liturgy, music, art and architecture, philosophy and theology, literature, and education.

BUDDHISM

Here we shall focus on developments within the Buddhist monastic tradition after its founding; in particular, on the monastery as an educational institution, and the monk as teacher, reformer, and—above all—exemplar. We shall study Nalanda, the most famous Buddhist university on the Indian subcontinent, and then explore the ways in which the Asian Buddhist monastic traditions have depicted the exemplary nature and role of the monk.

THE MONASTERY AS UNIVERSITY

From the time of the Buddha, the Buddhist monk and the Buddhist monastic community performed the role of teacher-educator. The early Buddhist texts portray the Buddha and his followers primarily as teachers of the *dharma*. In time, Buddhist monks in India and elsewhere throughout Buddhist Asia became one of the most literate groups within their particular societies. They created and memorized scriptures, wrote commentaries and treatises, and taught others, both fellow monks and laity. They continue to perform these tasks, although in most Asian countries monastic university education has been superseded by private and government institutions.

When the Buddhist monastic fellowship became a settled community it became a "university" or educational center.[1] Indeed, the Buddhist coenobium arose in part to abet and enhance the educational teaching function of the monk. Pious lay men and women donated permanent residences; communal activities expanded; individual monks developed special expertise in particular types of literary genre and religious practice; both monks and laity sought out the "experts" in such subjects as philosophy, monastic discipline, astrology, and so on. Furthermore, as different Buddhist schools emerged over the years, they developed their own unique scholastic traditions over against one another and in relationship to competing non-Buddhist schools.

Such factors encouraged the development of relatively specialized centers of learning that, in time, became the major universities of Asia. This occurred in all Buddhist cultures, although the most famous were the Indian universities, where major intellectual battles raged. From them some of the most renowned Buddhist missionaries found their way across Central and East Asia, and to them Buddhist monks journeyed from foreign countries. This development has been summarized as follows:

> Almost from its origin Buddhism had been organized in the dwellings of its monks, in monasteries. Under the conditions of an increasingly academic tradition, needing large libraries of non-Buddhist as well as Buddhist texts of every school for reference purposes and systematically training its students as professional philosophers, it was natural enough that some of the greater monasteries should develop into what in modern terms would be called universities. Smaller communities of monks no doubt remained closer to the conditions of early Buddhism, their members concerned more with meditation than with theory, but the magnetism of the great universities tended to draw the ablest scholars and the keenest philosophers to them.[2]

In short, the monastery as a university evolved from a small mendicant group bound together by belief in a common teaching (*dharma*) to a center of general learning and scholarship.[3]

Historically this shift had taken place by the Gupta period in India (300–550 C.E.), at a time when Mahayana Buddhism and a revived Brahmanism were flourishing. Monastic education was no longer confined to study of the doctrine and the discipline in order to produce the perfect monk. Rather, study entailed the five branches of knowledge typical of the Indian pattern of learning—grammar and philology, medicine, logic, the fine arts, and metaphysics—as well as the major classifications of Buddhist texts, namely *sutras* (dialogues of the Buddha), *vinaya* (monastic discipline), and *abhidharma* (scholastic philosophy). This broadening of the program of study promoted the purposes of spreading the faith, serving the laity, and entering into scholarly debate and disputation.[4] Eventually, the monastic universities served not only the religious communities of monks, but the laity as well. To be "learned" meant, in effect, to have studied at one of the famed monastic universities such as Nalanda.

Nalanda

Nalanda, south of Patna in Bihar state, appears to have been founded as a monastery during the first half of the fifth century C.E. It developed into a monastic university in the middle of the sixth century, and for over a century was an international center of higher learning. The Chinese pilgrim-monks, Fa-hsien, I-tsing, and Hsuan-tsang, from whom we learn so much about the condition of Buddhism in India and Southeast Asia from the fifth to the eighth centuries C.E., provide the most comprehensive information about Nalanda and other Buddhist monastic universities.[5] From them we learn that Nalanda had rigorous entrance qualifications and strict regulations. Although degrees were apparently not granted for a formal course of study as in a modern university, there were specialized schools of learning and discussions of Mahayana texts, the eighteen Hinayana sects, logic, philosophy, medicine, and Brahmanical philosophies. Eminent authorities on all these subjects taught at Nalanda. Hsuan-tsang's biographer writes:

> There are 1,000 men [at Nalanda] who can explain twenty collections of Sutras and Shastras; 500 can explain thirty collections, and perhaps ten men, including the Master of the Law [namely, Hsuan-tsang], who can explain fifty collections. Silabadra [the abbot during Hsuan-tsang's six-year stay] alone has studied and understood the whole number.[6]

Education at the great Indian Buddhist universities can be classified as spiritual, moral, literary, and technical.[7] The first included the study of Buddhist texts and doctrines as well as meditation and other spiritual techniques. Moral education fostered the study of etiquette and practical living as well as the rules of the discipline. Literary education meant not only the study of particular literary texts, but languages, grammar, and philology, especially Sanskrit. Finally, technical education had special reference to art, architecture, sculpture, and painting.

Such a large collection of students, teachers, and curricula obviously necessitated a sizable physical plant and a relatively complex organization. Nalanda had extensive boarding and lodging arrangements, lecture halls, hostel rooms for students, special chambers for distinguished professors, and a spacious library. Like the Library of Congress or Harvard's Widener Library, the Nalanda University library was the standard place to find copies of authoritative texts. I-tsing, for example, reports taking over four hundred Sanskrit manuscripts back with him to China from the Nalanda library.

Life at Nalanda was carefully regulated. The abbot was in charge of the academic program and was expected to be the most erudite person in the community. Other officials included a manager or supervisor of the facilities who looked after the physical well-being of the staff and students, and a director of admissions. The monastery also had an astronomical observatory, and an elaborate water clock by which the daily schedule was regulated. According to I-tsing, the routine of daily life was divided between study and the performance of religious rites, but it was the former that so impressed another Chinese traveler:

> The day is not sufficient for the asking and answering of profound questions. From morning till night they engage in discussion; the old and the young mutually help one another. Those who cannot discuss questions out of the Tripitaka [Buddhist scriptures] are little esteemed and are obliged to hide themselves for shame. Learned men from different cities, on this account, who desire to acquire quickly a renown in discussion, come here in multitudes to settle doubts, and then the streams (of their wisdom) spread far and wide.[8]

Nalanda was, of course, not the only renowned Buddhist university in India. Valabhi, contemporaneous with Nalanda, specialized in the study of the Hinayana Buddhist systems, and Vikramasila, founded around 800 c.e., was known as a center of Tantric Buddhist studies. These internationally famous universities illustrate one of the basic aspects of the Buddhist monastic system wherever it was established, be it the Theravada tradition of Sri Lanka and Southeast Asia, Tantrayana in Tibet and Central Asia, or Mahayana forms of Buddhism in China, Korea, and Japan.

Buddhist education today

Obviously the nature and role of Buddhist education within these countries varied greatly. Generally speaking, Buddhist universities on the model of Nalanda did not develop in East Asia, due partially to the identification of Confucianism with literary knowledge.[9] Recently the highly developed system of monastic education in Tibet has become more familiar to Americans through the establishment of Tibetan centers in various parts of the United States, as well as through the publication of autobiographical accounts of Tibetan monk-expatriates educated in traditional Tibetan monastic colleges.[10] In the modern period Buddhist monasteries throughout Asia have developed extensive educational programs that teach both religious and secular subjects to both monks and lay people.

In Japan local Buddhist temples have long been involved in the education of children, although the creation of universities such as Hanazona Buddhist University in Kyoto under the aegis of the Myoshin-ji Zen tradition is of more recent origin (see chapter 6). There Zen priests and laity study both religious and secular subjects toward a recognized university degree. In China the development of school departments within a monastic precinct occurred after 1912 as part of the republican government's program to improve education. Prior to the communist revolution, school departments were found in prominent monasteries throughout the country.[11]

In Theravada Buddhist countries such as Sri Lanka and Burma, the resurgence of Buddhism in the early nationalist periods was accompanied by the revitalization of Buddhist education. In Thailand a nationwide network of monasteries enabled the government to create a national educational structure around the turn of this century, using the monastery compound as a school and the monks as teachers. Two monastic universities in Bangkok have been the principal means through which monks have been educated in secular as well as religious subjects. Monastic educators believe that without such training monks will be deprived of the place they once held in Thai society. Said one university administrator:

> It is not that we are trying to secularize the Buddhist monk, rather, we are attempting to restore him to his traditional place as a religious leader and guide of the people. Besides their own peculiar duties to-

ward the goal of self-enlightenment, monks are bound with many social obligations to serve the community and to render reasonable services for the benefit of lay society.[12]

EXEMPLARS

The monastic contribution to community life was carried out by men and women dedicated to the monastic ideal. They, even more than the institutions they created, represented life betwixt and between the transcendent and the mundane, a life transformed by dedication to goals not defined by the calculations of worldly success, a life in which material poverty was a sign of spiritual wealth. Of the many features of the monastic life, none so typifies monasticism as the "holy wo/man," be it as ideal, symbol, artistic or literary portrait.[13] In particular, the monastery has generated countless stories of saints, patriarchs, reformers, and founders.

These stories perform different functions. Some inspire, others instruct, while yet others provoke. They often function as models or paradigms, narratives that humanize and exemplify the religious ideal, seeming to place it within the grasp of all who aspire to holiness and goodness. As such, the "lives of the saints" represent the essence of the religious life, not simply historical accounts of great men and women who influenced the development of a religious institution. In this section we shall study several monastic exemplars whose story, or episodes from whose story, illustrate the boundary or liminal nature of a religiously motivated life.

In many respects the legend of the Buddha represents the touchstone of the exemplary narratives of all "transformers and transmitters," a journey, universal in structure, of renunciation, realization (Nirvana), and return. Yet, each story of a saint, reformer, or founder uniquely represents a particular aspect of the Buddhist tradition and plays a particular role within a given culture, be it that of Tibet, China, Japan, or Sri Lanka. We shall focus our discussion on Tibet.

Buddhism was established in Tibet in the eighth century C.E. by Padma Sambhava, a Tantric master from northern India. From this time the Tantric tradition dominated the religious history of Tibet and much of Central Asia. Its full-blown metaphysics, intricate techniques of logical argumentation, elaborate pantheon of Buddhas, consorts, gods, and goddesses provided a complete religious system capable of competing with an entrenched Tibetan animism, but it was also able to appeal to a ruling elite.[14]

In Tibet the entire range of Buddhist scriptures—Hinayana, Mahayana, Tantrayana—was preserved. Its finest monastic colleges were renowned for their rigorous and extensive courses of instruction, and various sectarian traditions flourished under brilliant founders and reformers.[15] These leaders figure prominently in the legendary history of Tibetan Buddhism narrated through their life stories. This tradition of holy persons or fully realized human beings assumes a metaphysical dimension in the Tibetan Buddhist lineage of incarnate Buddhas, epitomized by the Dalai Lama who ruled the country as a theocratic state prior to the Chinese Communist takeover in 1958.

Among the best known stories of Tibetan Buddhist saints or exemplars are those of Padma Sambhava, Milarepa, and Naropa.[16] While the details of their legendary life stories vary considerably, they share a common structure: renunciation, preparation-study, testing, initiation, and subsequent teaching. We shall examine these stories for what they tell us about the monk as exemplar within the context of Tibetan Buddhism, and briefly contrast this picture with that of the great fifteenth-century reformer, Tsong-Kha-Pa.

Padma Sambhava

Both Padma Sambhava (fl. 750 C.E.) and Naropa (1016–1100 C.E.) are founders of monastic lineages. The former, considered the father of Buddhism in Tibet, is associated with the Nyingma sect; the latter, together with the Tibetan saint, Marpa, with the origin of the Ka-gyu lineage. In Padma Sambhava's legendary biography[17] his birth occurs as a divine gift of the Buddha Amitabha to King Indrabodhi, but, more importantly, as the fulfillment of the Buddha's prophecy of a "lotus-born one" (= Padma Sambhava) who would become the teacher of Tantric Buddhism in Tibet.

Raised in splendor, Padma Sambhava eventually leaves his princely life to be tested in a cemetery, where he subjugates many gods and demons. Having been successful at this stage, he is initiated into esoteric mysteries by four classes of witches. Following an extensive period of training and instruction, he journeys to Tibet, where he subjugates the guardian spirits throughout the land by his superior magical powers. In the legends Padma Sambhava appears as a miracle worker par excellence, a role downplayed in stories of the historical Buddha and his disciples:

When the Guru [Padma Sambhava] reached gNam-t'an'mk'ar-nag, the white fiendess of that place showered thunderbolts upon him, without, however, harming him. The Guru retaliated by melting her snow-dwelling into a lake; and, the discomfited fury fled into the lake, T'an-dpal-mo-dpal, which the Guru then caused to boil. But though her flesh boiled off her bones, still she did not emerge; so the Guru threw in his thunderbolt, piercing her right eye. Then came she forth and offered up to him her life essence . . . .[18]

The Padma Sambhava legend underscores the syncretic nature of Tibetan Buddhism—Buddhism conquered and incorporated Tibet's indigenous animism—and, furthermore, depicts the monk as one whose training endows him with supernatural powers. While such miraculous tales can be demythologized according to modern tastes, to do so undermines what must have been the normative popular perception of the Tibetan Buddhist monk as a semidivine being.

Naropa

Naropa's life, like that of Padma Sambhava, shares some elements with the biography of the Buddha. He, also, is a royal son whose birth is heralded by the prediction of his future greatness as either a world-ruler or religious leader. At twenty-five years of age he renounces the householder life to become a monk. The biography marks his spiritual transformation through twelve stages or acts of self-denial which, on one level, describe a process, and on another, summarize the teachings of the Buddhist Tantra.[19]

The narrative, consequently, functions as the framework for a more discursive and didactic mode of instruction. In this case, the monk, via his life story, exemplifies the content of the *dharma*, a pattern within the Buddhist monastic tradition inspired by the example of the Buddha. Naropa provides a balance to Padma Sambhava. While Padma Sambhava's legendary life emphasizes the esoteric nature of his training and his conquest over the indigenous Tibetan divinities, the Naropa narrative delineates the substance of the Buddhist path to the highest stage of self-realization. Thus, while the Buddhist monk may be a miracle worker, he is foremost one who has realized and teaches the truth about the nature of existence.

Milarepa

Unlike the legendary lives of Padma Sambhava and Naropa, the story of Milarepa (1040–1123 C.E.) does not begin with a miraculous or supernatural birth.[20] The son of a merchant who died when Milarepa was a young boy, he learned sorcery in order to punish relatives who derided his family's poverty. Filled with remorse after destroying their crops and leveling their house by means of magical powers, he sought out a teacher who would lead him along a "path of light." He met Marpa, known in Tibetan Buddhism as the founder of the Ka-gyu monastic lineage, who led Milarepa through an onerous six-year course of initiation to purge him of his past evil intentions, and to test his loyalty to his *guru* or teacher.

After his pupil successfully endured various trials and hardships, Marpa finally initiated and instructed Milarepa in a "middle way" representing a moral transformation of his destructive powers. Milarepa then embarked on a religious career of meditation and fasting, spending much of his time in mountain caves. Following the normative example of the Buddha, however, he completed his religious quest only after adopting a less extreme form of practice, once again confirming the ideal of moderation that informs the ethos of Buddhist monastic life.

Milarepa's fame as a monk-exemplar stems not only from the decisive role his life plays within the Ka-gyu lineage of Tibetan monastic Buddhism, but also from a large collection of poems attributed to him. Milarepa, like many Buddhist monks, represents a high level of cultural, not simply religious, attainment. He sets a literary as well as a spiritual standard to be emulated by those who consider themselves to be cultured and literate. The monk-exemplar, in short, represents a multiple set of values and ideals. The following poem conveys something of the magic of Milarepa's imagination:

This is the hermitage, called the "Palace of Enlightenment";
Above towers the high white glacier mountain of the gods;
Below are many faithful bringers of gifts;
Behind the mountain is a veil of white silk;
Before me grow the wish-fulfilling woods;
Meadows and green valleys stretch far away;
Over the lovely and scented water lilies,
Buzz and swarm the insect folk.
At the edge of the lake and pool,
Water fowl crane their shapely necks.
In the spreading branches of the trees,
Swarms of birds sing sweetly.
Moved by the wind, the bearer of scents,
The foliage dances in the air.
High in the crowns of the trees
The monkeys twist and turn.
On the soft green carpet of fields
The four-footed creatures browse,
Whilst the herdsmen their masters
Sing songs and pipe the melancholy flute.
Below the slaves of worldly greed
Busy themselves with their follies.
But I, the Yogi, look down on it all
From my perch on these glorious mountains
And take the inconstant world as a parable.
Earthly goods are to me as a reflection in water;
Life is the deceit of a dream.
And my pity goes out to the unenlightened.
The vastness of space is my banquet,
No distraction disturbs my meditation.
That all diversity is encompassed in my spirit,
That all the things of the three-world circle
Although irreal are yet visible, how wonderful that is![21]

Tsong-kha-pa

Within the Tibetan monastic tradition the unrivaled monastic reformer was Tsong-kha-pa (1357–1410 C.E.). The son of poor parents
in eastern Tibet, he was ordained a novice at the age of seven. Nine
years later he began studies in the great fathers of Mahayana Buddhist thought, for example, Maitreya, Dharmakirti, Nagarjuna, at

some of the famed monasteries in Lhasa and central Tibet. His scholarly acumen so outstripped that of his peers that within two years he was reputed to have mastered the five areas of study: logic, the doctrines of the Perfection of Wisdom (*prajnaparamita*), the teaching of Nagarjuna, the *Abhidharmakosha* of Vasubandhu, and the discipline of the monastic Order (*vinaya*).

Receiving his final or higher ordination at age twenty-five, Tsong-kha-pa continued scholarly studies, mastering medicine, mathematics, and the esoteric Tantric texts, especially the famed *Kalacakra Sutra* and the *Guhyasamaja*. He then proceeded to write two works that, more than any others, influenced the direction of Tibetan Buddhist thought to the modern period, the *Steps to Enlightenment* (1403 C.E.), and *The Great Stage Way to the Occult Sciences*.

Tsong-kha-pa's scholarship and moral example attracted more and more followers until he formed a new religious community called the Ge-lugs-pa (Sect of the Virtuous), known as the Yellow Hat Community, a reformed sect of the Ka'gdams-pa lineage. The Ge-lugs-pa monasteries were known for their strict adherence to the monastic discipline and their strong critical stand toward magical practices. The Ge-lugs-pa tradition eventually came not only to dominate the spiritual life of Tibet but to hold temporal power over the country as well. Thus, Tsong-kha-pa's monastic reform eventually developed into a theocratic state ruled by monks for over five hundred years.

Hui-neng

Monks as exemplars, reformers, and scholars—*transforming* the tradition and *representing* it to the world—typify Buddhist monastic traditions in all times and places, be it Southeast, Central, or East Asia. We have previously referred to the example of the abbot in the training of Ch'an/Zen monks (see chapter 4). Stories of the Ch'an/Zen patriarchs, furthermore, establish the distinctive ethos of the Chinese and Japanese monastic tradition as well. Among the tales of the Chinese masters, that of Hui-neng (638–714 C.E.), the sixth patriarch, has a normative significance for the School of Sudden Enlightenment.

Next to Bodhidharma, Hui-neng is regarded as the second and actual founder of the Sudden Enlightenment tradition of Ch'an/Zen

Buddhism. According to one of the major legendary accounts of Hui-neng's life (the *Liu-tsu-ta-shih-pa-pao-t'an-ching*), the sixth patriarch led an impoverished childhood after his father died when the boy was three years old. He and his mother eked out a meager existence collecting and selling firewood. One day while sitting in the local market Hui-neng overheard a recitation of the *Diamond Sutra*, one of the Indian wisdom texts germinal to the development of the Ch'an/Zen tradition. So moved was he by the recitation that he decided to journey to the monastery of Hung-jen (601–674 C.E.), the fifth patriarch of Ch'an/Zen Buddhism, who was famed for his knowledge of the *Perfection of Wisdom*.

Young and uneducated, Hui-neng arrived at Hung-jen's monastery in north China only to be set to the menial tasks of cutting wood and grinding rice. Several months after Hui-neng's arrival, the abbot decided to choose his successor by devising an exercise designed to indicate the degree to which a monk's enlightenment qualified him to bear the patriarchal mantle. The test was to compose a verse or *gatha*. Shen-hsiu, the foremost monk of the community and expected successor, wrote:

> The body is the Bodhi tree [enlightenment],
> The mind is like a clear mirror standing,
> Take care to wipe it all the time,
> Allow no grain of dust to cling.[22]

Publicly Hung-jen praised the verse, but privately told his disciple that it lacked insight, that the lines were "devoid of logical contradiction and could be interpreted readily by resolving the two allegories." Hui-neng heard Shen-hsiu's stanza, but since he could not write, he had his own verse written on the monastery wall by a fellow monk:

> The Bodhi is not like a tree,
> The clear mirror is nowhere standing.
> Fundamentally not one thing exists;
> Where, then, is a grain of dust to cling?

Recognizing the profound nature of Hui-neng's enlightenment, Hung-jen called the boy into his quarters at night, designating him as his successor in secret for fear that the ire of the senior monks might be aroused. In the *Platform Sutra* the episode is recorded as follows:

> The Fifth Patriarch waited till midnight, called me to come to the hall, and expounded the Diamond Scripture. As soon as I heard this, I understood. That night the Law [*dharma*] was imparted to me without anyone knowing it, and thus the method of sudden enlightenment and the robe were transmitted to me. "You are now the Sixth Patriarch. This robe is the testimony of transmission from generation to generation. As to the Law, it is to be transmitted from mind to mind. Let people achieve enlightenment through their own effort."[23]

While the historicity of this legend is much in question, its paradigmatic significance for the Ch'an/Zen tradition is beyond dispute. Hui-neng's life contrasts enlightenment-knowledge with knowledge acquired gradually through study and discipline. This tradition of Ch'an/Zen Buddhism became known as the Sudden Enlightenment school, noted for its iconoclastic orientation toward the tradition and its radical monastic training techniques designed to induce "abrupt enlightenment" (see the story of I Hsuan or Lin Chi in chapter 4). In short, the story of Hui-neng defines the distinctiveness of a particular Buddhist monastic lineage over against other Buddhist traditions.

Exemplary nuns

For the most part the founders, reformers, and exemplars within the Buddhist monastic tradition are men, but there are exceptions. Exemplary nuns do appear. In the Theravada tradition, the *Songs of the Sisters* (*Therigathas*) provide inspiring examples of women who attained to the highest state of self-fulfillment (Nirvana), and the *Gandavyuha Sutra* relates the story of a nun, Simhavijrmbhita, a religious teacher, spiritual friend, and presumed *bodhisattva*, who assists Sudhana, the quintessential religious pilgrim, along his path to salvation.

Furthermore, women were known to have founded monasteries. For example, tradition claims that King Asoka's daughter, Sanghamitta (third cent. B.C.E.), established an Order of nuns in Sri Lanka. While the *bhikkhuni* Order died out in India and Southeast Asia, a women's monastic Order was sustained in China, Taiwan, and Tibet. The Council of Religious and Cultural Affairs of H.H. the Dalai Lama in Dharmasala claims that prior to 1959 there were over twelve thousand nuns residing in 618 nunneries in Tibet.[24]

Stories of exemplary nuns in the early centuries of the spread of Buddhism are found in a wide variety of Asian contexts. Women were ordained in China as early as the fourth century C.E., and a separate female Order was established in the fifth century. The *Pich'iu-ni chuan*, compiled by Pao Ch'ang in 576, relates stories of sixty-five female monks. Although in general the tales are modeled after Mahapajapati (see chapter 4), Pao Ch'ang delineates four different types of exemplars: "ascetic, contemplative, faithful and steadfast, and the teacher of great influence."[25]

The story of Tao-Kuei, a Ch'an (Zen) nun, tells of an exemplary female monk who brings Ch'an Buddhism to China in 516 C.E., several years prior to the arrival of the reputed founder of the tradition, Bodhidharma. In Japanese Zen, as well, stories of nuns appear. In the thirteenth century, Zen master Dogen claimed in his *Rohai Tokuzui*, "If a nun appears who has acquired the Way, who has acquired the Dharma, the monk who is seeking the Dharma should become her disciple. . . . It is like looking for drinking water when you are thirsty."[26]

CHRISTIANITY

From the Buddhist perspective, the Gospel accounts of the activity of Jesus look quite familiar. The sage, who achieves enlightenment through a period of intense spiritual self-scrutiny (the Temptation in the Wilderness), gathers round himself a collection of followers who come to him seeking to learn his secret, and who with alarming frequency fail to get the real point of what he is saying because it is so radically at odds with what they are accustomed to expect. The original story appears to be that of a spiritual teacher who attracts disciples and expects those who are serious to renounce worldly ties in the interests of gaining true enlightenment. Jesus proposes a going forth from the householder life—"We have left everything to follow you," say the disciples—to discover a new family context. A Buddhist reading the New Testament might well assume that what needs legitimizing is not Christian monasticism, but any other form of organized Christian life.

CHRIST THE TEACHER

In the Book of Acts the apostles do virtually everything Jesus had done, and teaching would have been one of their essential functions. Jesus was a spiritual parent to his disciples, and to the extent that monks/nuns served this function they were true heirs of the apostles who had carried on Jesus' work. Athanasius introduces Antony's long address to the monks in a way reminiscent of the beginning of many of Jesus' speeches: "Now, one day when he had gone out, all the monks came to him and asked to hear a discourse."[27]

Palladius, who lived about a century after Athanasius, at the beginning of his own account of the origins of monasticism emphasizes the role of Christ as a teacher whose words have cogency because of the life that lies behind them and guarantees them:

> Now those who think they need no teacher, or those who do not believe those who teach them in the way of love, are afflicted with the disease of ignorance, which is the mother of overweening pride. They are preceded in the way of destruction by those who have fallen from the heavenly path, the demons who fly about in the air, having left their heavenly teachers. For words and syllables do not constitute teaching—sometimes those who possess these are disreputable in the extreme—but teaching consists of virtuous acts of conduct, of freedom from injuriousness, of dauntlessness, and of an even temper. To all this add an intrepidity which produces words like flames of fire.
>
> For if this were not so, the Great Teacher would not have told his disciples: "Learn of me, because I am meek and humble of heart." He did not use fine language when teaching them, but he required rather the formation of their character, causing grief only to those who hate the word and teachers as well. For the soul being trained to act in accord with God's plan must either learn faithfully what it does not know, or teach clearly what it does know.[28]

Christ the Great Teacher, his teaching designed primarily to form character, his authority coming from virtuous acts that teach more than words and syllables—in these fifth-century remarks are embedded some of the deepest tensions within the Christian monastic tradition. A case can be made that abbots/prioresses in their function as teachers of monks/nuns are as fully in the line of apostolic succession as are bishops when they preside at the Eucharist. But in monastic history there have been voices warning repeatedly that learning is a snare, a distraction from the true monastic vocation.

THE MONASTERY AS SCHOOL

Christian monasticism has played a decisive role in the shaping and transmission of Western culture. The popular image of medieval monks faithfully and laboriously copying manuscripts, not only of the Bible and Christian writers but also of the Greek and Latin classics, reminds us how much of the past we owe to them. Familiarity with monastic tradition makes clear, however, how odd it is that such accomplishments should be monks' chief claim on our gratitude.

Many of the early monks were illiterate, and unashamed of the fact. Indeed, their lack of learning gave their biographers an opening for marvel at the power of God, who could inspire the unlettered to such feats of physical mortification and spiritual insight. As we saw in chapter 3, one of the arguments used by early Christian spokespersons for the truth of Christianity was the capacity of their doctrine to enlighten and reform even the simplest of people. St. Jerome, a man of prodigious learning and a missionary for the monastic life in the early fifth century C.E., reports a dream in which he was brought before the judgment seat of God, and when "asked what my rank was, I replied: 'A Christian.' But the one who presided said: 'You lie. You are a Ciceronian, not a Christian. For where your treasure is, there will your heart be also.' "[29] His unconscious life was haunted by the suspicion that one could not be learned in the tradition of Cicero and Vergil and, at the same time, a good Christian, let alone a good monk.

Despite this undertone of suspicion, however, the roster of learned Christian monks and nuns is long and illustrious. The basic teaching function of the abbot/prioress, and, by extension, of other monks/nuns, lies at the base of this development. Reinforcing that function are the place given to work (*labora*) in the monastic hierarchy of values and the historical anomaly that most monks have also been priests. Priests must, at a minimum, be able to read, and their effectiveness is enhanced if they can compare and critically study texts and analyze theological options as they prepare their sermons, instruct converts to the faith, and dispute with heretics. As more and more monks assumed priestly responsibilities, monks more and more looked to study as their work, their service to God.

The schoolteachers of Europe

Among the casualties of the decline and fall of the Roman Empire was a system of education at least a thousand years old. In the course of time the scheme of study and learning had become rigidly fixed. Attention was concentrated on a set of classic texts, primarily the poetry of Homer in Greek and, in Latin, the poetry of Vergil and the prose of Cicero. Emulation of the past rather than innovation for the future was the goal of every student, and the measure of a teacher was the student's success in measuring up to the ancient ideal.

The monasteries fell heir to this social and cultural function. The monks had the Christian classics, preeminently of course the Bible, to transmit to coming generations, and it did not take long for the writings of the early Christian centuries, beyond the time of the Bible, to acquire a classic status. Thanks to the efforts of Christian thinkers who explained how the great geniuses of Greek and Latin literature had been Christians in intention if not in fact, monasteries also took responsibility for transmitting the treasure-trove of style and substance to be found in pagan writings. The very teaching of language itself was a cultural force of extraordinary consequence, for Latin became the common tongue of Europe only by sustained effort of monks and nuns over many generations.

From the fifth century to the twelfth the work of elementary and secondary education was carried on almost exclusively in monasteries. The eighth and ninth centuries saw a flowering of creativity, known to historians as the Carolingian Renaissance, orchestrated by the Emperor Charlemagne, who prided himself on his role as patron of learning and the arts and who made the momentous decision to impose the Rule of Benedict on all monasteries in his dominions. He was determined that his educational program succeed, and the network of monasteries provided the necessary personnel and organization.

Within a generation of Charlemagne's death (814 C.E.) his empire lay in fragments, and for centuries his educational program was a lingering memory of a distant golden age. The period from 850 to 1050 C.E. is the time when the monasteries were doggedly preserving a culture that was in grave danger of disappearing entirely.

The decline of monastic influence in education

In the story of Buddhist monasticism and culture universities take pride of place. The same is not true of Christian monasticism. When historians talk about the rise of universities in the West, they usually preface the story with an account of the declining influence of monasteries. There were certainly monks among the masters who taught at Oxford and Paris, but these new institutions were not bound to monastic foundations. The primary loyalty of the masters, even those who were monks, was to the new academic institution, and there was an exhilarating feeling among many of the teachers that a new age had dawned, an age new precisely because no longer held in bondage by monastic tradition. The Renaissance of Charlemagne's time had depended on the monasteries for its viability. Many in the twelfth century would have argued that their own Renaissance presupposed the decline of monastic influence.[30]

From the High Middle Ages to our own time, higher education under monastic control has been far less significant for Christianity than for Buddhism. In the eleventh and twelfth centuries an entirely new impulse from classical antiquity shaped culture and learning. The scientific and philosophical works of the ancients, especially Aristotle, came into Latin by way of Arabic, and the literary tradition passed on in the monasteries was swamped in the tide of this new learning. From that time to the present, academic curricula and the training of teachers in the West have taken their cue from traditions other than those of the monasteries. Even today a frequent subject of dispute within faculties of colleges and universities run by monks/nuns is whether and how the monastic school is in any essential way different from secular or other church-related institutions, and, specifically, whether a college or university can have a recognizable monastic character as distinct from a general churchly or Christian one.

On occasion a monk or nun who is a professor will be heard to ask, Ought we to be in this higher education business at all? The question may be simply a prudential one: when there are so many academic institutions competing for a decreasing number of students, does it make good business sense for us to be fighting to keep our place in the running? But the question may go much deeper, resonating with a debate about the place of learning in the monastic life that has continued unabated almost since the beginning.

We saw early in this chapter that Jesus functioned as a teacher, but we saw also that virtuous example and formation of character were understood to be, respectively, the means and the end of true education. The relation of painstaking study, of prolonged and erudite research, to this ideal of education is not self-evident. If the monk/nun works hard at learning, is there not a danger that he/she is doubting the sufficiency of the wisdom God freely grants? And what of the threat of pride, the chief enemy of the supreme monastic virtue of humility?

LEARNING: VOCATION OR SNARE?

These questions can be found lurking beneath the surface in nearly every age of Christian monasticism, but they came forcefully and classically into full view in the seventeenth century in a debate between Armand-Jean de Rancé (1626-1700 C.E.), founder of the Cistercians of Strict Observance ("Trappists," the order to which Thomas Merton belonged), and Jean Mabillon (1632–1707 C.E.), one of the greatest of historical scholars. Their arguments are all the more convincing because the two men had high and genuine regard for each other.

Rancé and Mabillon: the debate over monastic studies

Rancé was self-consciously a reformer of a reform, or rather, a restorer of a restoration. The Cistercian order originated in the twelfth century as an attempt to recover the pristine purity of Benedict's vision over against what the reformers considered to be the corruption and distortion prevalent in their day. The Cistercians might well have called themselves "Benedictines of Strict Observance." Five hundred years later Rancé concluded that the Cistercians themselves had fallen prey to the same temptations as the earlier Benedictines, and he set about to recover the original Cistercian recovery of the original Benedictine way.

Since the claim to be the best Cistercian was in effect a claim to be the best Benedictine, it was inevitable that Rancé would tangle with the best-known Benedictines of his day, the Congregation of St.-Maur. The Maurists had already established a reputation for thorough, accurate, and brilliant scholarship, especially in their research of the traditions of lives of the saints, and in Mabillon they had produced their star. When Rancé started saying publicly that one could not do what the Maurists do and be a true monk, he was bound to get a reply.

The most striking feature of the debate between Rancé and Mabillon is the extent of their agreement. They share a devotion to the Rule of Benedict and its ideals. Neither of them claims that the Rule is an outmoded document that must be reinterpreted in light of "modern" conditions. Their disagreement is almost entirely over strategy. How, for example, can the monk guard his humility?

But to say the disagreement is strategic is not quite right. The argument is carried by images as well as by terms, and the governing images used by Rancé and Mabillon have sufficiently different implications to suggest discrepancies in ends as well as in means between the two protagonists. For example, while some monastic writers see Christ the teacher as model for the monk/nun, Rancé focuses attention on Christ in another role:

> This it was that made the holy Abbot Pynufe say that the renunciation and engagement of the religious is no less than a public testimony by which he proves to all that he is crucified and dead . . . exemplifying in all his actions that state in which his Redeemer was when he hung on the saving Tree. . . .
>
> [Christ] gave his body up to the austerities of a mortified life. . . . We are well informed of his fastings, retirements, and silence. [Then follows an account of the Temptation story.] . . .
>
> In a word, he continually suffered the whole sum of his passion. . . .

> [The religious] ought to live in a holy sadness, in a profound humility, and in rigorous austerity.[31]

In Rancé's view Christ is a teacher, to be sure, but the teaching is exclusively by example and the example is determined entirely by the Passion. It can hardly be said that Rancé is accurately recovering the clear meaning of the Rule of Benedict, for Benedict's system is marked by moderation. Even Benedict, however, admires desert monastics of the centuries preceding his own, and Rancé might well claim simply to be restoring the standard Benedict really wanted but had not stated because he judged his own contemporaries were not up to it.

The conclusion Rancé drew from his convictions about monastic imitation of Christ was a frontal assault on everything the Maurists stood for: "Now it is certain . . . that monks have not been appointed for study, but for doing penance; that their condition is to weep and not to teach." He goes on to explain that God may on occasion have called a monk to be learned, but we must not substitute the exception for the norm.[32] Rancé is of course not saying that learning and teaching are inessential activities for the church. Rather, they are inappropriate in monasteries.

Mabillon's counterargument subtly grants some of Rancé's assumptions.

> Saint Paul was very correct when he said that learning divorced from any love makes a person proud. But it is just as true that helped by grace nothing is better suited than study to lead us to humility, since nothing makes us realize more our corruption, our misery, and our nothingness.[33]

Furthermore, Mabillon was an honest historian as well as a learned one, strengthening Rancé's argument by pointing out it was a mistake to think the first monasteries were founded as schools:

> A holy contempt for the things of this world and a desire to escape the corruption of the world were the real motives behind the establishment of the first monastic centers. As Saint Bernard pointed out, it was the desire to follow Christ in abandoning all things and the remark of Saint Peter, "See how we have left all things to follow you," which led to the populating of the deserts and the cloisters.

Mabillon quotes with approval St. Gregory of Nazianzus, who said the point of learning is to be able to scorn it, and St. Vincent of Vulturne: "If I am not capable of possessing both knowledge and virtue, I readily consent, my Savior, to forego knowledge rather than virtue." And in a gesture that would be suspected of sarcasm in a less generous-spirited man, Mabillon says that if all abbots were as Rancé, there would be little need for monastic studies, for "the superior himself would supply all the learning that [the monks] would otherwise have to obtain through study."[34]

What, then, is the rationale for monastic learning? Beyond the humility that comes to anyone who discovers the infinitely receding horizon of knowledge, there is a positive contribution to what Benedict prescribes as the chief motive of the monastic life—to seek God:

> If undertaken from the right motives, study will enable you to understand yourselves better, foster humility and the desire to escape the recognition of the world. Study will aid you to know God more fully, to love God more deeply, and serve God more effectively.

Mabillon even confronts the argument that concentrating on study amounts to distrust of God's power to teach us what we need to know:

> We would be tempting God if we were to discontinue our studies as a means of acquiring an understanding of Sacred Scripture under the pretext that God has granted this gift of wisdom to some saints and may grant it to us.[35]

In addition to these arguments, which go to the heart of monastic motivation, Mabillon adds some practical considerations from his storehouse of historical knowledge. Abbots and monks have attended the great councils of the church in the past, and they would have appeared ridiculous among all the august and learned bishops if they had been boorish and unlettered. What would have been the plight of those abbots who at various times were called on to serve as interim bishops if they had been unable to make the kinds of distinctions and judgments that are the fruit of scholarly training? Most important of all, as monks have been increasingly sought out by the laity to oversee confession and penance, monks have had their learning tested, for "it is impossible without adequate learning to prescribe the correct remedies to the illnesses of the penitents."[36]

If Mabillon and Rancé were at sharp odds over the means to their agreed goal of humility, they also had deeply divergent views of the role monks play in the overall spiritual economy of the church. Mabillon wants monks to be skilled at measuring the faults of the laity and calculating the penalties. Rancé considers that monks, through their own penitential life, are to make up for the deficiencies of the laity. The church is in terrible danger, Rancé says, because monks, partly as a result of the diversion of study, have failed in their primary task:

> Nothing is more capable of drawing down the indignation of the Lord on whole empires than the disorder of monasteries and the licentious conduct of monks. . . . When those who ought to cover the sins of the people by the innocence and merit of their lives and stand between them and the justice of God, have themselves become objects of God's wrath, then there is nothing more to solicit and move God's compassion or to stem the fury of God's vengeance. . . . The desolation of states, the persecutions of the church, and the ravages of infidels in every Catholic country, are the unhappy consequences of [the monks'] infidelities to God.[37]

In the interests of keeping monks from thinking too highly of themselves because of their learning, Rancé has here escalated the importance of monasticism until the spiritual condition of the monks becomes the determiner of the general welfare of the entire church, even of the whole society.

The debate between Rancé and Mabillon was prefigured five centuries earlier in the dispute between St. Bernard of Clairvaux and Abbot Suger of St.-Denis over the proper role of art in monastic life. The parallels are more than fortuitous, since Bernard was among the earliest Cistercians, so Rancé looked to him as one of his ancestors, and, as we have seen above, Mabillon quoted Bernard with approval. As in the seventeenth-century arguments over studies and learning, so here the scope of discussion covered a wide range of monastic ideals and practices, theories, and history.

Suger and Bernard on monastic art

By the beginning of the twelfth century C.E. the form of Benedictinism associated with the abbey of Cluny and its hundreds of allied houses had become the norm. Monasticism had become unimaginably wealthy and intricately woven into the complex social and political fabric of European life. A movement of reform, centered at Cîteaux (hence the name Cistercian) and stamped indelibly with the strong personality of St. Bernard of Clairvaux (1090–1153 C.E.), challenged the Cluniac tradition as a gross distortion of Benedictine asceticism.

Just as Rancé and Mabillon, though deeply respecting one another, disagreed sharply over the meaning of monastic vocation, so Bernard and Abbot Suger of St.-Denis (ca. 1081–1151 C.E.) were friends whose ideas of monasticism clashed. Bernard demanded that Suger reform his monastery, and his sharp criticism had an effect. Bernard wrote to Suger congratulating him: "Even those who have not known you, but have only heard how great has been the change from what you were to what you are, marvel and praise God in you." It would have been enough, Bernard says, if Suger had simply changed his own behavior: "The whole and only thing that upset me was the pomp and splendor with which you travelled. This seemed to me to savor of arrogance." But Suger had undertaken a general reform of St.-Denis, reducing its social centrality ("They say the cloister of the monastery was often crowded with soldiers, that business was done there, that it echoed to the sound of men wrangling, and that sometimes women were to be found there") in favor of silence, discipline, and liturgy.[38]

Bernard's critique extended beyond the routine and style of monastic life, into the realm of aesthetics. Cistercian manuscripts are characteristically devoid of illuminations; Cistercian churches are plain and unadorned, though they are designed with careful attention to mathematical proportion. Bernard's problem with the florid artistic traditions that were so much part of monastic life was partly that they distracted the mind and spirit, partly that they diverted funds and energies that ought to be expended on serving the poor. Aesthetics could not be treated in isolation from ethics.

On this point, Suger and Bernard did not come together. Gothic art and architecture, which were born at St.-Denis during Suger's tenure as abbot, certainly partake in some measure of Cistercian spirit, but Suger's account of the building of the Abbey Church breathes a continuing love of splendor and public recognition that would cause Bernard to wince. Suger writes his treatise

> to save for the memory of posterity, in pen and ink, those increments which the generous munificence of Almighty God had bestowed upon this church, in the time of our prelacy, in the acquisition of new assets as well as in the recovery of lost ones, in the multiplication of improved possessions, in the construction of buildings, and in the accumulation of gold, silver, most precious gems and very good textiles.[39]

He misses no opportunity to highlight his own initiative and accomplishment, and the spectacle of the church's dedication, attended by gloriously robed archbishops and bishops and the king himself, is the occasion for enthusiastic prose.

Monastic art and architecture, like monastic scholarship, is a cultural inheritance of inestimable value. Monks and nuns bring with them into the monastery their gifts and their talents. Thomas Merton was always fearful that his abbot at Gethsemani would impose on him, as an ascetic discipline, a ban on writing, but the abbot never did. Yet Merton's fear was an authentic expression of a tradition that goes back to his Cistercian ancestors, Bernard and Rancé. At some level, probably, Merton recognized in his obsessive creation of words a severe threat to the openness, the transparency to God that was his chief religious goal.

There is no right answer to the debates between Rancé and Mabillon, Bernard and Suger. Their confrontations are classic and clear illustrations of polarities, creative tensions built into monastic tradition. We should hardly be surprised to find conflict in—to use Merton's graphic phrase—the belly of a paradox.

EXEMPLARS

The monastic tradition is carried on in studies and in arts that have transmitted and transformed cultures. At the heart of monastic tradition, however, are exemplary characters, embodiments of the ideal. A purely theoretical argument could be constructed according to which the truly good monk/nun would not be known at all, since the ultimate in humility would be self-denial so thorough that the individual would come to no one's notice. The argument would be absurdly abstract, but it does highlight an anomaly in the role monks/nuns play as exemplars, whether for other monastics or for laypersons. Fame itself, even fame for humility, distorts "pursuit of perfect charity after a monastic manner of life"—distorts it both for the monk/nun and for those who look to his/her example for inspiration. This irony, that the pursuit of perfect charity has a built-in trap (pursuits can reach goals, be successful, and hence corrupt perfect charity), reminds us that any discussion of the monk/nun as exemplar needs to be carried on with tongue in cheek and fingers crossed.

We have already encountered the monastic tendency to look to predecessors as intimidating models. Antony tries to emulate Elijah, the Desert Fathers try to emulate Antony, Benedict laments the decline in commitment since the time of the Desert Fathers, and then reform after reform in subsequent monastic tradition justifies itself as a return to the fervor of an earlier age.

The monastic penchant for looking back in order to find the way forward generated from a very early period the most characteristic form of monastic literature, the saint's life. There is a stylized pattern to many of these texts. The childhood of the holy person is presented either as foreshadowing adult sanctity or, conversely, as a time of frivolity and license from which God must call the individual by a more or less dramatic conversion. Seldom is the future saint presented as a mixture of both good and bad. The author of a saint's life wants to fire the reader's spirit of emulation without dampening the reader's hope that "I, too, with sufficient effort can achieve what that great person did."

Four figures out of hundreds will serve to illustrate the role of monk/nun as exemplar in Christian tradition.

Benedict

Pope Gregory the Great (590–604 c.e.), himself a monk, wrote a Life of Benedict (known as Gregory's *Second Dialogue*) that has been through the centuries one of the most popular Christian books. It is the only biographical material about Benedict from anywhere near his own time, and it is highly problematical as a historical source. But what matters for our discussion is the portrait Gregory draws of Benedict, not the degree of correspondence between that portrait and historical fact.

Benedict, as Pope Gregory portrays him, would have agreed with Rancé in the debate with Mabillon. Benedict's parents sent him to school in Rome:

> but when he saw many of his fellow students falling headlong into vice, he stepped back from the threshold of the world in which he had just set foot. For he was afraid that if he acquired any of its learning he, too, would later plunge, body and soul, into the dread abyss. In his desire to please God alone, he turned his back on further studies, gave up home and inheritance and resolved to embrace the religious life. He took this step, well aware of his ignorance, yet wise, uneducated though he was.[40]

Benedict's spiritual wisdom is manifest immediately. Even before he takes on the monastic habit he miraculously puts back together a tray his nurse has broken, and the rest of the *Dialogue* is full of stories of similar feats, including recovery of a scythe blade lost in a deep lake, Benedict's knowing in detail events that happen long distances away, and bringing dead people back to life. As Gregory's dialogue partner points out, nearly every wonder that Benedict performs has a parallel in the Bible, and Gregory indicates that is just the point—God is actively present in the world now as then.

Pope Gregory complained about the way his papal duties distracted him from the life of prayer and contemplation he thought was his true calling, so there is a kind of ambivalence in his portrayal of Benedict, a recognition of the tension between Benedict's desire for solitude and his almost constant involvement in larger affairs.

Gregory, like Benedict, was a reformer, and when in the *Dialogue* we read about a group of monks who ask Benedict to be their abbot and shortly afterward regret their decision because their actions clash with his standards, we sense that Gregory knows from experience what he is talking about. This particular group of monks, who "could not see why they should have to force their settled minds into new ways of thinking," did not simply grumble behind Benedict's back. They "decided to poison his wine." The glass shattered when Benedict made the sign of the cross over it. "Why did you conspire to do this? Did I not tell you at the outset that my way of life would never harmonize with yours? Go and find yourselves an abbot to your liking. It is impossible for me to stay here any longer."[41]

Benedict faces opposition not only from disgruntled monks, but also from the devil in person, and from a nearby priest, and Gregory shows how Benedict overcomes all obstacles. However, the most poignant moment in the *Dialogue* occurs when Benedict is found weeping. Asked why, the abbot replies, "Almighty God has decreed that this entire monastery and everything I have provided for the community shall fall into the hands of the barbarians. It was only with the greatest difficulty that I could prevail upon God to spare the lives of its members."[42] Gregory presents Benedict as *knowing* his creation will be destroyed, yet the remainder of the *Dialogue* gives no sign that the abbot despaired or became lethargic. Gregory's Benedict exemplifies dramatically the conviction that what God expects is faithfulness, not success.

The *Dialogue* culminates in an extraordinary vision, a classic instance of the clarity and perspective that are the fruit of ascetic discipline:

> In the dead of night he suddenly beheld a flood of light shining down from above more brilliant than the sun, and with it every trace of darkness cleared away. Another remarkable sight followed. According to his own description, the whole world was gathered up before his eyes in what appeared to be a single ray of light.

Gregory's dialogue partner is puzzled: "I have never had such an experience. How is it possible for anyone to see the whole universe at a glance?" Gregory replies:

> The light of holy contemplation enlarges and expands the mind in God until it stands above the world. In fact, the soul that sees God rises even above itself, and as it is drawn upward in God's light all its inner powers unfold. . . . Of course, in saying that the world was gathered up before his eyes I do not mean that heaven and earth grew

small, but that his spirit was enlarged. Absorbed as he was in God, it was now easy for him to see all that lay beneath God.[43]

There is only one bit of *Dialogue* text between this story of Benedict's vision and the account of his death:

> With all the renown he gained by his numerous miracles, the holy man was no less outstanding for the wisdom of his teaching. He wrote a Rule for Monks that is remarkable for its discretion and clarity of language. Anyone who wishes to know more about his life and character can discover in his Rule exactly what he was like as abbot, for his life could not have differed from his teaching.[44]

We often enough hear people say, Do as I say, not as I do, to wonder at Gregory's confidence that "his life could not have differed from his teaching," but the important point here is the narrative move the pope makes: if you want to know how to live now according to the example set by Benedict, who was so obviously on familiar terms with God, his Rule is where to look. In short, the monastery is where "the soul's inner powers unfold" and "spirits are enlarged."

Hildegard of Bingen

Benedict was fashioning a new form of life at a time when an ancient civilization was crumbling. Hildegard of Bingen (1098–1179 C.E.) lived at a time when Benedict's institution had become culturally so significant that modern historians can refer to the period as the monastic centuries, and from that base she took a leading part in a cultural opening that is frequently referred to as a renaissance.

Hildegard of Bingen has become better known in recent decades than at any time since her own twelfth century. She was a figure of great renown among her contemporaries. Her extant correspondence includes letters to a virtual Who's Who of the European ecclesiastical and political worlds. A pope read aloud from her works to an assembled council. But not long after her death her memory faded, largely because women just were not taken seriously as transformers and transmitters of the Christian tradition. Recently, though, Hildegard has become the focus of intense interest, partly because she is a woman, but even more because her understanding of the-

ology as an integrative activity of heart and head is appealing and
salutary in our fragmented culture.

Hildegard is an astonishing genius: mystic, biblical commenta-
tor, musician, poet, painter, physician, scientist. In all the current
excitement over her rediscovery, however, there is danger of for-
getting that her primary identity was that of Benedictine nun—
dedicated to that life as a tithe by her parents at her birth (she was
their tenth child), entering the community at age eight, and at thirty-
eight, in 1136 c.e., becoming prioress, a position she held until her
death forty-three years later. "The stunning originality of her for-
mulations must not be allowed to obscure her fundamental orthodoxy or her classic Benedictine approach to the spiritual life."[45]

The story of Hildegard's life—of her visions, which began when
she was a child, of her struggles to achieve and then maintain the
autonomy of her monastery from the efforts of nearby abbots to control her and her sisters, of her preaching expeditions up and down
the Rhine—is a classic study of the Benedictine polarity between worship and work (*ora et labora*). She criticized those who wanted to
give up the latter in order to concentrate on the former. To a prioress who wants to retire to the eremitic life Hildegard writes:

> O daughter born of the side of man, and figure formed in the build-
> ing of God: why do you languish so that your mind shifts like clouds
> in a storm, now shining like the light and now darkened? . . . You
> say, "I want to rest and seek a place where my heart can have a nest,
> so that my soul may rest there." Daughter, before God it is useless
> for you to cast off your burden and abandon the flock of God, while
> you have a light to illumine it so that you can lead it to pasture. Now
> restrain yourself, lest your mind blaze in that sweetness which would
> greatly harm you in the vicissitudes of the solitary life.[46]

And the work into which Hildegard threw herself with enormous
energy was not just the sustenance of her community, but the activity of reform of thought and structures in monastery, church, and
state, all of which was part of the cultural revolution known to
historians as the renaissance of the twelfth century.

Very near the end of her life Hildegard faced a crisis that brought
into sharp focus many of the concerns that had shaped her ex-

perience through more than four decades of leadership in a religious community.

In 1178 the canons of Mainz Cathedral ordered Hildegard to exhume the body of a young man buried in the monastery's cemetery just a few days before, on the grounds that the man had been excommunicated and therefore should not be buried in consecrated ground. Why they demanded this is not clear, but Hildegard knew that the man had been restored to the church on his deathbed. Instead of digging the body up, she blessed the grave with her prioress's staff. In response to her refusal, the canons of Mainz imposed an interdict on Hildegard's monastery, forbidding the celebration of the Eucharist in the monastery, and, further, prohibiting the chanting of the office, the "Work of God."

Hildegard wrote to the canons, justifying her action, and pleading for a lifting of the interdict. She appeals to direct communication from God as the source of her confidence, but beyond this special revelation the reader can also hear in her letter the special sadness of a Benedictine, whose spirit has been formed by multiple daily repetition of the Psalms from age eight to age eighty, at an ecclesiastical censure that has cut the nerve of Benedictine identity. She turns the tables—the canons have accused her and her sisters of devilish action, she in turn says they are doing the devil's work:

> With his never-stopping, evil, lying chatter he thinks and seeks unceasingly to bring to disharmony, and even to ban, God's praise and the beauty of spiritual songs. He works at this not only through evil temptations, impure thoughts, and a variety of diversions springing from human hearts, but also, wherever he can, through discord, arguments, or unjust persecution.[47]

Through further maneuverings, which brought in the authority of the archbishop of Cologne to counterbalance that of the archbishop of Mainz, Hildegard succeeded in having the ban removed, and during the last six months of her life this exemplary Benedictine was able to express by her prayer life her conviction about the fundamental meaning of Christian theology:

> So remember: just as the body of Jesus Christ was born by the Holy Spirit from the spotless Virgin Mary, so too the singing in the church of God's praise, which is an echo of the harmony of heaven, has its

roots in that same Holy Spirit. But the body is the garment of the soul and it is the soul which gives life to the voice. That is why the body must raise its voice in harmony with the soul for the praise of God.[48]

Zossima

Our third exemplary figure is a fictional character, Father Zossima, whom we met in the Introduction to this book. Fashioned after the historical Staretz Amvrosy (1812–91 C.E.), Dostoevsky's Father Zossima is a portrayal of the ideal Russian monk. He has an uncanny insight into the spiritual state of all the persons who come to him seeking advice, and accounting for that insight is one of the marks of Dostoevsky's genius.

We meet Father Zossima at age sixty-five, just a few days before he dies. His cell is a point of reference, a center of stability in the midst of the swirling, tempestuous, sensual, lacerating life of the Karamazov family and the region in which they live. As we come to know Zossima better, however, through the recollections of his last conversations that were put to paper by the youngest of the Karamazov brothers, Alyosha, it becomes clear that Zossima's effectiveness as a spiritual guide depends on his knowing at first hand the extremities of emotion of those who come to him for counsel: ''He sometimes astounded and almost alarmed his visitors by his knowledge of their secrets before they had spoken a word.''[49]

In scene after scene, with peasants, with children, with rich persons, with his own spiritual sons in the monastery, Zossima demonstrates an insight that is at the same time unexpected and very simple. To the coarse, bombastic Fyodor Pavlovich Karamazov, father of the clan, Zossima says, within minutes of meeting him: ''Do not trouble. Make yourself quite at home. And, above all, do not be so ashamed of yourself, for that is at the root of it all.''[50] Fyodor Pavlovich instantly recognizes a truth about himself that no one had ever articulated before.

It is only much later in the novel, in the final speech to the monks, that Zossima reveals the origin of his broad human sympathy and understanding. When he was a young military officer, he fell in love with a young woman who married someone else. ''I was filled with sudden irrepressible fury." Zossima contrived to insult her husband in order to provoke a duel. The night before the duel:

> something happened that in very truth was the turning-point of my life. In the evening, returning home in a savage and brutal humor, I flew into a rage with my orderly Afanasy, and gave him two blows in the face with all my might, so that it was covered with blood. He had not long been in my service and I had struck him before, but never with such ferocious cruelty. And, believe me, though it's forty years ago, I recall it now with shame and pain.

The next morning Zossima is overcome with the horror of his act: a human being beating a fellow creature. "I stood as if I were struck dumb, while the sun was shining, the leaves were rejoicing, and the birds were trilling the praise of God." To his own astonishment, and even more to the astonishment of Afanasy, Zossima, on his way out the door to the duel, bows to the ground before his orderly and begs forgiveness. At the dueling site Zossima's opponent gets the first shot, which misses; then Zossima tosses his own gun away. The other officers are appalled at the "disgrace" to their regiment, but soon they are saying "there's something else in this, something original." Zossima resigns his commission, and enters a monastery.[51]

This "originality" of Zossima underlies his spiritual genius. His sense of his own sinfulness, and of everyone's responsibility, sounded clearly in an earlier speech to the monks—"every one of us is undoubtedly responsible for all persons and everything on earth, not merely through the general sinfulness of creation, but each one personally for all humankind and every individual person"[52]—is the fruit not of some abstract reasoning, or even of meditating on the Bible, but of intense reflection, over a lifetime, on a momentous experience that brought him face up against his own capacity for destructiveness and chaos. Because he recognizes he can destroy the world and at some level wants to, the monk can truly and effectively live for the sake of the world.

Francis of Assisi

Saint Francis of Assisi (1181/2–1226 C.E.), our fourth exemplar, was not in the strict sense a monk. The Franciscan Order, which he founded, is centrally organized, and far from demanding stability of its members, expects them to move about freely and often. Still, Francis drew much of his inspiration from previous monastic experience, and ever since his time he has been venerated as expressing better than anyone else the full meaning of Christian asceticism. That he was not technically a monk is a nice debating point for scholars; that ever since the thirteenth century he has been among the most effective exemplary monastic figures is simply a fact.[53]

If Gregory presents Benedict as holy from the beginning, Thomas of Celano, Francis's first biographer, portrays Francis as someone in need of a radical conversion. "Almost up to the twenty-fifth year of his age, he squandered and wasted his time miserably. Indeed, he outdid all his contemporaries in vanities and he came to be a promoter of evil and was more abundantly zealous for all kinds of foolishness." The conversion itself is reminiscent of that of the Buddha. Francis became ill, and "began to think of things other than he was used to thinking upon." His first reaction to a request that he join a military expedition against a neighboring town is excitement, but meditation raises questions, and a period of intense private self-scrutiny leads to a radical break with convention that comes as a stunning shock to Francis's friends and family. He gives everything away:

> When those who knew him saw this, they compared what he was now with what he had been; and they began to revile him miserably. Shouting out that he was mad and demented, they threw the mud of the streets and stones at him. They saw that he was changed from his former ways and greatly worn down by mortification of the flesh, and they therefore set down everything he did to exhaustion and madness.[54]

Francis's father imprisons his son in his own house, but Francis's mother releases him when her husband is away. The father's fury finally abates when he recovers some of his money, and in a kind of desperate capitulation to his son's determination he takes Francis to the bishop. There Francis impulsively divests himself of *everything*, including all the clothes he is wearing, in what amounts to a complete ascetic renunciation, so that "only the wall of flesh should separate him from the vision of God."[55]

Immediately Francis began to live his new conviction of solidarity with the suffering and needy. He who had previously stayed miles away from the houses of lepers now lived among them, "and washing all foulness from them, he wiped away also the corruption of the ulcers." He lived an austere life, but within a few years he heard the Gospel reading about the conditions in which Jesus sent the disciples forth to preach, and his renunciation became more thorough: "He immediately put off his shoes from his feet, put aside the staff from his hands, was content with one tunic, and exchanged his leather girdle for a small cord."[56]

It was not long before others started living with Francis, following his example of selling all and giving to the poor, and being taught by him "to walk with undeviating steps the way of holy poverty and blessed simplicity." As the nascent order grew, its fame spread and, according to Thomas of Celano, the exemplary character of the friars had an immediate effect: "There was also great wonder among the people of the world over all these things and the example of humility led them to amend their way of life and to do penance for their sins." And the example was one of an extraordinary freedom: "Followers of most holy poverty, because they had nothing, loved nothing, they feared in no way to lose anything. . . . They were, therefore, everywhere secure, kept in no suspense by fear." Francis "wanted to have nothing to do with ownership, in order that he might possess all things more fully in God."[57]

Francis is famous, and justly so, for his delight in creation, but his world-affirmation did not rule out some traditional ascetic austerities. If assailed by a sexual temptation, "he would hurl himself into a ditch full of ice, when it was winter, and remain in it until every vestige of anything carnal had departed." "Cooked foods he permitted himself scarcely at all or very rarely; and if he did allow them, he either mixed them with ashes or destroyed their flavor with cold water." Having succumbed to the temptation to eat a bit of chicken, Francis had himself dragged through the city by a friar who shouted, "Behold the glutton who has grown fat on the meat of chickens which he ate without your knowing about it."[58]

As we saw in chapter 3, Bishop Athanasius of Alexandria, writing the biography of Antony, the first Christian monk, was careful to insist that Antony was a loyal son of the church. Thomas of Celano does the same in his story of Francis: "He revered priests and he had a great affection for every ecclesiastical order." Francis twice appeared before popes, both of whom must have been puzzled by him but both of whom recognized the supreme importance of keeping Francis's new form of religious life within the church. At the second of these appearances, before Pope Honorius III in 1223 C.E., Francis behaved with a spontaneity and hilarity that must be very rare in the annals of papal audiences: "He began to speak fearlessly. Indeed, he spoke with such great fervor of spirit, that, not being able to contain himself for joy, when he spoke the words with his mouth, he moved his feet as though he were dancing."[59]

In the stories of all these exemplary characters there is something elusive, a quality of life, experience, insight, an originality, that can only be hinted at—Benedict's seeing everything in true perspective, Hildegard's knowledge of the interconnectedness of music and the incarnation, Zossima's uncanny understanding of what was really going on in other people, Francis's dancing before the pope. Each of these characters is more fully alive, more available for the sake of the world, than the rest of us, but for just that reason they seem to come from somewhere else. The amazement they all generate is perhaps best captured by Thomas of Celano as he tries to account for the impression made by Francis: "He seemed like a new person, one from another world."[60]

6

Monasticism and Modernity

BUDDHISM

Although the Asian settings of Buddhist monasticism differ significantly from the West, Buddhist monks face many of the same pressures and challenges as their Christian counterparts. Indeed, the dispassionate observer interviewing someone on the street in New York, Paris, Tokyo, and Bangkok might come to the conclusion that monasticism—whether Christian or Buddhist—has a problematical future at best as it attempts to come to terms with the dramatic challenges of the twentieth century.

In the case of Buddhism these challenges have been brought about through the impact of colonialism, in particular, and the influence of the West in the areas of education, economics, politics, and in reshaping sociocultural values. In some cases—China, Cambodia, Vietnam—revolutionary political change has undermined the stability and cultural importance of monastic institutions, while in others—Thailand, Japan—traditional values associated with monastic Buddhism seem to be overwhelmed by secularism and materialism.

It would be overly dramatic for our interviewer to predict the demise of the Buddhist ascetic/monastic ideal and its accompanying institutions in today's world, but it would be naive not to recognize the profound challenge to traditional monastic life. To be sure,

181

outside large urban centers, somewhat protected from the pressures of rapid social, economic, and political change, traditional monastic life continues much as in the past, but in many instances the monastery has lost its vitality or is in the process of significant reformation and transformation.[1]

We shall look at two flourishing religious centers, one in Japan and another in Thailand, as case studies of large modern monastic centers; then we shall explore two diverse aspects of Buddhist monasticism today—varied dimensions of the revival of the monastic/ascetic ideal, and the relationship between the monastery and its rapidly changing sociopolitical environment.

THE ZEN MONASTERY OF MYOSHIN-JI

Myoshin-ji, founded in Kyoto in 1342 C.E., is the largest branch of Rinzai Zen in Japan. This Zen tradition is noted for its emphasis on training and claims the illustrious seventeenth-century reformer, Hakuin Zenji, as one of its leaders. Myoshin-ji was founded on the site of the Emperor Hanazona's palace, and throughout the history of the tradition there has been a close connection with the Imperial Household. Kanzan, the founder, was noted for his simple style of life, the severity of his teaching and practice, and his disdain for formalities and ritual.

Myoshin-ji has had a distinguished history.[2] Among the best-known religious centers associated with this tradition is the rock and gravel meditation garden, Ryoan-ji, built in the fifteenth century. An irregular collection of stones emerging from a bed of sand and gravel, the garden has been likened to a "visual *koan*" capable of guiding the meditator to enlightenment.

Myoshin-ji abbots have also played an important role in the development of Japanese Zen, although none surpasses the great Rinzai reformer of the Tokugawa period, Hakuin Zenji (1685–1768 C.E.). Best known as a Zen master of mystical intensity who spoke the language of the ordinary layperson, Hakuin was also a gifted poet and painter. He created a "living Zen" attractive to the Japanese religious spirit: on the one hand, espousing a rigorous form of meditation training, but, on the other, making Zen accessible to the masses rather than a religion for the elite. Hakuin's method of *koan* training was systematized by his disciples, becoming the normative practice in the Rinzai Zen tradition by the early nineteenth century. In the West, teachers of Zen often try to discuss the nature of the *koan* using Hakuin's "What is the sound of one hand clapping?" This mental conundrum points to the difficulty of "discussing" the *koan* in a conventional, rational manner.

Today, while there are thirty-five hundred temples of the Myoshin-ji lineage scattered throughout Japan, the headquarters, with one of the fifteen monastic training centers, remains in Kyoto. The Myoshin-ji compound follows the classical pattern of Chinese Zen temples. Arranged in a straight line from south to north with the front gate at the foot and the lecture hall at the heart, the major buildings can be diagrammed as follows:

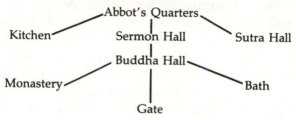

One enters the compound through a massive gate with three entrances symbolizing the cardinal Zen principles of Emptiness, No-Sign, and Non-active Action.[3] The Buddha hall enshrines a large image of Shakyamuni Buddha flanked by two of his disciples—Ananda and Mahakasapa. Buddhist *sutras* are chanted in this hall every morning. Sermons are delivered in the lecture hall and meetings of various kinds are held there, including meditation (*zazen*) practice for the laity. Flanked on the front sides are the training monastery or meditation hall (*sodo*) and kitchen. The *sutra* hall to the rear is, in fact, the library, housing over five thousand volumes of Mahayana texts.

The priests who serve Myoshin-ji and its subtemples spend most of their time officiating at various religious ceremonies and are expected to be a moral example for the laity. If the parish is poor, they may be compelled to find supplemental employment as well. Before ordination Zen priests must spend at least two to three years in monastic training. During this time they will study the major texts of the tradition, memorize chants for religious services, and practice meditation (*zazen*). Once outside the monastery, however, the typical parish priest will practice *zazen* only if exceptionally motivated. Thus, while there are Zen monks who observe a monastic discipline and practice, most lead lives similar to those of Christian ministers and priests and Jewish rabbis. As we observed in chapter 3, in Central and East Asia Buddhist monastic life changed and diversified. In particular, a priest/monk distinction developed similar to that in the Christian West, and, as in Myoshin-ji Zen, a period of monastic training became part of the preparation for ordination into the priesthood.

The Myoshin-ji Zen center has a specifically monastic dimension for those training to be priests, but in the broadest sense it functions as the focus of religious life for its parish or lay adherents. The main ceremonial and ritual events at Myoshin-ji are the following: (1) quarterly seasonal sermons in the sermon hall, (2) the emperor's celebration on the first and fifteenth days of every month, (3) the Buddha's birthday (April 8), enlightenment (December 8), and death (February 15), (4) Bodhidharma Memorial Day (October 5), (5) Founder's Day (December 12), (6) Emperor Hanazona's Memorial Day (November 1), (7) an annual ceremony honoring the Perfection of Wisdom Sutras, (8) the Obon Festival in honor of the ancestors, and several other memorial-type services. The educational role of Myoshin-ji also figures as a very prominent part of its life; in particular, it sponsors schools up through university level.

Religion in Japan in the contemporary period faces a continuing crisis of secularization. Surviving this challenge will require both the strength of the traditional resources of Zen Buddhism and modern adaptations. It has been argued that the practice of traditional Rinzai Zen is no longer viable in a society as modernized as Japan's, and that the people do not have the leisure time or the inclination to be devoted to its teachings and practices. Myoshin-ji must certainly adapt itself to changing circumstances while at the same time maintaining the tradition of Kanzan Zen.

Much can be said about Zen as an institution in contemporary Japan by looking at a major temple-monastery complex like Myoshin-ji located in the religious and cultural heart of Japan, Kyoto. In the first instance, the visitor to Myoshin-ji is struck by a sense of sacred space. In the midst of the din and rush of crowded Japan, Myoshin-ji offers a refreshing oasis, a special sense of place, a moment of quiet, an awareness of Japan's religious history, a reference point transcending space and time. Myoshin-ji provides a sense of place both time-full in terms of its rich history, and time-less in relationship to the ideals of Zen.

Part of the uniqueness of Myoshin-ji is its art and architecture. The Japanese government has designated it as a cultural treasure. The Taizo-in garden, the founder's hall, the *sumei* paintings of Kano Tannyu, even the layout of the main buildings of the temple itself, are reminders of the development of the Japanese artistic tradition with its roots in China. In a day when the impact of modernity is radically transforming many of Japan's cultural traditions, Zen headquarters such as Myoshin-ji are important conservators of Japan's rich religious and cultural heritage.

But Myoshin-ji stands for much more than a physical place, gardens, buildings, and paintings. It represents the centrality of Zen monastic training, namely, meditation or *zazen*. Kanzan, the founder of Myoshin-ji, was noted for his emphasis on meditation training rather than buildings or rituals. While in practice this tradition might not always have been borne out, it remains important as an ideal. Whether for monk, laywoman, or layman, the practice of *zazen* represents the religious way par excellence. On weekends Zen meditation and training sessions for the laity are held at Myoshin-ji, and at noontime Hanazona high-school students can be seen practicing *zazen* in the sermon hall. As we have noted, every ordained priest has practiced *zazen* as part of his training. Zen training involves more than meditation, however. Myoshin-ji also emphasizes the development of the intellect, as evidenced by the fact that Myoshin-ji has established the only Rinzai Zen university-level education in Japan.

Myoshin-ji is, above all, a lineage of Zen masters beginning with Kanzan, the founder. Hence, Myoshin-ji stands for a "transmission of the Zen mind." This transmission has both personal and institutional referents. On the one hand, it represents the certification by a Zen master that his student has reached an acceptable level of religious or spiritual attainment. On the other hand, it makes the institution responsible to the individual and the individual responsible to the institution. Here is no isolated priest or monk carrying out his duties at a particular temple or monastery. Rather, the individual personifies the way of Kanzan Zen, perpetuated and propagated by the institutions of the Myoshin-ji line.

Finally, a comment needs to be made about the relationship between Zen and the state. Myoshin-ji has had a curiously ambivalent relationship to the secular powers of Japan. While it owes its very existence to the Emperor Hanazona, it is proud of a long tradition of independence from political authority. Today, when government policy regarding religion provides less support for religious institutions than in the past, Myoshin-ji's tradition of independence will help it survive.

WAT HARIPUNJAYA, LAMPHUN, THAILAND

The traditions of the monastery known as Wat Haripunjaya in Lamphun, northern Thailand, go back to the middle of the eleventh century C.E.[4] According to northern Thai chronicles, the monastery (Thai: *wat*) was founded by Adittaraja, the ruler of a Mon kingdom known as Haripunjaya. The king built the monastery in honor of the discovery of a Buddha relic, which he enshrined on the compound of his royal palace and then donated to the *sangha* or monastic Order. Hence, from its origin Wat Haripunjaya has had important political connections, first with the princely families of Lamphun and Chiangmai, and later with the Thai monarchs who ruled the country from Bangkok. Furthermore, since pilgrimage to reliquary sites has constituted one of the main forms of popular Buddhist piety, Wat Haripunjaya has been an important center of lay devotional life for over seven hundred years.

Thus, far from being a quiet retreat from the hustle and bustle of town life, Wat Haripunjaya has been at the center of northern Thai social, political, and religious life. We shall examine this important monastic center as a sacred space, as an educational center for training Buddhist monks, as a link within a national "monastic-church," and, finally, as a focus of religious life for the community on local, regional, and national levels.

Sacred space

Like Myoshin-ji, Wat Haripunjaya's physical layout reflects ancient and hallowed traditions of monastic architecture. (See figure on p. 188.) In the case of the Haripunjaya monastery, the reliquary mound or pagoda provides the physical and symbolic focus for both the physical space and the activities that take place on the monastery compound. Symbolically it represents the axis of the universe, the cosmic mountain at the center of the world, the point of orientation for everything seen and unseen. Buddhists worldwide come to Wat Haripunjaya on pilgrimage to make simple offerings at one of the altars located at the four cardinal directions situated in the wall surrounding this sacred space. Or they may come on the Buddhist sabbath day, when monks conduct a chanting ceremony in one of the four temples enshrining Buddha images that encircle the reliquary. The heart of the monastery compound, in sum, represents the Buddha and is known, literally, as the "place of the Buddha." Consequently, the reliquary and the image halls around it provide the place for lay religious practice.

Surrounding the "place of the Buddha" we find the "place for the monks." While at one point in history four separate monasteries were on the periphery of the reliquary, today they constitute four divisions of a single monastic structure under the authority of the abbot of Wat Haripunjaya and his assistant abbots. These four units contain dormitories for the monastic population, usually numbering about one hundred, and various buildings for specifically monastic use, such as ordination ceremonies, the fortnightly ritual recitation of the 227 rules of monastic training, and classroom buildings. While this distinction between two parts of the total monastery compound is relatively informal, it provides an important separation between those activities limited to the monastic community, for example, the ritual recitation of the monastic rules, and those that include the laity, for example, sabbath ceremonies. Thus, the physical structure of the monastery provides an insight into the two dimensions of the life of the monks at Wat Haripunjaya—one specifically focused on the discipline, practices, and ceremonies of the monastic community, and the other including the laity.

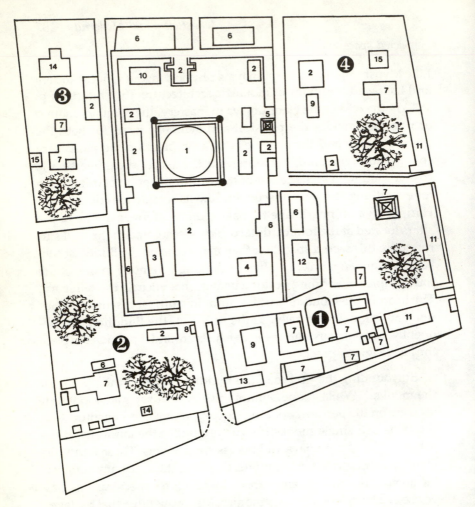

DIAGRAM OF WAT HARIPUNJAYA

Bold numerals 1–4 designate the four divisions of the Sanghavasa.
Other structures include the following:

1. Relic *ceitya*
2. Vihara
3. Library
4. Bell tower
5. *Ceitya*
6. Open verandah
7. Monks' quarters
8. Guardian lions
9. Ordination hall
10. Lamphun museum
11. School buildings
12. Office of the school principal
13. Pond
14. Drum
15. Kitchen

Diagram reprinted with permission from Donald K. Swearer, *Wat Haripunjaya* (Scholars Press, 1976).

An educational center

Education at Wat Haripunjaya constitutes one of its central activities. Roughly speaking, education at the monastery can be divided into religious and secular studies. Enlightened Thai monarchs at the end of the nineteenth century utilized the network of Buddhist monasteries throughout the country as the backbone of the development of a nationwide educational system. While government schools gradually became independent of their religious roots, many monasteries continue to provide government-sponsored education for boys and girls, especially in rural areas.

Wat Haripunjaya has a boys' school founded in 1946 with an enrollment of about fifteen hundred students. Nearly one-third of the student body are novice monks, most of them ordained primarily to receive an elementary and secondary education. As monks, their studies, room, and board are free, and the great majority of them come from relatively poor farming families. Having completed their education, most of these novices will then leave the monastic Order. Students of Thai Buddhism have observed that the monastery in Thailand, specifically the monastery school, provides the most important avenue for social advancement for the rural poor.

Students at the boys' school are required to study Buddhism. Known as "ethics," the curriculum is set by the Department of Religious Affairs of the Ministry of Education and is standard for all schools throughout the country. Novice monks at the boys' school are required, in addition, to take further work in Buddhist studies and the Pali language of the Buddhist canon in preparation for monastic exams. It might be said that religious and ethical instruction at the Wat Haripunjaya boys' school attempts to provide a moral-ethical base for Thai society by teaching the essential interrelationship between Buddhism and Thai culture and by stressing those values in the Buddhist world view that are most conducive to social harmony and cohesiveness.

In addition to the boys' school, which teaches the required government curriculum in all subjects, Wat Haripunjaya has an academy exclusively for Buddhist studies. Monks and novices who study at the Pali School devote all of their formal education to religious studies, especially the Pali language. A much higher percentage engage in serious preparation for the standard monastic examinations, which include three levels of Buddhist studies—history, doctrine, liturgy—and nine levels of Pali language exams. Only a few monks are able to pass all of these examinations successfully. Those who do pass achieve an honorific title, and many of them become active leaders in the Thai monastic Order or "monastic-church" at national, regional, or provincial levels.

Part of a "monastic-church"

Thailand is unique in the Buddhist world today in having a nationally organized monastic Order or "monastic-church." The following diagram outlines its formal structure:

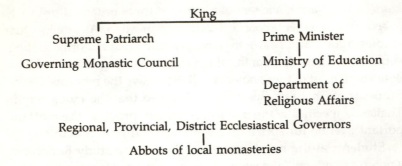

This diagram points to two striking facts about the Thai monastic Order: (1) The king has formal authority over the religious realm as well as the sociopolitical realm, and while the Thai constitution supports religious toleration the king is also designated as the protector of the Buddhist faith. (2) The monastic Order is a hierarchical organization paralleling the structure of the state, headed by a supreme patriarch (*sangharaja*) and a governing monastic council, with a subordinate set of ecclesiastical officials at regional, provincial, district, and subdistrict levels. For example, the abbot of Wat Haripunjaya is also the ecclesiastical governor of the northern region, and his two assistant abbots hold positions of leadership at provincial and district levels. Thus, while Wat Haripunjaya functions in many respects as an autonomous monastery, it is part of a national religious system that sets guidelines for monastic discipline, education, and monastic administration.

A religious center for laity

Finally—and this is in many respects the most important aspect of monastic life at Wat Haripunjaya—the monastery serves the entire Buddhist community as a religious center where the faithful observe the Buddhist sabbath, celebrate the major Buddhist festivals and holy days, and come on pilgrimage. Ceremonies at Wat Haripunjaya may involve only the monks, as do morning and evening chanting services in the main image hall, but most also involve the laity. Even ordination ceremonies are major events for family and friends. Furthermore, in mid-July and mid-October, at the beginning and end of the monastic "rains retreat" (a period when monks engage in more intensive study and meditation), there are several rituals involving extensive lay participation. Major festivals celebrated at Wat Haripunjaya include Thai New Year, which occurs in April; the Loi Kratong festival in November honoring the spirits of the ancestors; and, usually in May, the annual festival in honor of the founding of the monastery and the celebration of the Buddha's birth, enlightenment, and death.

Major religious festivals at Wat Haripunjaya include an extensive level of lay involvement. As with religious festivals worldwide, part of the celebration is pure carnival—an opportunity to socialize or for those who operate a local food or gift stall to make some extra money. Hence, during major religious holidays, Wat Haripunjaya will be crowded with vendors, families, and friends simply having a good time. This more secular part of the festival blends in with pious religious acts, which may include making food offerings to the monks, listening to lengthy sermons and many hours of monastic chanting, and—most important at Wat Haripunjaya—circumambulation of the reliquary.

Some monks participate informally in some of these activities, appearing to enjoy the festivities as much as the laity who crowd into the compound of the monastery. Others, however, seem to be removed from the noise and activity, participating only when required, chanting, and preaching. In short, at a major religious center like Wat Haripunjaya the monastery and the monk play many different roles, and lines between priestly and monastic functions or even between secular and sacred are not easily drawn.

Challenge and Revival

In the preceding sketches of two major Buddhist centers in East and Southeast Asia we have described traditional monastic life as we might find it in actual practice. These sketches omit the extent of the challenge to this relatively traditional picture and also various responses to the challenge. Such political changes as those in China, Tibet, and Cambodia have significantly undermined the traditional role of the monastery in these societies and the nature of monastic life itself. But, on a more subtle level, the challenge of modern, secular world views to a traditional Buddhist way of understanding the world has had an equally profound impact on the nature and role of Buddhist monasticism. A barefoot, saffron-robed monk walking with downcast eyes along a commercialized, crowded, noisy, polluted Bangkok street seems a living contradiction in terms!

How can a tradition like Buddhism, which espouses the ideals of equanimity, calm, compassion, and non-egoism, survive in a world so apparently dominated by opposing values? Must Buddhism itself become aggressive and commercial if it is to compete? Or are there ways in which the Buddhist monastic tradition can reform and reformulate so that its ideals can provide a realistic critique and viable alternative to "the way of the world"?[5] Can a Buddhist monastic world view realistically address the moral and ethical issues raised by modern science and technology, or respond effectively to the social critiques of contemporary feminist and liberation thinkers?

The modern challenge to a traditional Buddhist monastic way of life has created a conservative, if not reactionary, response among some Buddhists, that is, an attempt to preserve—and in some cases create—forms of monastic Buddhism associated with an idealized Golden Age. The Buddhist revival in Sri Lanka in the modern period can be characterized as a resurgence rather than a reformation of the Buddhist monastic traditions.[6] Conservative or reactionary response to the genuine confusion created by rapid social change is, of course, universal, and not unique to Buddhism. But there have been other, more creative initiatives taken by Buddhist monks throughout Buddhist Asia. For example, training in meditation, once thought to be the special domain of the monk, is being much more widely practiced among the laity. As a consequence, new forms of

meditation are developing and being integrated into modern thera-
peutic and psychoanalytical techniques.

Buddhist monks in various countries, furthermore, are reinter-
preting the Buddhist world view and creating new institutions in
order to give the tradition a new currency and relevance. In particular, Buddhist monks have added a strong voice to the peace movement; they have developed programs to address poverty and such
major social problems as prostitution and drug abuse; and, while
Buddhist societies are still largely patriarchal, contemporary
feminists have found support in the tradition for a less sexist and
more egalitarian vision of the human community.[7] We shall focus
our discussion on a reformist Thai monk, the abbot of Suanmokh,
a meditation monastery in southern Thailand, who has inspired
Buddhists there and elsewhere by both his example and teaching.[8]

BHIKKHU BUDDHADASA

Buddhadasa was born in 1906 in Chaiya, southern Thailand. Ordained a monk at age twenty, he proved to be a serious student
of the tradition and at an early age was made the abbot of an old
and famous monastery in his home town. Buddhadasa was not content simply to fit into a conventional leadership role in the Thai
monastic Order, however, and soon founded a meditation monastery on a 125-acre tract of land about five kilometers outside of town.
There he proceeded to establish one of the most interesting Buddhist monasteries in the country, a betwixt-and-between place, syn-
thesizing the poles of solitary practice and involvement in the social
and political issues of the day. The fifty-some monks in residence
there live in simple wooden cottages and spend a good deal of time
in individual study and meditation. Some work at painting murals
on the walls of a large building called a Spiritual Theater, which is
also used to show slides and films. Other monks spend afternoons
making castings of bas reliefs from the ancient Indian Buddhist sites
of Sanchi and Barhut to be sent to other monasteries in the country. And a few teach meditation to the scores of Westerners who
come to train there.

Buddhadasa himself may often be found lecturing to groups of
students who come to receive instruction from him. On the one

hand, he teaches them about the highest ideals of Buddhist self-perfection—Nirvana and Emptiness. Yet, on the other hand, he spells out a Buddhist social ethics and political philosophy he calls Dhammic Socialism.[9] He criticizes institutional Buddhism in Thailand for excessive attention to self-serving ceremonials and for a preoccupation with the form rather than the substance of the tradition. He urges his listeners to return to the essence of the teachings of the Buddha: a quest for personal self-transformation, the attainment of wisdom, and the courage to act for the well-being of the whole rather than out of self-centered interest.

Bhikkhu Buddhadasa embodies a reformist Buddhism that aims to recapture what is universally true in the Buddhist monastic tradition. He advocates a simple style of life for both monk and layperson, a way-of-being-in-the-world based in the recognition of the essential interrelatedness of everything in the world. While he lives a relatively secluded life, he strives to influence others by both his example and teaching. Thus, he is not only a critic of conventional Thai social and religious life. He also articulates an egalitarian social and political vision that he believes is closer to the authentic teachings of the Buddha.

BUDDHIST NUNS TODAY

Women as well as men will contribute to the shaping of Buddhism in the contemporary world. In the past few years there have been efforts to revive a *bhikkhuni* Order in Sri Lanka and Thailand, and to establish an international Order of Buddhist women monastics. The first International Conference on Buddhist Nuns was held at Bodh Gaya, India, in February 1987, attended by over a thousand nuns and laypersons from twenty-four countries. With the establishment of *Sakyadhita*, an international organization of Buddhist women, more attention will be given to women in Buddhism, and the exemplary role of Buddhist nuns will take its rightful place in our understanding of the history of Buddhist monasticism.

The contribution of women to the reshaping of Buddhism will be more than simply the recovery of their own role within the history of Buddhist monasticism, however. Women are playing active leadership roles within Buddhist monastic institutions throughout the world as lay practitioners, nuns, and even founders of new Orders. Jiyu Kennett, for example, is prioress of Shasta Abbey, an active, stable Zen center in California. Vorami Kabilsingh, from Thailand, sought *bhikkhuni* ordination in Taiwan and has established a monastery for women outside of Bangkok. Nuns like Manseong Sunim of Korea were known for their diligence and insight. Women as well as men are seriously involved in Buddhist practice at various centers throughout Europe and America.

Impetus for reform within the Buddhist monastic tradition is occurring not only in Asia, but in America and Europe as well. Zen monasteries and meditation centers are located throughout the United States, and two Tibetan monastic lineages have headquarters in California and Colorado. In more recent years over one hundred Theravada monasteries have been established in the United States, primarily to serve growing Southeast Asian populations in this country. Within the coming years distinctive Western forms of monastic Buddhism will be developed. Undoubtedly, some of these forms will be short-lived, but others, like the efforts of Bhikkhu Buddhadasa and other monastic leaders in Asia, hold the promise of helping to make monasticism a vital and viable force in today's world.

THE MONK AND THE POLITICIAN

An important aspect of Buddhist monastic life and the world has been and continues to be the relationship between the monastery and politics, in particular the role played by the Buddhist monastery as the countries of Asia emerged from the colonial period as modern nation-states.[10] From the outset Buddhist monasticism has been closely associated with political rulers. Indeed, at Siddhartha Gotama's birth his greatness as either a Buddha or a world ruler was predicted, and Buddhist chronicles are filled with stories of monarchs who supported the monastic Order, which, in turn, helped to legitimate their rule. In the modern period this close relationship between religion and the state has continued, although in forms reflecting different political circumstances. On the one hand Buddhism has contributed decisively to the development of new Asian nation-states. On the other hand, the Buddhist monastery has sought to resist the pressures put on the tradition by the new governments and their policies. And, in some cases, the state has done its best to restrict or repress the monastery and the Buddhist values it upholds.

Sri Lanka and Burma

In the former colonies of Great Britain, Sri Lanka (Ceylon) and Burma, the early nationalist movement was fed by strong Buddhist sentiments. Buddhists in both countries felt that British attitudes toward their religion were demeaning, and that British policies undermined the traditionally close relationship between Buddhism and the state. Toward the end of the nineteenth century, aggressive monks in Sri Lanka began speaking out against Christianity and British rule. Their efforts gained momentum with the support of the American theosophist, Henry Steel Olcott, who came to Sri Lanka and helped to found Buddhist colleges. This resurgence gained momentum through the early part of the twentieth century and was led, in part, by the Anagarika Dharmapala, who founded various Buddhist lay organizations, such as the Mahabodhi Society, and devoted much energy to the restoration of Buddhist monastic and pilgrimage sites in India.

Finally, spurred on by the celebration of the 2500th anniversary of the birth of the Buddha in 1956 and the simultaneous publication of the Report of the Buddhist Committee of Inquiry with strong anti-British sentiment, S. W. R. D. Bandaranaike and the Sri Lanka Freedom Party were swept into power on a ticket that promised restoration of Sinhalese Buddhist institutions and values. Buddhist monks participated actively in political campaigns and continue to do so today. While this active involvement by monks in electoral politics has been criticized by some Buddhist leaders in the country, it reflects the monks' concern for the political and social well-being of their country as well as the symbiotic tension that exists between the monk and the politician.

In Burma the early nationalist movement was also fed by Buddhist sentiments. As in Sri Lanka, Buddhism represented the only widely accepted symbol able to focus the accumulated economic, social, and psychological grievances of the people. In the early decades of this century the nationalist cause was led by such politically active monks as U Ottama and U Wisara. When U Nu became prime minister of a newly independent Burma in 1948, he pledged himself to make Burma into a Buddhist state. In particular, he attempted to strengthen the monastic Order in Burma by creating a national monastic committee, and by calling an ecumenical council in Rangoon in honor of the 2500th anniversary of the birth of the Buddha. One of the council's major tasks was to produce a new edition of the Pali canonical scriptures of Theravada Buddhism. In short, U Nu, the modern politician, attempted to restore the Buddhist monastic vision to a central place in the lives of the Burmese. While in many respects he failed, there can be no doubt that the monastery plays a vital role in Burmese society today.

Thailand

Thailand provides another example of the relationship between Buddhism and the state. There Buddhism and the monarch continue to function as the most visible symbols of national unity. In addition, the government has carefully designed a number of national development programs utilizing Buddhist monks. Two of these, the Dhammadhuta and Dhammacarika, organized during the 1960s, train monks to work in politically sensitive areas in the northeast bordering Laos and Cambodia, and among the animistic hill tribe peoples in northern Thailand. Both programs aim to encourage national loyalty among people whose affiliation rests more strongly with a regional ethnic group or tribe. More recent government programs have encouraged monks to take leadership roles in rural economic development such as rice and buffalo banks, and vocational training in nonagricultural jobs such as electrical repair, sewing, and weaving to supplement family and village income.

Prospects

There are, of course, numerous instances during the past fifty years when the Buddhist monastery and the state have not been so mutually supportive. One of the most dramatic was the protest of Vietnamese monks against the Diem regime in the 1960s, including several instances of self-immolation. In Burma and Thailand there have been monks who have actively resisted pressures brought by the government to standardize monastic rule and practice. On the other side, there have also been instances where the state has discouraged Buddhism or has taken active steps to disestablish the monastery. The best-known cases are those where communist regimes have come into power—China, Tibet, Vietnam, Laos, and Cambodia. The policies of these governments have varied greatly, however. The most devastating anti-Buddhist periods were the Cultural Revolution in China and the reign of Pol Pot in Kampuchea (Cambodia). But even in these countries Buddhist monastic life, while curtailed and modified, survives.

Buddhism and its monastic traditions have been severely tested in the modern period. As we have seen in the examples of Myoshin-ji and Wat Haripunjaya, in the face of this challenge the monastery continues to embody the ascetic ideal in an environment where self-aggrandizement, rather than self-transformation, often seems to be the norm. To be sure, Buddhist monastic traditions must necessarily change in order to survive in an increasingly secular ethos, and to challenge the assumptions of secular materialism. While Buddhist monks may, in some instances, have pursued their own institutional self-interest in supporting nationalist causes in the early twentieth century, or have been too uncritically supportive of their government's policies of economic and political development, today monks like Bhikkhu Buddhadasa mediate a different way of being-in-the-world. They embody what the monastic ideal has always been—a betwixt-and-between state, one which is to the fullest extent in the world, and for this very reason can never be fully of it; that paradoxical state of individualism and selflessness where one is truly oneself in being for the sake of the world.

CHRISTIANITY

One way to get round the difficult question of monasticism and the modern world is the way of complete open-mindedness: monasticism, like everything else, is fine for people who want to do that sort of thing. The life of the monk or nun is simply one of countless options open to people. In this view, what characterizes the modern world is precisely its tolerance, its abandonment of norms, its exaltation of individual autonomy and its acknowledgment of the authority of individual feelings. To invite a monk to one's cocktail party is a stroke of social genius, for the most entertaining gatherings bring people of many different life styles together. "Oh, you are a monk. That must be *very* interesting! Tell me all about it."

The recruitment brochure for a contemporary Christian monastery suggests a disconcerting answer to the query, Tell me all about it. "The monk is a sign of contradiction."[11] Of course the brochure does not presuppose that the monastic life is for everyone, but it does not suggest, either, that the monastic life is justified as a social niche into which people who favor a particular life style can fit themselves. Monks and nuns are not just "doing their thing." If they are a sign of contradiction, they are defined in part by what they are contradicting, but the contradiction is not simply a minus sign placed before the whole modern world equation. "The monk/nun is a sign of contradiction" has been a true statement throughout the history of monasticism, even in those centuries that are designated monastic by historians. The relation between monasticism and any specific modern world is complex, with influences moving in both directions.

One way to pose the question about monasticism and the modern world is this: Do Father Zossima's assertion, that a monk is what every person ought to be, and the recruitment brochure's declaration, that the monk is a sign of contradiction, mean the same thing? Another way to pose the question is this: Have both statements— Father Zossima's and the brochure's—been replaced by the conviction that the monk/nun is what people *used to think* all persons ought to be, and by the judgment that the monk/nun is now a sign of irrelevance?

AGGIORNAMENTO

"As we sit around reminiscing about our life in the 1950s and early 1960s, we ask ourselves repeatedly, 'Was it *really* like that? Did we *really* do those things?' It was, and we did. Unbelievable." Among contemporary Roman Catholic religious, especially nuns, the question of monasticism and the modern world is the very antithesis of an abstract academic debate. It is the stuff of heartache and division, of rage and liberation, of loss of bearings and new solidarity. The issues are personally intense, and many who are involved have the clear impression of having lived through many decades in a brief period. The changes that have occurred since the mid-1960s are so extensive and so pervasive as to defy the belief of participants that it can really have happened. The maintenance of a sense of continuity requires an act of imagination as well as an act of will.

The Decree on Renewal of Religious Life

No historical movement can be attributed to one isolated cause, but most of the commotion in contemporary Catholic monasticism can be traced to a single occasion: the promulgation of *Perfectae caritatis*, the Decree on the Appropriate Renewal of Religious Life, by the Second Vatican Council on October 28, 1965. The Council Fathers summed up the whole scope of renewal in the following succinct sentence:

> The appropriate renewal of religious life involves two simultaneous processes: (1) a continuous return to the sources of all Christian life and to the original inspiration behind a given community and (2) an adjustment of the community to the changed conditions of the times.

The decree gives some specification of each element in this sentence. The "sources of all Christian life," that is, the Scriptures, are frequently cited, and Jesus is put forth as the supreme example of life lived in poverty, chastity, and obedience. The "original inspiration behind a given community" is distinguished from the deposit of subsequent legislation and tradition that may have distorted what the founder of a particular order intended: "Hope for renewal lies more in greater diligence in the observance of the rule and constitutions than in the multiplication of laws." Finally, "the changed conditions of the times" are spelled out in a very general way when the decree indicates that the modern world is not to be merely an outward adornment of the religious, but rather an internal appropriation:

> Lest the adaptation of religious life to the needs of our time be merely external and lest those whose rule assigns them to the active ministry should prove unequal to the task, they should be properly instructed—each according to his/her intellectual calibre and personal

bent—concerning the behavior-patterns, the emotional attitudes, and the thought-processes of modern society. The elements of the education should be so harmoniously fused that it will help to integrate the lives of the religious.[12]

The final sentence of the quotation is deceptively simple. The Vatican Council declares the goal of education for religious to be personal integration. But the most notorious failure of education in our time is its inability to provide just such an integration. Fragmentation of knowledge and territorial imperatives of academic disciplines reflect and reinforce the pathologies that afflict "the behavior-patterns, the emotional attitudes, and the thought-processes of modern society."

Has the Council, in its general program of *aggiornamento*, updating the church, eroded the contradiction character of the religious life? *Perfectae caritatis* does not, of course, intend such an erosion. It is full of admonitions to traditional spirituality, and insists that coming to terms with the modern world is a means to more effective apostolic work. But is modern society sufficiently flexible to let itself be taken seriously by those whose fundamental purpose is to contradict it? The capacity to be in the world but not of the world presupposes that the world in which you are will not co-opt you.

It did not take the Council Fathers long to learn how momentous their call for renewal was. Tumult became the steady state of religious life throughout the church, but nowhere was the sense of revolution more acute than among women religious in the United States.

The revolution among American monastic women

In 1968, three years after the conclusion of the Vatican Council, an American bishop wrote to the president of the Federation of Saint Scholastica, an organization of twenty-three North American Benedictine convents:

> To become concerned about the implementation of the Decree [more accurately, the Pastoral Constitution] on the Church in the Modern World [*Gaudium et spes*] will distract the Sisters from their assigned area of concentration: the Council Decree addressed to Religious [*Perfectae caritatis*].

It all seemed so clear and simple, back during the days of the Council. . . . Now, three years later, it is not nearly so simple.[13]

Perfectae caritatis had of course clearly implied that religious should be concerned with the matters specified in *Gaudium et spes*, but the bishop in his alarm is warning the sisters to pay strict and undivided attention to their "assigned area of concentration," the directions he and his fellow bishops in Council gave to *them*.

The old problem of monastic independence, implied already in Athanasius's portrayal of the obedient Antony in the fourth century and dealt with peremptorily by Justinian's legislation in the sixth century, had suddenly become sharply pointed once again. The ancient problem now had an added dimension—the determination of women not to submit passively to direction from men. But while opposition to ecclesiastical sexism is unmistakable among women religious, it would be both superficial and historically uninformed to think that feminism is the basic explanation for the recent ferment. The fundamental issue is this: If the church as a whole and the religious institutes within it both undertake to relate to the modern world, what happens to the relation between the church and the institutes? In all human relationships triangles are notoriously troublesome, and the same may be true in institutional life as well.

The issues posed by adaptation to the conditions of modern society range right across the spectrum of the monastic life. At one end of the spectrum are unexceptionable decisions. No one could seriously question the provision of typewriters or word processors as a functional equivalent of the pens allowed by Benedict.

Somewhere in the middle of the spectrum are such questions as the number and length of gatherings for communal worship (e.g., how to balance the traditional sevenfold daily *opus Dei* against the need of monks and nuns who are university professors to spend adequate time preparing for their classes), and the means of providing monastic meals (e.g., what should be done if it costs more to have Benedict's one or two frugal meals a day than to sign the monastic refectory onto the meal plan of the dining service in the monastery's college?). These middle-range questions generate discussion but not much controversy.

At the other end of the spectrum come the profound questions of identity and purpose in the monastic life, questions that affect both the inward spirits and the outward behavior of monks and nuns. It is at this end of the spectrum that appearances can be most deceptive. For instance, to the outside observer monastic dress might seem a superficial issue, yet no single feature of renewal has been more hotly debated—"*the* one change recognized by everyone and the most controversial of all the changes"[14]—and the intensity of discussion should alert us to the serious inward confusion of which the dress debate is an outward and visible sign.

Changing Catholic culture

The Vatican Council, when it admonished religious to inform themselves about modern society, was confirming fact as well as projecting for the future. Up until the middle of the twentieth century the Catholic church had quite effectively fought off all sorts of modern onslaughts, and the majority of religious had been formed, prior to their novitiates, in a Catholic culture that had reinforced its social isolation by its own school system. Many a monk and nun had first been attracted to the religious life by the example of a particularly beloved parochial school teacher. In the United States, at least, this whole cultural situation began to change dramatically in the 1950s.

But it was not just social integration into the American mainstream that altered the context for monasticism. Pope Pius XII, who appears in retrospect to have been one of the most revolutionary of Peter's successors, called on religious to become more professionally competent for their apostolic work. Just as he opened the door for Catholic biblical scholars to make the most of modern critical scholarship, so he propelled Catholic religious into secular colleges and universities to get their training.[15] Monasteries and convents began discouraging professions prior to an individual's completion of college education. In short, the new recruits to the religious life were bringing the modern world with them into the cloister. The operative question was not whether to relate to modern society, but how to do so.

As long as Catholics lived in their own world, it was possible for the official Scholastic theology, with its relatively static categories and its relatively clear-cut picture of human perfection, to permeate all levels of Catholic society. Monks and nuns were living a style of life that had been sanctioned as holy by the church. In theory, at least, perfection was absolute and uniform. If a religious felt uneasy or rebellious, it was because the flesh was weak, and perhaps even because the spirit was unwilling—not because the monastic institution itself was proposing an inadequate or distorted ideal.

When defections are sporadic, it is plausible to conclude that a few unworthy candidates have slipped through the screening net. In the words of *Renew and Create*, the 1969 renewal charter for many American Benedictine monks:

> Some monks, in fact, including some superiors, consider the problems which beset our communities to be simply a matter of the personal failure of individual monks. Such problems are considered to be no more than signs of the inevitable gap between practice and the ideal. The gap can be lessened, it is said, and things will return to normal, if the monks will just shape up, become more obedient, and observe the rules.

When defections become a stampede—for example, between 1963 and 1969 four hundred sisters, or 20 percent of the membership, left the priories of the Federation of Saint Scholastica—suspicion is apt to switch from the individuals to the ideal and the institution:

> It is clear, however, that our communities experience not only the inevitable gap between practice and ideal but also serious disagreement about the identity of the ideal itself. Further, the monks in our communities today are not responsible for many of the options which the houses of the Congregation made in the past in response to the earlier needs of the Church. Nor are they responsible for the radically changing cultural conditions of our own times. But it is precisely from the confrontation of today's changed conditions with the options and practices of the past that many of our problems arise.[16]

The "modern persons" who, from the early 1950s, came to the religious life brought with them many challenges to the assumptions of Catholic culture. "Those who have come to the monastery in recent years have brought with them a mentality quite different from that of their older brothers in religion."[17]

Among the challenges, none cut deeper than the pervasive *developmental* model of individual and community life. The disciplines of history and psychology had been profoundly shaping the surrounding culture for several generations, replacing the Scholastic and Enlightenment models of natural law and self-evident truths with evolution and growth, and setting up an ideal of maturity in the place formerly held by perfection. Authority figures were increasingly suspect, as more and more people began to consider themselves the only authoritative arbiters of their own values and ideals. ''In post-Vatican [II] religious life it will have to be discovered how to make self-direction compatible with community.''[18] The ''experts'' who continued to wield influence were those who argued that identity is a personal achievement, not an external prescription. ''Authenticity'' had become the goal of life, and did not necessarily coincide with what had become the traditional understanding of holiness.

> Neither the scholastic notion of religious life as a state of perfection in this life nor a 19th century understanding of it as a collectivity whose members lived a uniform existence was adequate to speak to the 20th century aspiration for human community.[19]

The monastery as it used to be

When religious today look back with incredulity on the way they used to live, what they are attempting to recreate in imagination is a world in which everything was sure, everything was in place. Of course the monastic world was never perfectly ordered, but in the pre-Vatican II period there was an acquiescence in authority and a uniformity of behavior that undergirded a monk's or nun's confidence: What l am doing today I will also be doing on the day I die. To have made it to the religious life was the main achievement, and once you were there, individual responsibility was no longer necessary and might even be dangerous to your spiritual health. Not every convent posted a notice each autumn indicating the day on which sisters should start wearing shawls, and another notice in the spring when the shawls were to be put away, but such regulating of the details of everyday life, by which an individual's obedience became synonymous with a virtually total abdication of personal responsibility for even trivial decisions, was extreme only in degree, not in kind.

The development of monasticism had taken an ironic twist. The Protestant Reformers had attacked the institution on the grounds that it was the most blatant expression of Catholic "works-righteousness." Luther condemned the vow itself as an intolerable burden which the church held out as a guarantee of salvation. In other words, Luther accused the church of making entry into the monastic life a "meritorious work." In subsequent centuries, that taking of the vows came to be seen as the acceptance of a challenge more than the achievement of a status, but the challenge itself was met by a view of human nature more traditionally, if not entirely accurately, associated with Protestantism. It was assumed that the individual will, left to its own devices, would go astray, so the monastic superior, functioning in the place of Christ, became a law-giver with a thoroughness reminiscent of Calvin's Geneva. Far from "working out their own salvation," monks and nuns asked what they should do and did what they were told.

Benedict had, to be sure, laid on them a requirement of total, ungrudging obedience, even in face of "impossible" demands, though discernment by the superior and participation by the community in discussions prior to the making of decisions are built into the Rule. But by the beginning of the twentieth century a "Catholic" legalism, which makes sense only when grounded in a relative optimism about human nature, had come to be grafted onto a "Protestant" pessimism about the possibilities for human accomplishment. The model for obedience was no longer what it had been for Benedict, the self-emptying of Christ, but the child's asking the parent's permission to buy a new toothbrush.

The problem of the monastery and the modern world, then, was doubly complex. Not only did an ancient institution have to come to terms with a new cultural situation, but also the institution itself had internalized one of the deepest splits in Christian consciousness. Any solution to the external problem that did not include an address to the internal one would be temporary and unstable. If it was important for monks and nuns to understand "the behavior-patterns, the emotional attitudes, and the thought-processes of modern society," it was even more important for them to understand the sources of coherence in their own monastic way of life. The "adjustment of the community to the changed conditions of the times" was clearly a call for new directions. What the Vatican Council Fathers perhaps did not fully realize was that "continuous return to the . . . original inspiration behind a given community" was just as revolutionary, maybe even more so.

AD FONTES — TO THE SOURCES

As pressures built for fundamental changes in religious life, many monks and nuns considered specifically historical work on origins and rules to be an unaffordable luxury and an untimely diversion. It was self-evident that the current problem resulted from slavish adherence to an outmoded past, and the Vatican Council's call for a "return to the . . . original inspiration" seemed a classic instance of Rome's taking away a concession—the "adjustment of the community to the changed conditions of the times"—which had just been given.

But the past can be very surprising territory, particularly when it ceases being an undifferentiated burden and appears in its complexity, a complexity fully as intriguing and ambiguous as that of the life we ourselves experience in the here and now. The overcoming of history by history happens often enough to put to rest the suspicion that history is a form of escapism. The religious who were most adamant for reform soon learned that the reforming potential of historical scholarship surpassed in some ways even the power of their own indignation.

Historical research came to two particularly disconcerting conclusions. First, the past to which monasticism was being faithful turned out to be a recent, nineteenth-century past, a past that had been shaped by an almost desperate defensiveness in nearly every corner of the Catholic Church, a past in which the modern world had been summarized and denounced in Pope Pius IX's *Syllabus of Errors* of 1864. The "options and practices of the past" to which *Renew and Create* refers were those of the time of our grandparents, not those of the time of "our Holy Father Benedict."

Second, the founding documents of Western monasticism presupposed the various developments of the ascetic life in the time from Antony to Benedict, and to look *with* the Rule of Benedict rather than *at* it is to gain a fresh perspective with new possibilities. "The elements [of Benedictine life] are set forth as certain time-tested characteristics of a monastic tradition reaching back to, or even beyond, the Rule of Benedict."[20] What is raised here is no less a question than that of the function of a rule—is it of the nature of rules to be the letter that kills, or can they be vehicles for the spirit that gives life?

There is a perfectly plausible explanation for the dependence on a foreshortened history, a history extending back only into the previous century. By the end of the eighteenth century there was hardly any Christian monasticism left, so the nineteenth-century development of monasticism was literally almost a new beginning. The *theoretical* continuity with the whole sweep of monastic history was of course intact, but in practical terms the story line had been broken.

The one area where monasticism retained a hold, and was able slowly to revive, was Germany. Until the time of Bismarck (Chancellor of the German Empire, 1871–90 C.E.) and Prussian domination, Germany remained a loose collection of fragmented states, and within such a context the systematic assault on monasticism that could be mounted, for example, in a unified France was impossible. Moreover, German Catholic piety had been much less eroded than the French by Enlightenment skepticism, and it was in Germany that the Romantic reaction began, with its exaltation of the emotional and its nostalgic regard for the past, even a medieval past that was largely a construct of the Romantic imagination.

Monasticism, as it revived, assimilated itself to patterns of political and paternal authority, and even authoritarianism, which are not unique to Germany but which have for a long time been especially acute there. The condition of women religious was further shaped by widespread assumptions about female weakness, and by even more deeply rooted, unconscious fears of female power and destructiveness. Virginity was considered the heart of identity for female religious, but not for the men. (It was of course required of the men, but was not regarded as the hallmark of their monastic identity.) Monks and nuns might have appeared to the casual observer to be signs of contradiction, but they were on the verge of becoming vivid expressions of some of the more problematical features of German culture.[21]

The Rule of Benedict can certainly give aid and comfort to an authoritarian personality, whether one that wishes to exercise authority or one that wishes to be subjected to authority. The abbot/prioress has complete charge, and the monk/nun is instructed to be obedient. However, when the Rule is read in context, it becomes a striking moderation of authoritarianism and an indirect attack on scrupulousness.

It is important, first, to note that Benedict, according to Gregory the Great, had initially practiced severe austerity—three years alone in a cave with little to eat; throwing himself into a bed of nettles and briers to quell a vision of a woman—and the Rule suggests strongly that Benedict in his maturity rejected such extreme measures. Second, while we cannot know the whole range of monasticisms with which Benedict was acquainted—the very success of Benedictinism led to the suppression or simple disappearance of the records—we do know of some in which the crushing of the individual will by a harsh and stern abbot was the declared ideal. Third, the Rule of the Master, which Benedict certainly knew and of which his Rule is almost certainly a self-conscious revision, legislates for the details of life with a minuteness on the order of the notice about when to wear shawls and when to put them away.[22] It seems clear that Benedict knew of such scrupulosity and wanted no part of it.

To those monks and nuns who were studying this history—and that nuns were studying it was itself revolutionary—it became increasingly apparent that they were signs of contradiction not primarily because they were living the gospel life within a secularized world, but because they were abiding by a nineteenth-century ideal in the middle of the twentieth century. The contradiction was more chronological than theological.

Sister Joan Chittister, O.S.B.

Opponents of monastic change turned the reformers' own argument against them. The argument can be reconstructed as follows: You, who accuse us of being locked into a bygone culture, are yourselves selling out our heritage to the fads of this present culture. You, like our nineteenth-century predecessors, are looking at the Rule and treating it as a mirror. Our culture suspects all authority, so you turn the abbot/prioress into an "enabler." Our time is obsessed with "autonomy," so you set up every individual religious as the arbiter of what the Rule means for her or him in a particular case—indeed, the whim of each religious becomes the norm of interpretation of the Rule. You transform Benedict's admonition to the abbot, to take seriously individual temperaments and abilities, into negotiations and bargaining; it can hardly be otherwise when the assumption is granted that everybody knows what is best for themselves. You apply up-to-date ethical schemes—for example, "contextual," "situational"—to the monastic life, and the result is chaos. One of the most effective and articulate of current monastic reformers has said of her own initial attitude toward the proposed changes:

> I was ready to leave the convent, because I thought a few weak-willed Sisters, lacking any real vocation, were changing the whole pattern of religious life to make things easier for themselves; in fact, I saw it not as my leaving religious life, but as religious life leaving me.[23]

What then happened to Sister Joan Chittister, O.S.B., is a paradigm of the convergence of *aggiornamento* and *ad fontes*, of coming to terms with the modern world and with the original inspiration of the Benedictine Order. She who was ready to leave religious life because it was being radicalized was sent by her prioress to Pennsylvania State University to work for a Ph.D. in communication:

> I started studying the social sciences, particularly social psychology, and I realized that my vocation was really "to seek God," not in withdrawal or perfectionism, but in social communal forms that enable personal growth and obligate a response. Consequently, my life and faith have taken a great turn: to liturgy, but not to formalism, to sacrifice but not to masochism. The renewal of religious life made the Order a place where the problems of credibility and risk that have entered my life can be dealt with. My faith has been stripped to the core; the easy answers are gone, and when that happens, a person is left nowhere and everywhere, and that is where I am.[24]

Sister Joan can recall a time shortly after she had entered the convent when she was permitted to go with her parents to a relative's funeral, but on the way back she refused to go into her parents' new home because she had not obtained prior permission to do so. She stood on tiptoe outside and looked in. She, and a whole religious culture, believed that was a holy renunciation. Sister Joan and a large part of that religious culture now believe such an action was a grotesque distortion of what Benedict had in mind when he wrote:

> Listen carefully, my son/daughter, to the master's instructions, and attend to them with the ear of your heart. This is advice from a father who loves you; welcome it, and faithfully put it into practice. The labor of obedience will bring you back to God from whom you had drifted through the sloth of disobedience.[25]

Sister Joan has been near the center of reforming efforts for two decades. She was president of the Federation of Saint Scholastica during the years 1969–74, when delegates from all the Federation's convents met regularly to act on the Vatican Council's mandate, and in the process "had effected by 90 to 100 percent majorities the most sweeping policy changes ever to shape religious life in a single decade."[26] For part of that time she was also president of the National Leadership Conference of Women Religious, and as such was official spokesperson for the approximately 125,000 women within the many different Catholic orders in North America. For several years recently she has been prioress of her own community of about 140 sisters, Mount Saint Benedict, in Erie, Pennsylvania, where she has responsibility for making specific to that place and those sisters the general reforms over which she presided. The challenge she faces can be put succinctly: What happens when a Ph.D. in social science finds herself with the responsibilities of Benedict's abbot/prioress?

MONASTERY AND CHURCH

The full implications of the reforms for an understanding of monastic life in the modern world would be material for at least a whole book. When the current situation is seen in the perspective of all of monastic history, one issue seems particularly familiar. As religious put more and more emphasis on the experience of community itself as both the value for them and the main message for others in the religious life, is there not a real and present danger that the monastery will become a substitute for, not a part of, the church? A bishop writing a biography of Sister Joan Chittister could tell about her loyalty to the hierarchy, as Athanasius said about Antony, but that would be only part of the story. Such a biographer would overlook Sister Joan's deep agonies about the church's persistent insensitivity to some social issues, especially its effective disenfranchisement of women. Such a biographer would have to suppress Sister Joan's clear conviction that if it were not for the faith community she experiences with the sisters, she could not in conscience remain in a church that marginalizes women and sees only half of human creation as fully "good."

Another current form of the perennial tension between monastery and church—the predilection of the laity for turning to monks as spiritual advisers—received national attention in 1975. Saint John's Abbey Press in Collegeville, Minnesota, published a *Book of Prayer for Personal Use: A Short Breviary, Abridged and Simplified by Monks of Saint John's Abbey from the Liturgia Horarum*, that is, based on the official four-volume Roman Liturgy of the Hours. The Press had no reason to believe that such a publication for private use would be banned. However, as soon as the Press sent a complimentary copy to each American bishop, the hierarchy ordered that distribution cease for six months, pending the appearance of an officially sanctioned version. The day before the six-month waiting period ended, the bishops declared that in the interests of unity of text the *Book of Prayer for Personal Use* could not be sold to Catholics in the United States. There was of course an element simply of business conflict in this episode, but there was also the old question of who has effective spiritual authority in the church.

The fundamental question posed by Sister Joan, by the *Book of Prayer*, and in countless other ways is this: Can the church continue to include within itself a reformed monasticism, which is not only a sign of contradiction to the world but also a sign of contradiction to the church?

There is, of course, a prior question: Can monasticism itself, even in its reformed state, survive? As we have noted before, the burden of the argument is on those who doubt monasticism's future. The centuries have come and gone, and living monasteries are still to be found. But the monks and nuns themselves have warned that unless the fundamental problems of monastic identity—What is a monk/nun? What is monasticism? Does being a monk/nun have a value in itself, or is it simply a framework for engaging in priestly and educational work? Where are we going? What interpretation and valuation should be given to our heritage, and what goals should we set for ourselves?—are faced squarely and answered persuasively, "the judgment of those who suggest that our monasteries cannot and will not survive the critical period of history in which we now find ourselves" may prove correct.[27]

FORMATION

All these questions converge on *formation*—the processes and procedures by which men and women are introduced to the monastic life and instructed in its ways. Renewal discussions and actions are largely concerned with formation, both directly and indirectly. The issues range all the way from criticism of the guidebooks traditionally put in the hands of novices to claims that formation is nothing less than the whole activity of the community experienced over a lifetime.

The problem is acute. The guidebook approach can mislead the novice by presenting the religious life as an easily comprehended and closed system that can be "learned" and then "done." This courts the danger that the monastery will appear to be a "steady-state environment," and the monk or nun may later be caught off-guard by the unanticipated "rag-tag consequences of personal growth patterns."[28] Then the complaint, I was never warned it would be like this, would be legitimate. But if the novice can be tricked by a formation that is foreshortened and deceptively complete, the whole lifetime formation—"formation in a Benedictine community is a lifelong process which takes place in the very center of the community's life"[29]—makes it difficult to decide after a few years that the monastic life is for me—and for keeps.

What is monastic formation? is a question complex enough to test the ingenuity of any abbot or prioress, but its complexity is compounded by other questions that used to be easier to answer than they are now. One of the questions is limited to male monastics, at least for the foreseeable future: What is priestly formation? Another applies to nuns as well: What is professional formation? In earlier generations these two questions were relatively straightforward, since there was widespread agreement on what priests were for and what professionals (in most cases among the religious, teachers) were for. A monk who was tongue-tied when asked, What is your purpose as a monk? could give a confident, clear response when asked to explain his identity as priest or professor. Indeed, such an explanation would seldom have been asked for, since a whole culture shared the answer. More recently, however, priestly identity has become almost as problematical as monastic identity, and neither teachers nor the society they serve consider the value of education any longer to be self-evident.

PROTESTANT MONASTICISM

There can be few more striking illustrations of the irony of history than the renewal of monastic life in our time. The recovery of the past of Benedictinism has been more deeply revolutionary than the adjustment of monasticism to the modern world. We may, however, be seeing the beginnings of an irony of history that could surpass even the wistful bafflement of the bishop who wrote to the sisters in 1968, "It all seemed so clear and simple, back during the days of the Council. . . . Now, three years later, it is not nearly so simple."

In chapter 3, concerning the historical road of monasticism, we noted that the Protestant Reformation made a decisive break in the monastic story. Luther's attack on the ideals that had given rise to the life of monks and nuns was as thoroughgoing as King Henry VIII's dissolution of monastic institutions. The very term "Protestant monasticism" causes heads to turn and jaws to drop. Yet there *are* Protestant monasteries—about forty of them, in Germany (both West and East), Sweden, France, Switzerland, Austria, Korea, Cameroon, and the United States.[30]

These communities are of many different sizes and express a variety of religious and social ideals. Their connection with the official churches is tenuous. But they are places where an authentic religious witness is centered, and they may become sources of renewal for the wider life of the church. At a time when Catholic monks and nuns are wondering where the recruits will come from to continue "the monastic manner of life," Protestants, who have inherited from the sixteenth century a strong antipathy to that manner of life, seem hungry for it. Might it be that Catholic monastics need to study the reasons Protestants are creating monasteries, in order to find new ways to sustain their own? The very fact that the question is not preposterous is itself a sign of history's strange turns.

7

Habits of the Monastic Heart

He is a good monk. She is a good nun. Monks and nuns will say such things about others of their company, but if asked to say what they mean by "good" when used in this way, they become more vague. At one level this is simply the problem anybody has in explaining an experience from within the world of that experience. Well, I just know a good monk/nun when I see one. But the difficulty persons in religious life have in finding words to express who they are goes deeper than the average human communication problem. There is something essentially elusive about monasticism.

The fact that people—both within and outside—are always faced with the conclusion, No, that comes close but is not it exactly, shows that monasticism exists not only in a realm between this world and another world, community and isolation, detachment and commitment, but also between categories, terms, constructs by which we conventionally parcel out the world in order to understand it. The trouble people have had and continue to have in *naming* monasticism, that is, in getting their thinking about it clear and straight, neat and tidy, may help explain the extraordinary staying power of this institution. If we know the true name of something we control it, and what we control we usually succeed, sooner or later, in killing. Our repeated failures to name monasticism are a hint that a mystery lodges in the heart of this form of life.

"THE SECRET SITS IN THE MIDDLE"

Comparative studies help deepen the perspective of our view of monasticism. It takes two eyes to perceive three dimensions. But as what we see becomes more rounded, the mystery becomes even more tantalizing. Buddhist and Christian monks and nuns can talk at length about what distinguishes them from each other in terms of belief and tradition and practice, but the more they do this the more they feel their undeniable and inexpressible unity. One of the current projects of interreligious understanding is a specifically monastic program with the intentionally paradoxical title "Dialogue of silence." Our own work on the comparative study in this book has brought us time and again, and finally, up against the truth in a couplet by Robert Frost: "We dance round in a ring and suppose,/ But the Secret sits in the middle and knows."[1]

While we cannot unlock the secret, we can provide a few more clues to its solution. A recent study of American values suggests an angle of approach to social, cultural, and religious riddles. *Habits of the Heart* draws on Alexis de Tocqueville for its governing image. Tocqueville, trying in the nineteenth century to express for a European audience his profound sense of the fundamental newness of the American experience and experiment, coined the phrase "habits of the heart" to signify those convergences of feeling, attitude, belief, custom that motivate people and shape their behavior more deeply than conscious decision and considered plan.[2]

Habits of the heart by their very nature are hard to specify. The evidence for them is not on the surface, but is in nuance, accent, image, and emphasis, as much in what people do not say as in what they say. To catch the habits of the heart we have to pay attention to the "how" of people's expression as well as to the "what." The analyses of various aspects of monastic theory, history, and practice in the previous chapters of this book have suggested indirectly some of the habits of the monastic heart. In this concluding chapter we attempt more directly to address the question.

The most compelling conviction one derives from concentrated study of monasticism over a long period of time is this: monks and nuns experience their lives as intricately bound in a network of human connections. Even hermits, who have cut all formal and visible traces with the larger human community, nearly always retain, often with heightened intensity, a sense of their responsibility for the spiritual welfare of others. Thomas Merton in his hermitage, loving the world and having a deep impact on the world, is not an anomaly, but a vivid example of the paradox of withdrawal and engagement that can be illustrated in every age of monastic history.

Monastic rules, and monastic lore more generally, are mostly about how to keep groups of people who have covenanted to live together living together in some sort of harmony. Monasteries are communities of memory (something *Habits of the Heart* says American culture desperately and dangerously lacks),[3] and the substance of the memories are the lives of the saints, both those who are officially canonized and those who live only in the stories, usually embellished, that are told and retold about them. If the "Secret" of monasticism "sits in the middle and knows," the middle of the Secret is the stories, the tales, the anecdotes, the legends that monks and nuns tell about what has happened in their home. You do not begin with He is a good monk or She is a good nun, and then explain it. You tell a story, and then at the end, maybe, you will say, Yes, he's a good monk, she's a good nun.

The monastic world, then, is an intensely human world, full of faces, voices, sounds, people doing things. It is, on the whole, a more ordered world, a more rhythmical world, than the one most other people inhabit, but the order and the rhythm do not produce a single type. Quite the contrary, there is a stunning variety of human characters in any monastery, suggesting that communal commitment, not individualism, is a precondition for true individuality:

> My dear novices: . . . You've probably been surprised to discover the assortment of monks that make up a monastery. One might think that a life patterned after a definite rule would produce one single kind of monk, one line of thought, one attitude toward life. Some disillusionment stems from the discovery that vows do not destroy personality and individuality.
>
> Perhaps only God understands how such an array of individualities can rub elbows in the same community and yet produce a unity of purpose. It's a miracle how one roof can cover such diverse characters and maintain the name of family. The Abbot is one father who can honestly say, "No two of my children are alike."[4]

HABITS OF THE MONASTIC HEART

We can detect within the human world of the monastery several features of attitude and style of life that count as habits of the monastic heart. There are undoubtedly many others, but these seem especially significant because they run counter to the habits that seem to direct the hearts of most people today. If the joint claim that monks/nuns are signs of contradiction and that monks/nuns are not special sorts of persons, but simply what every person ought to be, merits our attention, then these countercultural habits of the monastic heart are food for thought, perhaps even stones to stumble over.

Things take time

A nun who had ventured out with several other sisters to start a new community was asked how long it would be before they decided whether the new enterprise would succeed. "About twenty-five years." To allow a quarter-century to decide on the viability of anything is unheard of in our culture, which usually expects a definitive answer in about a quarter of a year. But even more striking is this nun's unflustered response to the follow-up exclamation, "But you will probably be dead before then!" "Yes, I know." What she did not need to know before starting the project was whether it would last, nor did there even need to be a good chance that she would eventually know.

Monastic tradition itself reinforces this habit of the heart. In a community whose memory extends back across scores of generations, the pressing concerns of this day or even of this decade lose something not of their importance but of their ultimacy. Decisions about what really matters are made not on the basis of catchy headlines, but in the context of classic stories. The benchmark for action is set not by the latest poll, but by the accumulated wisdom of the saints.

Things must be done together

"Togetherness" is for most of us a means to an end. The end is determined by our individual desires and preferences. I decide what I want, and then calculate whether my achievement of that is enhanced or hampered by my engagement with others in its pursuit.

If, after joining with others, I decide that the joint character of the enterprise is getting in my way, I will simply disengage, since the commitment to common effort was not of the essence of my goal but simply a tool to make the goal easier to reach.

The place assigned to communal life as such within monastic tradition, both Buddhist and Christian, is certainly not uniform. Indeed, monastic writings record sharp controversy over just this question. "Fare lonely as rhinoceros," "Go and sit in your cell, and your cell will teach you everything"—these contrast sharply with the *sangha's* strict regimen and with Basil's insistence that one cannot be a Christian, much less a Christian monastic, alone. But even the most isolationist of monks/nuns are a far cry from the individualists of our culture, for the hermits and the wanderers are taking their cues from an ancient tradition; they acknowledge the authority of guidelines. They are improvisers, not inventors, composers of variations on a theme, not practitioners of aleatory music (where the performer simply decides from moment to moment what to do next).

In short, the human world that is revealed in countless ways by monks and nuns in their writings, their rules and constitutions, their conversation, their humor, is not accidental, not simply a byproduct of the life they have chosen. That human world is part of their definition of themselves. The meaning of "I am on the way in company with these brothers/sisters" is identical to the meaning of "I am on the way." In the words of Sister Joan Chittister, O.S.B., "We live religious life together in community and that community itself leads us to conversion."[5]

Habit breaks habit

To many outsiders, the most distinctive feature of monastic life appears to be its regulation. Monks and nuns do not "do their own thing," but what is set down in a rule. At its most severe, the regulated monastic life can be an unrelenting assault on all self-generated activity. According to the Rule of Columbanus (end of the sixth century C.E.):

> The mortification of the monk is threefold: he must never think what he pleases, never speak what he pleases, never go where he

pleases. . . . He shall not do what pleases him; he shall eat what is set before him, clothe himself with what is given him, do the work assigned to him, be subject to a superior whom he does not like. He shall go to bed so tired that he may fall asleep while going, and rise before he has had sufficient rest.[6]

But while some practices can become almost pathological in their assault on the will, there is even in milder regimens an underlying conviction that the only force powerful enough to change habits is habit itself.

For the Buddhist, the habit that dissipates, fritters away, even obliterates life is diversion, the random motion of an attention distractable by the slightest activity on the horizon of consciousness. For the Christian, the habit that enslaves human beings is pride, wanting to be like God, sovereignly free and not responsible to any other. In one way or another virtually every element of monastic rules is designed to extricate people from the bondage of these habits. There is no magic wand, no formula to make it all happen, but there is a patient subjection to routine, to sitting and meditating hours on end, to praying three (or four or seven) times a day whether you want to or not, and to doing this day after day after day after day.

One of the fundamental and irreducible differences between Buddhist and Christian monasticism reveals itself here. While there is much variety on this point, as on all points, within each tradition, Buddhists are much readier than Christians to claim a definitive breakthrough to a state beyond the debilitating habits. "Enlightenment" is as various in its meanings within Buddhism as "salvation" is within Christianity, but most Buddhists would agree that once enlightenment is achieved (and it usually comes in a specific, datable moment) it is not lost. One continues in the new habits (e.g., meditation) that have broken the old habits not because the old habits are always lurking just around the corner ready to pounce, but because the new habits simply now come naturally, and also, perhaps, because compassion requires that one help others by setting an example.

There is certainly within Christianity a strong tradition of datable conversion experience, the moment before which one was blind and after which one sees, and many Christians who claim to be "born again" insist that there is no slipping back. But Christian monastic tradition has on the whole shied away from such a model of religious life. There must be few formal acts in the whole human repertoire that more winsomely reveal a habit of the heart than the renewal of vows pronounced by fifty- and sixty-year jubilarians on the Feast Day of St. Benedict. After all those decades of seeking God they say exactly what they did when they first committed themselves to "pursuit of perfect charity after a monastic manner of life." In chapter 4 we quoted Theophan the Recluse, "Progress in our spiritual journey ends with the cessation of our natural breath." Many Christian monks and nuns would hesitate even to say that much, insisting that by the time of the cessation of their natural breath they would expect at most to have made a good beginning.

Despite these differences—the Buddhist assumption that the goal will be reached, the Christian assumption that the goal will keep beckoning as long as we live—the two monastic traditions share an assumption that doing something over and over again is the only effective way to fight our tendency to do other things over and over again. The traditions know that habit will trump spontaneity every time, and rules are the precondition for freedom. Cocktail party behavior, both individual and group, is actually far more predictable and stereotyped than the behavior of monks or nuns. We who pity them the restrictions of their calendar might well envy them the consequent freedom of their character.

Things are seldom what they seem

This habit of the heart, which could also be called "we have an almost limitless capacity for fooling ourselves," follows closely on the previous one, though that previous one was related more directly to behavior while this one has to do with how reality is perceived.

That we are bombarded with illusions all the time can hardly be unknown to anyone today. Not every piece of public discourse is part of an intentional disinformation campaign, but only a fool would take at face value very much of what we hear. Politicians hoodwink us, advertisers hiddenly persuade us, sports luminaries mesmerize us, television evangelists ask us to send them money so God will not cause them to die. We have good reason to fear manipulation.

We know all this, yet so easily, so often, so contentedly we succumb to the illusions. The world constructed for us by the media
becomes our world, they construct it because we are willing to pay
for it, and we pay for it because we want it. One reason we want
that world is this: it is full of stuff, things we would like to have.
The monastic renunciation of wealth is an absolute prerequisite for
the shattering of illusion, for making real the monastic perception
that things are seldom what they seem. It is no accident that monks
and nuns are at the forefront of movements for protection of the
environment from the havoc we are wreaking. Because they do not
possess pieces of the world, they do not see the pieces as isolated
objects to be exploited, but as parts of the whole, held in fragile balance with everything else. Monks and nuns know that possession,
clinging, attachment is the first distorter of reality.

It would be preposterous to suggest that the whole world become a monastery, but it is not preposterous to point out that monks
and nuns remind all of us of an important truth: If we have not made
a monastic renunciation, we necessarily have a skewed view of the
world. Were asceticism simply nay-saying, turning the back on the
world of things and other persons, then asceticism itself would be
a dangerous illusion. But as we argued early in this book, asceticism is an attitude, a set of the self toward the world that lets what
is not-me be itself without always being interpreted in terms of its
value and use for me. St. Augustine's insight that we can truly know
only what we truly love presupposes that we know we can truly
love only what we do not grasp and cling to. There is no reason
to suppose that most people will practice monastic renunciation, but
the monastery as sign of contradiction can serve for the health of
everyone by reminding us that while it is all right to live with illusions, it is illusions we are living with.

CHALLENGES TO CONVENTION

These four habits of the monastic heart constitute an extraordinary
challenge to widespread conventions of social and individual behavior today.

Things take time confronts our expectation that results (whether
pleasure or victory or "the solution") will be quick, even instan-

taneous. It confronts our constant reference to polls and ratings, whose authority so overwhelms us that we respond to a drop of a few percentage points by abandoning a project or a program, or even a solemn commitment, as though it were plague-infested. If things take time, we can expect the past to contribute much wisdom to our enterprises, against the prevailing drive for the new, the unprecedented, the different. To be sure, there is something stultifying about the tendency of monks and nuns to insist that they are saying nothing new; the hand of the past can be deadly. But there is something bizarre about our tendency to dismiss previous thought because we have moved beyond all that into the modern world. The monastic tradition knows how many modern worlds there have been, and how they have all proved in retrospect to be variations on the same old world.

Things must be done together confronts our instinctive preference for going it alone, our admiration of those who single-handedly face and overcome all obstacles. Bellah and his coauthors have shown how pervasive this individualism is in American society. The Americanization of world culture, apparently unhindered by recent shocks to American political and economic prestige, elevates the fact of American individualism to the status of worldwide crisis.

Our passion for the new and different spills over into our praise for the original. Such an attitude affects even our estimate of the past. Historical research that calls into question the full originality of the Buddha or of Benedict is resisted by many as a threat to the authority of the venerated founder. We hardly stop to ponder whether the pedigree really makes any difference. Perhaps our criteria for originality need to be changed. Selection from traditional materials to create a new pattern (or even to refurbish an old one) is as much an act of imagination as is dreaming up an entirely new work.

Everyone recognizes the historically demonstrable truth that in earlier ages a sense of communal identity was stronger than it is today. Many of us, however, because the idea of progress has shaped the habits of our hearts, assume that today's reigning individualism is better than the earlier collective identity. We conclude that institutions like monasticism, rooted in that earlier form of identity, are being left behind and will eventually wither away, lacking cultural nurture and sustenance. But what if the later is not better? What if what we have come to is about to do us in? Is the great interest evoked by *Habits of the Heart* a signal that people are longing for a recovery of the monastic knowledge that things must be done together?

Have you tried this? Have you tried that? Ours is an obsessively experimental culture. We are willing to try anything, but nothing for very long. *Habit breaks habit* simply does not fit our pattern, the pattern of miracle three-week diets, get-rich-quick lotteries, promises that the deficit will be eliminated in four years. Not only are we willing to try anything, but we are also eager to believe that if there is not a solution now, one is just around the corner. Hard, patient work, a "spirituality for the long haul"[7]—this we do not recognize as a demand placed upon us.

At the root of the problem lies our inability to recognize that our action, which we experience as spontaneous, is governed by convention, routine, habit. As debunker of this illusion Buddhism stands supreme among religions. The Buddha's perception that we are trapped by convention is unrelenting, unnerving, dazzling in its clarity. Our myth of individualism, and our worship of originality and the new, shape our conviction that we are unbounded, our own masters, doing it our way, when in fact we are the prey of forces, passions, illusions that have us entirely at their mercy—so entirely that we do not even acknowledge their presence. Christian monasticism is not so thorough in its critique of our usual thinking and feeling, largely because the Christian view of the world does not begin with so fundamental a philosophical critique of the world and our experience as we find in the Buddha's teaching. But the difference itself heightens the similarity, for despite its more positive evaluation of the world (the good, though fallen, creation of a good God rather than a realm of suffering grounded in misperception), the Christian monastic tradition shares with the Buddhist the practical conviction that only habitual action can cure our spiritual maladies. An old monk, fifty years in the monastery, asked some of the novices why one of their number had left. "He didn't like it." "Who *likes* it?"

The monastic habit of the heart that instinctively recognizes that *things are seldom what they seem* is in one sense the least startling of them all, since nearly everyone acknowledges the truth that illusion is rampant. For just this reason, however, the monastic shattering of illusion is all the more troubling. Although we know that things are seldom what they seem, we try to get away with the assumption that what we see is what we get, and what we get is what is there. In other words, when monks and nuns renounce possessions they are acting radically on knowledge we share but repress. Their example catches us in our bad faith, our largely successful tricking of ourselves. Householders who are harried beyond bearing by the thousand details of readying possessions for a move from one house to another are not just joking when they envy the monk or nun who could get everything into one or two suitcases, or who even has only robe and begging bowl. The envy is not just a reflex of frustration, though there is certainly an element of that. It is also a glimmer of recognition that clarity about the true nature of things may be simply impossible for one burdened with too many things.

We may also come to have too high an opinion of ourselves. Father Zossima knew he was not what he seemed to others—he knew he had savagely beaten another person because of his own internal anger. Ironically, it was his recognition that he was not what people thought he was that made him what they thought he was. In this, Zossima is much like an ancient monk, Macarius:

> They used to tell of the Abba Macarius that if a brother came to him with fear, as to a holy and great old man, he would say nothing to him. But if any of the brethren said to him, as if setting him at naught, "Abba, when you were a camel-man, and used to steal the natron and sell it, didn't the wardens beat you?"—if anyone said this to him, he would gladly talk to him on whatever he asked.[8]

As we said earlier in this chapter, habits of the heart are hard to get at directly. They are revealed in undertones and overtones, in images and contexts. A familiar text, read dozens of times, will suddenly yield up unexpected treasure, a doctrine or a rule will assume the contours of a human face or the resonance of a human voice. More often than any expert would care to admit, a student's spontaneous reaction to a document seen for the first time gets closer to the heart of that text than the scholar's own painstaking research. Most important, the interpreter of a cultural institution, in this case monasticism, will wake up to the fact that the real meaning of the form of life is carried in exemplary stories, the accounts people tell of those who, for myriad reasons, are judged by their successors, and sometimes even by their contemporaries, to embody what all are striving for. In their directness, simplicity, and paradoxicality these stories challenge the assumptions of our getting-and-spending world where status too often masquerades as competence, and competitiveness leaves little room for compassion.

A story from the Zen tradition illustrates our point:

> Nan-in, a Japanese master during the Meiji era (1868–1912), received a university professor who came to inquire about Zen.
>
> Nan-in served tea. He poured his visitor's cup full, and then kept on pouring.
>
> The professor watched the overflow until he no longer could restrain himself. "It is overfull. No more will go in!"
>
> "Like this cup," Nan-in said, "you are full of your own opinions and speculations. How can I show you Zen unless you first empty your cup?"[9]

As we saw with Thich Nhat Hanh, Chao-Chou, Thomas Merton, Francis of Assisi, Joan Chittister, Tsong-kha-pa, Hildegard of Bingen, and other monks and nuns who have demanded our attention throughout these pages, the monastic ideal has a way of emptying our cup, of recalling us to what we really are or what we might become.

MONASTICISM AND THE FUTURE

We have suggested—no, more, asserted—that there are some monastic habits of the heart that could heal what ails our social and cultural and religious life. Two questions linger.

First, does monasticism simply attract people who already have these habits of the heart, or do the monastic traditions, with their history, their rules, their skills in teaching and learning, their ambivalent encounter with the contemporary world, actually form these habits in the hearts of monks and nuns? There must be born monks and nuns just as there are born tennis players, but both the Buddhist and Christian monastic traditions operate on the theory that people must be formed—to become what they are. In other words, Father Zossima's dictum that a monk/nun is not a special sort of person but simply what every person ought to be is paradoxical, since to become what one ought to be (or, to put it another way, what one essentially is) requires such a careful, lengthy, patient formation that such persons are rare and very special. Few persons have awakened to what they are.

Second, can the habits of the monastic heart among monks and nuns themselves survive the onslaught of the habits of the modern heart? Expecting instantaneous results, saluting individualism as the apex of human achievement, trying everything once and nothing for long, living in a limbo of illusion-detected-and-accepted: this way of being in the world is so strongly set among us that we can wonder whether another way, even one that has survived the decline and fall (and rise) of cultures, revolutions, the blandishments of patrons, and the attacks of enemies, can withstand the tidal wave of current forces. Nostalgia is not enough. Monasticism as a museum piece, a quaint reminder of bygone habits of anthropological interest, would have no staying power in a world of shrinking resources. Monasticism's vitality comes precisely from its betwixt-and-between location, its links to an ideal world and the world of everyday experience. Should the perception ever become widespread that only in the past could these links be simultaneous, monasticism will die.

It could happen. We think it will not, for two reasons. First, the obituary of monasticism has been written many times before. There have been other modern worlds whose habits of the heart have been dissonant with the monastic habits, especially the eighteenth-century world of the Enlightenment. Monasticism was dismissed as not only irrelevant, but also as ridiculous, even pernicious. The trajectory of culture was leaving it behind, forever.

About 150 years after the definitive "death" of monasticism, a book called *The Seven Storey Mountain* sold half a million copies within a few months. Thomas Merton's autobiography is the story of a person who lived to the hilt and reveled in the modern world that had been heralded by the Enlightenment and elaborated in dozens of subsequent cultural movements, most of which were equally inhospitable to monasticism. The story culminates in this person's entry into one of the most severe, austere, forbidding forms of monastic life. Even early in his career Merton had a way of suggesting, what the remaining years of his life demonstrated so dramatically, that entering the monastery was not an escape from the world but an escape into the world, for the sake of the world.

This is our second reason for thinking that the habits of the modern heart will not obliterate the habits of the monastic heart, even in face of the statistics that show decline in the numbers of monks and nuns. We do not believe that habits of the heart are entirely the product of cultural formation, infinitely malleable and without any core of essential human character. Father Zossima's "what every person ought to be" presupposes a standard, an exemplary outline, against which particular kinds of persons can be appropriately assessed.

The range of possibilities is far greater than many observers in earlier ages thought. Modern communication, travel, and cultural anthropology have stunningly widened our sense of how many kinds of persons there are, how many different habits of the heart have been shaped and transmitted by cultures of extraordinary diversity. But it is worth remembering that Dostoevsky, the creator of Father Zossima, is one of the broadest of artists. His appreciation of the variousness of the human heart has not been surpassed. And he detected at the core of all the variety a standard, a "what every person ought to be."

Monasticism has survived, and will continue to live, for the simple reason that it has hold of a truth. That truth is not easy to articulate, because it is in a sense an unstable truth, a truth about a time that is already but not yet, about a place that is betwixt and between. Just as soon as you have said that monasticism is a retreat from the world, you have to say also that it is a cleareyed, effective engagement with the world. Just as soon as you have said that monks and nuns are not obsessed with immediate results and the latest thing, you notice that monks and nuns are at the forefront of efforts to stop injustice *now*. Recognition that the world is paradoxical is common. Living day in, day out on the basis of that recognition is rare. Habits of the heart of those who live in that way are a treasure for them and for all the rest of us.

If *Habits of the Heart* presents a cogent analysis of the current situation, another recent book with equally strong cultural relevance helps to explain how we have reached our current state. In *After Virtue: A Study in Moral Theory* Alasdair MacIntyre subjects the modern philosophical tradition, from the Enlightenment to the present, to a searching critique, all the more compelling because MacIntyre himself has been such a prominent advocate for and practitioner of that tradition. He asks how we have come to the point at which there is no effective common discourse on questions of value and ethics.

His argument is complex, though clear, and has countless nuances. But the conclusion of his book—literally the last sentence of the last chapter—suggests a shorthand answer. We have reached the current impasse because we have lost touch with habits of the monastic heart. As MacIntyre surveys future prospects and looks for signs of hope, he does not lapse into abstractions, academic sociological constructs, or even traditional philosophical categories. He turns to an exemplary figure. His choice from the literally thousands of characters he might have picked must come as a shock to anyone who, if thinking about monasticism at all, has dismissed it as a relic:

> What matters at this stage is the construction of local forms of community within which civility and the intellectual and moral life can be sustained through the new dark ages which are already upon us. And if the tradition of the virtues was able to survive the horrors of the last dark ages, we are not entirely without grounds for hope. This time however the barbarians are not waiting beyond the frontiers; they have already been governing us for quite some time. And it is our lack of consciousness of this that constitutes part of our predicament. We are waiting not for a Godot, but for another—doubtless very different—St. Benedict.[10]

"Doubtless very different"—perhaps so, probably so. But this new Saint Benedict, who may come from any part of the world, does not have to start from scratch. There is among us, for anyone who cares to look, a form of life that through centuries, even millennia, has practiced the formation of community for the sake of the world. The monastery is worth pondering, for it is a real home where real people dwell.

Notes

NOTES FOR INTRODUCTION

1. Fyodor Dostoevsky, *The Brothers Karamazov* (New York: Vintage Books, 1955), p. 194.

2. We are indebted to Victor W. Turner for the phrase "betwixt-and-between," spelled out in various ways in his discussion of ritual (see *The Ritual Process* [Chicago: Aldine Publishing Co., 1969]) and pilgrimage (see "Pilgrimages as Social Processes," chap. 5 of his *Dramas, Fields, and Metaphors: Symbolic Action in Human Society* [Ithaca, N.Y.: Cornell University Press, 1974], pp. 166–230).

3. Sylvia Whiteside, Swarthmore '81.

4. Oliver L. Kapsner, O.S.B., *Catholic Religious Orders. Listing Conventional and Full Names in English, Foreign Language, and Latin; Also Abbreviations, Date and Country of Origin and Founders,* 2d ed. enl. (Collegeville, Minn.: St. John's Abbey Press, 1957).

5. Indian Buddhist terms usually appear in their Pali rather than Sanskrit form unless otherwise dictated by context or reference/source. Notable exceptions are relatively well known terms, e.g., Nirvana, *karma, dharma.* Diacritical marks have been omitted from all foreign-language terms, proper names, and place names.

NOTES FOR CHAPTER 1

1. Writings by and about Merton are so numerous that there are independent Merton bibliographies. For a fine general study of Merton, see the first authorized biography, Michael Mott, *The Seven Mountains of Thomas Merton* (Boston: Houghton Mifflin, 1984).

2. Thomas Merton, *The Sign of Jonas* (New York: Harcourt, Brace & Co., 1953), p. 11.

3. Thomas P. McDonnell, ed., *A Thomas Merton Reader*, rev. ed. (Garden City, N.Y.: Image Books, 1974), p. 16.

4. Thomas Merton, *Thoughts in Solitude* (New York: Farrar, Straus & Ducahy, 1958), p. 13.

5. Thomas Merton, *The Silent Life* (New York: Farrar, Straus & Giroux, 1957), p. vii.

6. Thomas Merton, *Contemplation in a World of Action* (New York: Double-day Image Books, 1973), p. 159.

7. Merton, *Contemplation in a World of Action*, p. 161.

8. Merton, *Contemplation in a World of Action*, p. 161.

9. Thomas Merton, *The Asian Journal* (New York: New Directions, 1973), p. 296. Italics added.

10. Merton, *Asian Journal*, pp. 312–13.

11. Merton, *Asian Journal*, p. 143.

12. Thomas Merton, *The Wisdom of the Desert* (New York: New Directions, 1960), p. 11.

13. Merton, *Wisdom of the Desert*, pp. 6–8.

14. See Donald K. Swearer, "Three Modes of Zen Buddhism in America," *Journal of Ecumenical Studies* 10/2 (Spring 1973): 290–303.

15. Thomas Merton, *Zen and the Birds of Appetite* (New York: New Directions, 1968), p. 44.

16. Thomas Merton, *The Seven Storey Mountain* (New York: Harcourt, Brace & Co., 1948), p. 167.

17. Thomas Merton, *The Way of Chuang Tzu* (New York: New Directions, 1966), p. 30.

18. Merton, *Zen and the Birds of Appetite*, p. 27.

19. Merton, *Zen and the Birds of Appetite*, p. 25.

20. Merton, *Sign of Jonas*, pp. 97–8.

21. Merton, *Thoughts in Solitude*, p. 28.

22. Merton, *Midsummer Letter 1968*, quoted in Henri J. Nouwen, *Pray to Live: Thomas Merton: Contemplative Critic* (Notre Dame, Ind.: Fides/Claretian, 1972), pp. 56–57.

23. Parker J. Palmer, *In the Belly of a Paradox: A Celebration of Contradiction in the Thought of Thomas Merton*, Pendle Hill Pamphlet 224 (Wallingford, Penn.: Pendle Hill Publications, 1979), pp. 16–17.

24. Thomas Merton, *Selected Poems of Thomas Merton*, enl. ed. (New York: New Directions, 1967), pp. 126–27.

25. Merton, *Selected Poems*, pp. 125–26.

26. Merton, *Selected Poems*, pp. 116–17.

27. Thich Nhat Hanh, *Vietnam: The Lotus in the Sea of Fire* (London: SCM Press, 1967).

28. The following narrative is adapted from Thich Nhat Hanh, *The Miracle of Mindfulness: A Manual on Meditation* (Boston: Beacon Press, 1976), pp. 102–4.

29. For a presentation of the ten Ox Herding Pictures, see Paul Reps, *Zen Flesh, Zen Bones* (New York: Anchor Books, 1961), pp. 133–55.

30. For a contemporary interpretation of the mountains and rivers dialectic, see Thich Nhat Hanh, *Zen Keys* (New York: Anchor Books, 1974), chap. 4.

31. Nhat Hanh, *Zen Keys*, pp. 51–52.

32. Adapted from Nhat Hanh, *Miracle of Mindfulness*, pp. 4–5.

33. Nhat Hanh, *Miracle of Mindfulness*, pp. 13–14.

34. Nhat Hanh, *Zen Keys*, p. 41.

35. Thich Nhat Hanh, *The Cry of Vietnam* (Santa Barbara, Calif.: Unicorn Books, 1968), p. 20.

36. Nhat Hanh, *Miracle of Mindfulness*, p. 64.

37. Nhat Hanh, *Zen Keys*, pp. 148–49.

38. Palmer, *In the Belly of a Paradox*, p. 30.

NOTES FOR CHAPTER 2

1. The basic inspiration for this distinction is Max Weber, *Sociology of Religion*, trans. E. Fischoff (Boston: Beacon Press, 1963).

2. See, e.g., Robert Bellah, "Religious Evolution," in his *Beyond Belief* (New York: Harper & Row, 1970).

3. Peter Brown, "Approaches to the Religious Crisis of the Third Century A.D.," in his *Religion and Society in the Age of Saint Augustine* (London: Faber & Faber, 1972), p. 79.

4. Trevor Ling, *The Buddha: Buddhist Civilization in India and Ceylon* (New York: Charles Scribner's Sons, 1973), p. 62.

5. H. Kern, *Manual of Indian Buddhism* (Delhi: Indological Book House, 1968), p. 73.

6. See *Samannaphala Sutta, Dialogues of the Buddha*, pt. 1, trans. T. W. Rhys Davids, *Sacred Books of the Buddhists*, vol. 2 (London: Luzac & Co., 1956).

7. Henry C. Warren, *Buddhism in Translations* (New York: Atheneum, 1963), pp. 70–71.

8. *Samannaphala Sutta*, pp. 78–79.

9. Joseph Campbell, *The Hero with a Thousand Faces* (Cleveland and New York: Meridian Books, 1956), pp. 30ff.

10. See E. J. Thomas, *History of Buddhist Thought*, 2d ed. (London: Routledge & Kegan Paul, 1951), chap. 2.

11. *The Book of Discipline*, vol. 4, trans. I. B. Horner, *Sacred Books of the Buddhists*, vol. 14 (London: Luzac & Co., 1962), pp. 33–34.

12. *Dhammacakkappavattana Sutta,* in *Buddhist Suttas,* trans. T. W. Rhys Davids, *Sacred Books of the Buddhists,* vol. 2 (New York: Dover Publications, 1969), pp. 146–47.

13. See *Dhammacakkappavattana Sutta,* pp. 148–50, or E. A. Burtt, *The Teachings of the Compassionate Buddha* (New York: Mentor Books, 1955), p. 30.

14. See Paul Younger, "The Concept of Dukkha and the Indian Religious Tradition," *Journal of the American Academy of Religion* 37/2 (June 1969): 141–52.

15. *The Book of Discipline,* vol. 4, p. 45.

16. See Nalinaksha Dutt, *Early Monastic Buddhism* (Calcutta: Calcutta Oriental Book Agency, 1960), chap. 10.

17. *Samannaphala Sutta,* p. 83.

18. See S. J. Tambiah, *Buddhism and Spirit Cults in North-east Thailand* (Cambridge: Cambridge University Press, 1970), pp. 107ff., for a discussion of the relationship between ordination and the transcendence of sexuality, i.e., a neutral state beyond the distinction of male and female.

19. *Woven Cadences of the Early Buddhists (The Sutta Nipata),* trans. E. Hare, *Sacred Books of the Buddhists,* vol. 15 (London: Oxford University Press, 1945), pp. 6–10, stanzas 35, 36, 37, 39, 44, 65, 42.

20. Thomas, *History of Buddhist Thought,* p. 23.

21. Nur Yalman, "The Ascetic Buddhist Monks of Ceylon," *Ethnology* 1/3 (July 1962): 315–28.

22. Charles Drekmeier, *Kingship and Community in Early India* (Stanford, Calif.: Stanford University Press, 1962), chap. 6.

23. Matthew 24:42 (New English Bible).

24. 1 Corinthians 7:29–31.

25. Matthew 19:29/Mark 10:29–30/Luke 18:29–30; Matthew 16:24–26/Mark 8:34–37/Luke 9:23–25; Matthew 6:25–33/Luke 12:26–32; Luke 12:16–21; Matthew 4:18–22/Mark 1:16–20; John 18:33–38.

26. Mark 2:18–20; cf. Matthew 9:14–15 and Luke 5:33–35; Sabbath reference: Mark 2:27.

27. Galatians 4:4.

28. Matthew 11:18–19/Luke 7:33–34.

29. This statement needs to be qualified by reference to Jaroslav Pelikan, *Jesus through the Centuries: His Place in the History of Culture* (New Haven: Yale University Press, 1985), chap. 9, "The Monk Who Rules the World," pp. 109–21. Pelikan makes the point that in the Middle Ages, especially, monks tended to see themselves in the mirror of Christ, but the contrast with Buddhism, where the founder *was* a monk, can be highlighted by reference to Pelikan's remark that "by the time [the monks] were finished they were likewise patterning Christ after themselves" (p. 110).

30. Philippians 2:3–8.

31. Matthew 4:1–11/Luke 4:1–13. The characterization of the temptations as miracle, mystery, and authority is from the chapter "The Grand Inquisitor"

in Fyodor Dostoevsky, *The Brothers Karamazov* (New York: Vintage Books, 1955), pp. 292–314.

32. 1 Corinthians 11:1.

33. Romans 6:1.

34. *Gospel of Thomas,* Logion 56, in Edgar Hennecke, ed. Wilhelm Schnee-melcher, *New Testament Apocrypha,* vol. 1 (Philadelphia: Westminster Press, 1963), p. 516; Romans 8:22.

35. For a comprehensive study of this concept, see Helen North, *Sophrosyne: Self-Knowledge and Self-Restraint in Greek Literature,* Cornell Studies in Classical Philology, vol. 35 (Ithaca, N.Y.: Cornell University Press, 1966); chap. 9 (pp. 312–79) analyzes the development of *sophrosyne* in the early Christian centuries, and shows how the term and the ascetic movement influenced each other.

36. Ron Cameron and Arthur J. Dewey, trans., *The Cologne Mani Codex (P. Colon. inv. nr. 4780) "Concerning the Origin of His Body,"* Society of Biblical Literature Texts and Translations 15, Early Christian Literature Series 3 (Missoula, Mont.: Scholars Press, 1979).

37. For an account of the eastward spread of Manichaeism and its complex interactions with Buddhism and Taoism, see Samuel N. C. Lieu, *Manichaeism in the Later Roman Empire and Medieval China: A Historical Survey* (Manchester: Manchester University Press, 1985).

38. The literature on nearly every aspect of Augustine is immense. For a perceptive, provocative overview, see Peter Brown, *Augustine of Hippo: A Biography* (London: Faber & Faber, 1967), esp. chap. 5, "Manichaeism," and chap. 9, "The Platonists."

39. *Apostolic Canons* 51, in *A Select Library of Nicene and Post-Nicene Fathers of the Christian Church,* Second Series (Grand Rapids: Wm. B. Eerdmans, n.d.), vol. 14, p. 597 (slightly altered).

40. Athanasius, Letter 48, in *Nicene and Post-Nicene Fathers,* Second Series, vol. 4, p. 557. Council of Trent, Session 24, Canon 10, in H. J. Schroeder, O.P., *Canons and Decrees of the Council of Trent* (Saint Louis: B. Herder Book Co., 1941), p. 453 (Latin text).

41. Basil of Caesarea, *The Longer Rules* 7, in W. K. L. Clarke, *The Ascetic Works of Saint Basil,* Translations of Christian Literature, Series 1: Greek Texts (London: SPCK, 1925), pp. 163–65.

42. Romans 12:4–8.

43. Martin Luther, *The Babylonian Captivity of the Church* (1520), in Theodore G. Tappert, ed., *Selected Writings of Martin Luther,* vol. 1 (1517–20) (Philadelphia: Fortress Press, 1967), p. 429.

44. Luther, *Babylonian Captivity,* p. 430.

45. Luther, *Babylonian Captivity,* p. 428.

46. Weber's thesis, first articulated in 1904–5, has generated a flood of discussion and debate. A good selection of materials can be found in Robert W. Green, ed., *Protestantism and Capitalism: The Weber Thesis and Its Critics,* Problems in European Civilization (Boston: D.C. Heath, 1959).

NOTES FOR CHAPTER 3

1. *Rig Veda* 10.136; trans. Ralph T. H. Griffith, *The Hymns of the Rig Veda*, 3d ed., 2 vols. (Varanasi: Chowkhamba Sanskrit Series Office, 1963).

2. See Mircea Eliade, *Shamanism: Archaic Techniques of Ecstasy*, trans. Willard B. Trask (New York: Pantheon Books, 1964), chap. 11.

3. See *Hymns of the Atharva Veda*, vol. 2, trans. Ralph T. H. Griffith (Varanasi: Chowkhamba Sanskrit Series Office, 1968), pp. 197–98.

4. *The Thirteen Principal Upanishads*, 2d rev. ed., trans. Robert E. Hume (London: Oxford University Press, 1934), p. 98.

5. *Thirteen Principal Upanishads*, p. 240.

6. *Thirteen Principal Upanishads*, pp. 240–41.

7. Joseph Campbell, *The Hero with a Thousand Faces* (Cleveland and New York: Meridian Books, 1956).

8. Charles Drekmeier, *Kingship and Community in Early India* (Stanford, Calif.: Stanford University Press, 1962).

9. Drekmeier, *Kingship and Community*, p. 101.

10. Sukumar Dutt, *Early Buddhist Monachism*, 1st rev. ed. (Bombay: Asia Publishing House, 1960), p. 31.

11. See the *Samannaphala Sutta* for the teachings of various sectarian leaders, *Dialogues of the Buddha*, vol. 1, trans. T. W. Rhys Davids, *Sacred Books of the Buddhists* (London: Luzac & Co., 1956).

12. *Dialogues of the Buddha*, vol. 1, p. 232.

13. A. L. Basham, *History and Doctrines of the Ajivakas* (London: Luzac & Co., 1951), p. 110.

14. Basham, *History and Doctrines of the Ajivakas*, p. 111.

15. *Mahavagga* 6:10–11, *The Book of Discipline*, vol. 4, trans. I. B. Horner, *Sacred Books of the Buddhists*, vol. 14 (London: Luzac & Co., 1962), p. 13.

16. *Mahavagga* 7:5.

17. *Mahavagga* 10:1.

18. *Mahavagga* 20:17.

19. Dutt, *Early Buddhist Monachism*, chap. 3.

20. *Cullavagga* 6:1, in Henry C. Warren, *Buddhism in Translations* (New York: Atheneum, 1963), p. 411.

21. *Mahavagga* 22:16.

22. For a discussion of the formation of Buddhism as a popular religion see Sukumar Dutt, *The Buddha and Five After Centuries* (London: Luzac & Co., 1957), and for sectarian formation in India see André Bareau, *Les sectes bouddhiques du petit véhicule* (Saigon: Ecole française d'Extrême-Orient, 1955).

23. For a brief overview of the development of Buddhist monasticism, see Heinz Bechert and Richard Gombrich, eds., *The World of Buddhism: Buddhist Monks and Nuns in Society and Culture* (New York: Facts on File Publications, 1984).

24. John Cassian, *Conferences* 18.5, in Owen Chadwick, ed., *Western Asceticism*, Library of Christian Classics, 12 (Philadelphia: Westminster Press, 1958),

p. 266. Cassian, founder of monasteries near Marseilles (in what is today southern France), reports Piamun's remark in a treatise he is writing for the benefit of a nearby bishop who intends to found a monastery of his own. The reference is to Acts 2:42–47.

25. Philo of Alexandria, *On a Contemplative Life* 1, in Nahum N. Glatzer, ed., *The Essential Philo* (New York: Schocken Books, 1971), p. 311.

26. Eusebius of Caesarea, *Ecclesiastical History* 2.17.1–24, in *A Select Library of Nicene and Post-Nicene Fathers of the Christian Church*, Second Series (Grand Rapids: Wm. B. Eerdmans, n.d.), vol. 1, pp. 117–19.

27. Philo, *On a Contemplative Life* 2, 3, 4, 9, pp. 313–17, 319, 327.

28. Eusebius, *Ecclesiastical History* 6.3.9–13, p. 252.

29. These themes are frequent in Origen; see, e.g., *Contra Celsum* 3.50 and 3.58, in Henry Chadwick, *Origen: Contra Celsum* (Cambridge: Cambridge University Press, 1965), pp. 162–63, 167–68.

30. Athanasius, *The Life of Saint Antony*, trans. Robert T. Meyer, Ancient Christian Writers 10 (New York: Newman Press, 1978), chap. 7, p. 26.

31. The story of Elijah is the main theme of 1 Kings 17:1 to 2 Kings 2:12. New Testament references: John 1:21; Matthew 11:14; Matthew 17:3/Mark 9:4/Luke 9:30; Matthew 17:10–12/Mark 9:11–13.

32. See esp. the *Community Rule* in G. Vermes, *The Dead Sea Scrolls in English* (Baltimore: Penguin Books, 1968), pp. 71–94. This document is also known in English as *Manual of Discipline*.

33. Athanasius, *Life of Antony*, Prologue, p. 17, and Epilogue (chap. 94), p. 98.

34. Athanasius, *Life of Antony* 2–3, pp. 19–20.

35. Athanasius, *Life of Antony* 3–4, pp. 20–21.

36. Athanasius, *Life of Antony* 25, pp. 41–42.

37. Athanasius, *Life of Antony* 49–50, pp. 61–62.

38. Athanasius, *Life of Antony* 39, p. 52.

39. Athanasius, *Life of Antony* 67, pp. 76–77.

40. Athanasius, *Life of Antony* 69–70, pp. 78–79.

41. Athanasius, *Life of Antony* 46, pp. 59–60.

42. Athanasius, *Life of Antony* 47, p. 60.

43. Palladius, *The Lausiac History*, trans. Robert T. Meyer, Ancient Christian Writers 34 (New York: Newman Press, 1964), chap. 25 (concerning a monk Valens), pp. 84–86.

44. Palladius, *Lausiac History* 17, pp. 57–58.

45. Palladius, *Lausiac History* 18, p. 58.

46. Cited in Derwas J. Chitty, *The Desert a City: An Introduction to the Study of Egyptian and Palestinian Monasticism under the Christian Empire* (Oxford: Basil Blackwell, 1966), p. 28 (from chap. 120 of the *First Life of Pachomius* [Greek]).

47. Palladius, *Lausiac History* 32, pp. 92–95.

48. *The Sayings of the Fathers* 2.9, in Chadwick, ed., *Western Asceticism*, p. 42.

49. Chitty, *Desert a City*, p. 21 (from *First Life* of Pachomius, chaps. 24–25).

50. Chitty, *Desert a City*, pp. 22–23.

51. David Knowles, *From Pachomius to Ignatius: A Study in the Constitutional History of the Religious Orders* (Oxford: Clarendon Press, 1966), p. 3.

52. Basil of Caesarea, *The Longer Rules* 7, in W. K. L. Clarke, *The Ascetic Works of Saint Basil*, Translations of Christian Literature, Series 1: Greek Texts (London: SPCK, 1925), p. 163.

53. For a brief summary of Symeon's extraordinary career, based on a variety of sources, see Hippolyte Delehaye, *Les saints stylites*, Subsidia hagiographica 14 (Brussels: Société des Bollandistes, 1923), pp. xxiv–xxxiv.

54. Peter Brown, *The Making of Late Antiquity* (Cambridge: Harvard University Press, 1978), pp. 9–12. For an analysis of Brown's importance as an interpreter of this period, see Patrick Henry, " 'Master of the Stray Detail': Peter Brown and Historiography," *Religious Studies Review* 6/2 (1980): 91–96.

55. Brown, *Making of Late Antiquity*, pp. 10–11.

56. Brown, *Making of Late Antiquity*, p. 94; Athanasius, *Life of Antony* 14, p. 32.

57. Brown, *Making of Late Antiquity*, p. 15.

58. Brown, *Making of Late Antiquity*, p. 12.

59. For an elaboration of this argument, see Patrick Henry, "From Apostle to Abbot: The Legitimation of Spiritual Authority in the Early Church," in Elizabeth Livingstone, ed., *Studia Patristica*, vol. 18 (Oxford: Pergamon Press, 1982), pp. 491–505.

60. Galatians 3:28.

NOTES FOR CHAPTER 4

1. *Milindapanho* 76.23, adapted from Henry C. Warren, *Buddhism in Translations* (New York: Atheneum, 1963), p. 421.

2. Sukumar Dutt, *Buddhist Monks and Monasteries in India: Their History and Their Contribution to Indian Culture* (London: George Allen & Unwin, 1962), pt. 1, chaps. 2–3.

3. For issues of gender relative to the ordination of males, see Charles F. Keyes, "Mother or Mistress But Never a Monk: Buddhist Notions of Female Gender in Rural Thailand," *American Ethnologist* 11/2 (May 1984): 223–41.

4. *Mahavagga* 6:32, *The Book of Discipine*, vol. 4, trans. I. B. Horner, *Sacred Books of the Buddhists*, vol. 14 (London: Luzac & Co., 1962), pp. 18–19.

5. *Mahavagga* 1:12.5.

6. *Mahavagga* 1:28.3–5.

7. This description is based on Vajiranavarorasa, *Ordination Procedure* (Bangkok: Mahamakuta Buddhist Academy, 1962), chap. 3.

8. S. J. Tambiah, *Buddhism and Spirit Cults in North-east Thailand* (Cambridge: Cambridge University Press, 1970), p. 107.

9. Paul Lévy, *Buddhism: A "Mystery" Religion?* (New York: Schocken Books, 1967), p. 90.

10. Holmes Welch, *The Practice of Chinese Buddhism, 1900–1950* (Cambridge: Harvard University Press, 1967), p. 276.

11. J. Prip-Møller, *Chinese Buddhist Monasteries,* 2d ed. (Hong Kong: Hong Kong University Press, 1967), p. 312.

12. This is the thesis of Lévy, *Buddhism: A "Mystery" Religion?*

13. Vajiranavarorasa, *The Entrance to the Vinaya,* trans. Khantipalo and Suchin (Bangkok: Mahamakuta Buddhist Academy, 1969), p. 9.

14. *Mahavagga* 185–86, *The Book of Discipline,* pp. 247–48.

15. See Dutt, *Buddhist Monks and Monasteries in India,* pp. 71ff.

16. Vajiranavarorasa, *Entrance to the Vinaya,* chaps. 4–9.

17. See Richard A. Gard, ed., *Buddhism* (New York: Washington Square Press, 1963), pp. 161ff., for a description of the rules of a famous monastery in Kandy, Sri Lanka.

18. See Gard, *Buddhism,* pp. 169–72.

19. See Welch, *Practice of Chinese Buddhism,* p. 106, for the normative place of Pai-chang. See also Pai Chang, *Sayings and Doings of Pai Chang,* trans. Thomas Cleary (Los Angeles: Center Publications, 1979). For the Mahayana *vinaya,* see Samuel Beal, *A Catena of Buddhist Scriptures from the Chinese* (Taipei: Ch'en Wen Publishing Co., 1970); for the *Sutra of Brahma's Net,* see J.J.M. De Groot, *Le code du Mahayana en Chine* (Wiesbaden: Martin Saendig, 1967).

20. Welch, *Practice of Chinese Buddhism,* p. 145.

21. Lu K'uan Yu (Charles Luk), *Ch'an and Zen Teaching,* 2d series (Berkeley: Shambala Publications, 1960), pp. 85–86.

22. This account is found in the *Gradual Sayings* (*Anguttura Nikaya* 4.274) and the *Book of Discipline* (*Vinaya* 2.253). See the discussion in E. J. Thomas, *The Life of the Buddha as Legend and History,* 3d ed. (London: Routledge & Kegan Paul, 1949), pp. 107–11. Two major works on women in Buddhism are I. B. Horner, *Women under Primitive Buddhism* (London: George Routledge, 1938); and Diana Paul, *Women in Buddhism: Images of the Feminine in Mahayana Tradition* (Berkeley: Asian Humanities Press, 1977).

23. Thomas, *Life of the Buddha,* pp. 108–9.

24. Thomas, *Life of the Buddha,* pp. 110–11.

25. *RB 1980: The Rule of St. Benedict in Latin and English with Notes,* ed. Timothy Fry, O.S.B. (Collegeville, Minn.: Liturgical Press, 1981), chap. 73, p. 297. This edition of the Rule, produced for the sesquimillennium (480–1980 C.E.) of the birth of Benedict and his sister, Scholastica, presents the results of the immense scholarly efforts of recent generations that have been devoted to the Rule, its antecedents, its context, its language, and its continuing relevance. The volume includes a list (pp. 608–12) of all the Benedictine monasteries (46 for men, 56 for women) in North America. The listing does not include variations on Benedictinism, such as the Cistercians and Trappists.

26. *Rule of Benedict* 58, p. 269.

27. *Rule of Benedict* 58, pp. 267–69.

28. *Newsweek,* November 7, 1977, p. 111.

29. Athanasius, *The Life of Saint Antony*, trans. Robert T. Meyer, Ancient Christian Writers 10 (New York: Newman Press, 1978), chap. 5, p. 22.

30. A brief but comprehensive account of the scholarly efforts to explain the phrase is in *Rule of Benedict*, pp. 457–66. It is noted (pp. 457–58) that while stability, fidelity to monastic life, and obedience have been treated since the Middle Ages as the specifically Benedictine vows, they were not originally three distinct obligations. "If the very nature of a vow was still unclear at [Benedict's] time, . . . the concept of distinct 'vows of religion' was still more remote. It did not develop until the speculative theological ferment of the thirteenth century prompted analysis and definition of such questions. The ancient monks promised simply to live the full monastic life as it was practiced in a particular monastery and defined by a particular rule."

31. *Rule of Benedict*, Prologue, pp. 165–67.

32. *Rule of Benedict* 5.1, p. 187.

33. *Rule of Benedict* 7.7, p. 193, and 7.51, p. 199. Jacob's dream of the ladder is recounted in Genesis 28:12.

34. Palladius, *The Lausiac History*, trans. Robert T. Meyer, Ancient Christian Writers 34 (New York: Newman Press, 1964), Prologue, chap. 10, p. 26. *The Sayings of the Fathers* 10.111, in Owen Chadwick, ed., *Western Asceticism*, Library of Christian Classics 12 (Philadelphia: Westminster Press, 1958), p. 130.

35. *Rule of Benedict* 7.67-69, pp. 201–3.

36. *Rule of Benedict* 71.1-2, p. 293.

37. *Rule of Benedict*, 2.2, p. 173.

38. Matthew 28:18; Matthew 20:28/Mark 10:45; John 13:1–17; Philippians 2:5–8.

39. *Rule of Benedict* 2.38–40, 31–32, pp. 177–79.

40. *Rule of Benedict* 64.1, p. 281.

41. *Rule of Benedict* 3.1-6, pp. 179–81.

42. *Rule of Benedict* 43.1-3, p. 243.

43. Cuthbert Butler, *Benedictine Monachism: Studies in Benedictine Life and Rule* (1924; New York: Barnes & Noble, 1961), chap. 17, "Daily Life in St. Benedict's Monastery," esp. p. 287.

44. *Rule of Benedict* 18.22-25, p. 215.

45. *Rule of Benedict* 48, pp. 249–53, and 73.2-7, pp. 295–97.

46. *Sayings of the Fathers* 6.3, in Chadwick, ed., *Western Asceticism*, p. 77.

47. *Rule of Benedict* 57.7-9, p. 257. The italicized phrase is 1 Peter 4:11, which has for long been treated as a motto by Benedictines (*ut In Omnibus Glorificetur Deus*—IOGD).

48. *Rule of Benedict* 60, pp. 273–75. Butler, *Benedictine Monachism*, pp. 293–94, discusses the available data for the clericalizing of the monasteries. There is a good chance it was normal by the end of the eighth century c.e. for monks to become priests, and "by the year 1000, it became the established rule that monks should be ordained."

49. Alfred Deutsch, O.S.B., *Bruised Reeds and Other Stories* (Collegeville, Minn.: Saint John's University Press, 1971), p. 83. Deutsch's book is a delightful set of fictional stories about monastic life, fashioned out of his memories of a lifetime in Saint John's Abbey, Collegeville, Minnesota.

50. *Novellae* 5.7, in Rudolph Schoell and Wilhelm Kroll, eds., *Corpus Iuris Civilis*, 5th ed. (Berlin: Weidmann, 1928), vol. 3, p. 33.

51. P. R. Coleman-Norton, *Roman State and Christian Church: A Collection of Legal Documents to* A.D. *535* (London: SPCK, 1966), 3 vols. (continuous paging), Nos. 31, 147, 269, 484, 488, pp. 78, 322–23, 473–74, 835–39, 849–51.

52. Basil of Caesarea, *The Longer Rules*, in W.K.L. Clarke, *The Ascetic Works of Saint Basil*, Translations of Christian Literature, Series 1: Greek Texts (London: SPCK, 1925), Preface, pp. 145–51.

53. Basil, *Longer Rules* 21, p. 187; Jesus' admonition to take the lowest place is at Luke 14:7–11.

54. *Novellae* 123.36, p. 619.

55. Theodore of Studios, *Testament* 12, in J.-P. Migne, *Patrologia Graeca*, 99.1820c.

56. Theophan the Recluse, quoted in John B. Dunlop, *Staretz Amvrosy, Model for Dostoevsky's Staretz Zossima* (Belmont, Mass.: Nordland Publishing Co., 1972), p. 26.

57. Karl Holl, *Enthusiasmus und Bussgewalt beim griechischen Mönchtum: Eine Studie zu Symeon dem neuen Theologen* (Leipzig: J. C. Hinrichs'sche Buchhandlung, 1898).

58. Dunlop, *Staretz Amvrosy*, p. 38.

59. Bishop Kallistos of Diokleia, "Wolves and Monks: Life on the Holy Mountain Today," *Sobornost* 5/2 (1983): 60. Our account of the current state of Athos draws on the entire article (pp. 56–68), on sections of Timothy Ware (= Bishop Kallistos), *The Orthodox Church* (New York: Penguin Books, 1980), esp. pp. 140–43, and on Patrick Henry's recollections of two brief visits to Athos. For a personal and vivid evocation of the mystery of the Holy Mountain, see Nikos Kazantzakis, *Report to Greco* (New York: Simon & Schuster, 1965), chap. 19 ("My Friend the Poet. Mount Athos"), pp. 188–234.

60. *Rule of Benedict* 2.2–3, p. 173; 36.1–2, p. 235; 53.1–4, pp. 255–57.

61. Fyodor Dostoevsky, *Crime and Punishment* (New York: Modern Library, 1950), pp. 392–93.

62. See Patrick G. Henry, "Monastic Mission: The Monastic Tradition as Source for Unity and Renewal Today," *The Ecumenical Review* 39/3 (July 1987): 271–81.

NOTES FOR CHAPTER 5

1. Lal Mani Joshi makes the point that from its inception Buddhism was a teaching enterprise. See his *Studies in the Buddhistic Culture of India*, 2d rev. ed. (Delhi: Motilal Banarsidass, 1977), p. 122.

2. A. K. Warder, *Indian Buddhism* (Delhi: Motilal Banarsidass, 1970), p. 463.

3. Sukumar Dutt, *Buddhist Monks and Monasteries in India: Their History and Their Contribution to Indian Culture* (London: George Allen & Unwin, 1962), p. 319.

4. Dutt, *Buddhist Monks and Monasteries in India*, p. 323.

5. During this period over 150 Chinese pilgrim-monks went to India; see Samuel Beal, *Buddhist Records of the Western World* (London, 1906); and his *The Life of Hiuen-tsiang* (London, 1914); J. Takakusu, *A Record of the Buddhist Religion* (Oxford, 1896); and H. A. Giles, *The Travels of Fa Hsien* (Cambridge, 1923).

6. Quoted from *Life of Hsuan-tsang*, in Dutt, *Buddhist Monks and Monasteries*, p. 338.

7. Joshi, *Studies in the Buddhistic Culture of India*, p. 126.

8. *Buddhist Records*, p. 170, quoted in Dutt, *Buddhist Monks and Monasteries*, pp. 334–35. For a more extensive discussion of Nalanda, see H. D. Sankalia, *The University of Nalanda*, 2d rev. ed. (Delhi: Oriental Publishers, 1972).

9. Charles Eliot, *Japanese Buddhism* (London: Routledge & Kegan Paul, 1969), p. 192.

10. See Rato Khyongla Nasang Losang, *My Life and Lives: The Story of a Tibetan Incarnation* (New York: E. P. Dutton, 1977), and B. Alan Wallace, *The Life and Teachings of Geshe Rabten* (London: George Allen & Unwin, 1980), for an autobiographical description of traditional Tibetan monastic training.

11. J. Prip-Møller, *Chinese Buddhist Monasteries*, 2d ed. (Hong Kong: Hong Kong University Press, 1967), p. 139.

12. See Donald K. Swearer, "Recent Developments in Thai Buddhism," in Heinrich Dumoulin and John C. Maraldo, eds., *Buddhism in the Modern World* (New York: Collier Books, 1976), chap. 6, p. 100.

13. Although males predominate in the genre of "saints' lives" in Buddhism, women are not absent. See I. B. Horner, *Women under Primitive Buddhism* (London: George Routledge, 1938); and Diana Paul, *Women in Buddhism: Images of the Feminine in Mahayana Tradition* (Berkeley: Asian Humanities Press, 1977).

14. For Tibetan animism, see David Snellgrove, *The Nine Ways of Bon* (London: Oxford University Press, 1967); Helmut Hoffmann, *The Religions of Tibet* (New York: Macmillan Co., 1961), chaps. 1–3; and Giuseppe Tucci, *Tibetan Buddhism*, trans. Geoffrey Samuel (Berkeley: University of California Press, 1980).

15. For a discussion of Tibetan Buddhist sectarianism, see David Snellgrove, *Buddhist Himalaya* (Oxford: Bruno Cassirer, 1957).

16. See Lobsang P. Lhalungpa, *The Life of Milarepa* (New York: E. P. Dutton, 1977).

17. See W. Y. Evans-Wentz, *Tibetan Yoga and Secret Doctrines*, 2d ed. (London: Oxford University Press, 1958).

18. Quoted in L. Austine Waddell, *Tibetan Buddhism* (New York: Dover Publications, 1972), p. 382.

19. See Herbert V. Guenther, *The Life and Teaching of Naropa* (London: Oxford University Press, 1963).

20. For lives of Milarepa, in addition to Lhalungpa, see W. Y. Evans-Wentz, *Tibet's Great Yogi, Milarepa* (Oxford: Oxford University Press, 1951); and Garma C. C. Chang, *The Hundred Thousand Songs of Milarepa* (New York: Harper & Row, 1970).

21. Quoted in Hoffmann, *Religions of Tibet*, p. 154.

22. This verse is contained in the *Lu Tsu T'an Ching*, known as *The Platform Sutra* or *The Altar Sutra of the Sixth Patriarch*. See *The Platform Sutra*, trans. Wing-tsit Chan (New York: St. John's University Press, 1963), p. 35. Several translations of this important text exist in English, e.g., Lu K'uan Yu (Charles Luk), *Ch'an and Zen Teaching*, Third Series (London: Rider & Co., 1962).

23. *The Platform Sutra*, p. 41.

24. *The Newsletter on International Buddhist Women's Activities (NIBWA)*, No. 10, January–March 1987, p. 18.

25. Audrey McK. Fernandez, "Women in Buddhism: For 2500 Years, a Persisting Force," *Spring Wind* 6/1, 2, 3 (1986): 43–44.

26. Francis D. Cook, *How to Raise an Ox: Zen Practice as Taught in Zen Master Dogen's Shobogenzo* (Los Angeles: Center Publications, 1978), pp. 133ff. Quoted in Fernandez, "Women in Buddhism," p. 45.

27. Athanasius, *The Life of Saint Antony*, trans. Robert T. Meyer, Ancient Christian Writers 10 (New York: Newman Press, 1978), 16, p. 33.

28. Palladius, Letter to Lausus 2–3, in *The Lausiac History*, trans. Robert T. Meyer, Ancient Christian Writers 34 (New York: Newman Press, 1964), pp. 21–22.

29. Jerome, Letter 22.30, in J. Stevenson, ed., *Creeds, Councils, and Controversies: Documents Illustrative of the History of the Church* A.D. 337–461 (London: SPCK, 1966), p. 164.

30. There is an immense literature on the history of education in this period. See H. I. Marrou, *A History of Education in Antiquity*, trans. George Lamb (New York: Mentor Books, 1964); Pierre Riché, *Education and Culture in the Barbarian West from the Sixth through the Eighth Century*, trans. John J. Contreni (Columbia, S.C.: University of South Carolina Press, 1976); Charles H. Haskins, *The Rise of Universities* (New York: Henry Holt & Co., 1923), where it is noted that schools attached to cathedrals had, by the beginning of the twelfth century C.E., surpassed monastic schools as active centers of learning, and the origins of universities can be traced to cathedral schools (p. 19).

31. Armand-Jean de Rancé, *A Treatise on the Sanctity and the Duties of the Monastic State* 12, in Colman J. Barry, O.S.B., ed., *Readings in Church History*, vol. 2 (Westminster, Md.: Newman Press, 1967), pp. 304–5.

32. Rancé, *Monastic State*, Question 4, p. 306.

33. Jean Mabillon, *Treatise on Monastic Studies*, in Barry, *Readings*, vol. 2, p. 311.

34. Mabillon, *Treatise on Monastic Studies*, pp. 314–15.

35. Mabillon, *Treatise on Monastic Studies*, pp. 311, 318.

36. Mabillon, *Treatise on Monastic Studies*, pp. 319–21.

37. Rancé, *Monastic State*, p. 309.

38. Bernard of Clairvaux, Letter 80.1, 3, 4, in Bruno Scott James, ed., *The Letters of St. Bernard of Clairvaux* (Chicago: Henry Regnery, 1953), pp. 110–12.

39. Erwin Panofsky and Gerda Panofsky-Soergel, eds., *Abbot Suger on the Abbey Church of St.-Denis and Its Art Treasures* (Princeton: Princeton University Press, 1979), p. 41. On the complexity of the interrelation between Bernard and Suger, see Otto von Simson, *The Gothic Cathedral* (New York: Harper Torchbooks, 1964), esp. pp. 44–49 and 111–13.

40. Gregory the Great, *Second Dialogue*, in Odo John Zimmerman, O.S.B., trans., *Saint Gregory the Great: Dialogues*, Fathers of the Church 39 (Washington: Catholic University of America Press, 1959), pp. 55–56.

41. Gregory, *Second Dialogue* 3, pp. 61–62.

42. Gregory, *Second Dialogue* 17, p. 85.

43. Gregory, *Second Dialogue* 35, pp. 105–6.

44. Gregory, *Second Dialogue* 36, p. 107.

45. Barbara Newman, *Sister of Wisdom: St. Hildegard's Theology of the Feminine* (Berkeley: University of California Press, 1987), p. xvii.

46. Hildegard, Letter 100, quoted in Newman, *Sister of Wisdom*, p. 30.

47. Hildegard, Letter to the Prelates of Mainz, in Matthew Fox, ed., *Hildegard of Bingen's Book of Divine Works with Letters and Songs* (Santa Fe: Bear & Company, 1987), p. 358.

48. Hildegard, Letter to the Prelates of Mainz, p. 358.

49. Fyodor Dostoevsky, *The Brothers Karamazov* (New York: Vintage Books, 1955), p. 29.

50. Dostoevsky, *Brothers Karamazov*, p. 47.

51. Dostoevsky, *Brothers Karamazov*, pp. 354–60.

52. Dostoevsky, *Brothers Karamazov*, p. 194. In this same speech Zossima says, ''Monks are not a special sort of person, but only what all persons ought to be.''

53. Francis is the entire subject of chap. 11, ''The Divine and Human Model,'' in Jaroslav Pelikan, *Jesus through the Centuries: His Place in the History of Culture* (New Haven: Yale University Press, 1985), pp. 133–44, where the extraordinary cultural impact of Francis as exemplar of Christian asceticism in both his own time and since is clearly set forth.

54. Thomas of Celano, *The First Life of Saint Francis*, trans. Placid Hermann, O.F.M. (Chicago: Franciscan Herald Press, 1963), 2.3–5.11, pp. 3–7.

55. Thomas of Celano, *First Life* 5.10–6.15, pp. 6–9.

56. Thomas of Celano, *First Life* 7.17, p. 9, and 9.22, pp. 12–14.

57. Thomas of Celano, *First Life* 11.26, p. 15; 12.31, p. 17; 15.39, p. 23; 16.44, p. 25.

58. Thomas of Celano, *First Life* 16.42, p. 24, and 19.51–52, pp. 28–29.

59. Thomas of Celano, *First Life* 22.62, p. 33; 13.32–33, pp. 18–19; 27.73, p. 38.

60. Thomas of Celano, *First Life* 29.82, p. 41.

NOTES FOR CHAPTER 6

1. For a discussion of contemporary Buddhism, see Donald K. Swearer, *Buddhism in Transition* (Philadelphia: Westminster Press, 1970); and his *Buddhism and Society in Southeast Asia* (Chambersburg, Penn.: Anima Books, 1981).

2. In 1976 Donald Swearer was privileged to work with the Reverend Eshin Nishimura, a monk in the Myoshin-ji tradition and a professor at Hanazona University, on a study of Myoshin-ji. The discussion here is based on that research, which included field observation and study of the traditional histories of Myoshin-ji: Kozan Kawakami, *Myoshin-ji Shi* (History of Myoshin-ji), 2 vols. (Kyoto, 1917 and 1921); Amabuki Sesan, *Myoshin-ji Ryobyuku Menshi* (Six Hundred Year History of Myoshin-ji) (Kyoto, 1935).

3. The terms *emptiness, no-sign, non-action* express the paradoxicalness of the religious view of life encountered in the Zen tradition, whether it be in realms considered to be absolute or relative, or more particularly, in the area of morality and ethics.

4. Information about Wat Haripunjaya is based on Donald Swearer's research conducted in Thailand in 1972–73, and periodic visits since then. For a more detailed discussion see Swearer, *Wat Haripunjaya. A Study of the Royal Temple of the Buddha's Relic, Lamphun, Thailand* (Missoula, Mont.: Scholars Press, 1976).

5. See Donald K. Swearer, "Buddhism in Today's World," in Frank Whaling, ed., *Religion in Today's World* (Edinburgh: T. & T. Clark, 1986), pp. 53–74.

6. Donald K. Swearer, "Lay Buddhism and the Buddhist Revival in Ceylon," *Journal of the American Academy of Religion* 38/3 (1970): 255–75.

7. For Buddhist approaches to contemporary issues, see Fred Eppsteiner and Dennis Maloney, eds., *The Path of Compassion: Contemporary Writings on Engaged Buddhism* (Berkeley: Buddhist Peace Fellowship, 1985).

8. Bhikkhu Buddhadasa, *Toward the Truth,* ed. Donald K. Swearer (Philadelphia: Westminster Press, 1970).

9. Donald K. Swearer, *The Dhammic Socialism of Bhikkhu Buddhadasa* (Bangkok: Thai Interreligious Committee for Development, 1986).

10. See Swearer, "Buddhism in Today's World."

11. *A Monk?* A booklet published by St. Anselm's Abbey, Washington, D.C. (n.d.), p. 3.

12. *Perfectae caritatis* 2, 4, 18. The first quotation is from Walter M. Abbot, S.J., ed., *The Documents of Vatican II* (New York: Guild Press, 1966), p. 468; the second and third quotations are from Austin Flannery, O.P., ed., *Vatican Council II: The Conciliar and Post Conciliar Documents* (Collegeville, Minn.: Liturgical Press, 1975), pp. 613, 621.

13. Quoted in Joan Chittister, O.S.B., Stephanie Campbell, O.S.B., Mary Collins, O.S.B., Ernestine Johann, O.S.B., and Johnette Putnam, O.S.B., *Climb along the Cutting Edge: An Analysis of Change in Religious Life* (New York: Paulist Press, 1977), p. 73.

14. Chittister et al., *Climb along the Cutting Edge*, p. 24.

15. See Chittister et al., *Climb along the Cutting Edge*, p. 18, for the significance of Pius XII's action.

16. *Renew and Create*, A Statement on the American-Cassinese Benedictine Monastic Life, Thirty-Sixth General Chapter, Second Session, June 1969, 8–9, pp. 11–12. The American-Cassinese congregation comprises about half the Benedictine monasteries for men in North America.

17. *Renew and Create* 27, pp. 25–26.

18. Chittister et al., *Climb along the Cutting Edge*, p. 180.

19. Chittister et al., *Climb along the Cutting Edge*, p. 117.

20. *Renew and Create* 5, p. 9.

21. See Chittister et al., *Climb along the Cutting Edge*, pp. 73–78.

22. On the complex and much controverted question of the relation between the *Rule of the Master* and the *Rule of Benedict*, see *RB 1980: The Rule of St. Benedict in Latin and English with Notes*, ed. Timothy Fry, O.S.B. (Collegeville, Minn.: Liturgical Press, 1981), pp. 478–93.

23. Joan Chittister, O.S.B., in Patrick Henry and Thomas F. Stransky, C.S.P., *God on Our Minds* (Philadelphia: Fortress Press; Collegeville, Minn.: Liturgical Press, 1982), pp. 14–15. The passage, like all the others in the book, is anonymous, and is identified here as Sister Joan's with her permission.

24. Chittister, in *God on Our Minds*, p. 15.

25. *Rule of Benedict*, Prologue 1–2, p. 157.

26. Chittister et al., *Climb along the Cutting Edge*, p. 168.

27. *Renew and Create* 33, p. 30, and 104, p. 76.

28. Chittister et al., *Climb along the Cutting Edge*, p. 171.

29. *Call to Life*, Constitutions of the Federation of Saint Scholastica, 1974 (Erie, Penn.: Benet Press, 1974), p. 41. The Federation of Saint Scholastica comprises almost half the Benedictine monasteries for women in North America.

30. This enumeration leaves out of consideration Anglican (Episcopalian) monasteries, which have a different history. On Anglican monasticism, see David Knowles, *Christian Monasticism* (New York: McGraw-Hill, 1969), chap. 19, pp. 205–11. For the contemporary Protestant situation, see Linda K. Fischer, "The Geography of Protestant Monasticism" (forthcoming Ph.D. diss., University of Minnesota). See also François Biot, O.P., *The Rise of Protestant Monasticism*, trans. W. J. Kerrigan (Baltimore: Helicon Press, 1963).

NOTES FOR CHAPTER 7

1. Robert Frost, "The Secret Sits," *The Poetry of Robert Frost*, ed. Edward Connery Lathem (New York: Holt, Rinehart & Winston, 1967), p. 362.

2. Robert N. Bellah, Richard Madsen, William M. Sullivan, Ann Swidler, and Steven M. Tipton, *Habits of the Heart: Individualism and Commitment in American Life* (New York: Harper & Row, 1986).

3. Bellah et al., *Habits of the Heart,* pp. 152–55, concerning "communities of memory." A similar critique, from a psychological perspective rather than the more sociological approach of Bellah et al., is offered by M. Scott Peck, *The Different Drum: Community Making and Peace* (New York: Simon & Schuster, 1987), esp. in his analysis of "the fallacy of rugged individualism."

4. Alfred Deutsch, O.S.B., *Bruised Reeds and Other Stories* (Collegeville, Minn.: Saint John's University Press, 1971), pp. 193–94.

5. Joan Chittister, O.S.B., *Living the Rule Today: A Series of Conferences on the Rule of Benedict* (Erie, Penn.: Benet Press, 1982), p. 44.

6. Columban, *Monastic Rule,* in Colman J. Barry, O.S.B., *Readings in Church History,* vol. 1 (Westminster, Md.: Newman Press, 1965), p. 266.

7. The title of a book by Robert S. Bilheimer, *A Spirituality for the Long Haul: Biblical Risk and Moral Stand* (Philadelphia: Fortress Press, 1984).

8. Derwas J. Chitty, *The Desert a City: An Introduction to the Study of Egyptian and Palestinian Monasticism under the Christian Empire* (Oxford: Basil Blackwell, 1966), p. 13.

9. Paul Reps, *Zen Flesh, Zen Bones: A Collection of Zen and Pre-Zen Writings* (Tokyo and Rutland, Vt.: Charles E. Tuttle Co., 1957), p. 19.

10. Alasdair MacIntyre, *After Virtue: A Study in Moral Theory,* 2d ed. (Notre Dame, Ind.: University of Notre Dame Press, 1984), p. 263.

Suggested Reading

Monasticism looms large in all general studies of both Buddhism and Christianity, and specialized treatments of monasticism are numbered in the thousands. We suggest here a few titles of various sorts for readers who wish to move to the next level in their knowledge of one or more of the subjects we have discussed in this book.

As we have noted often, Buddhism was founded as a monastic movement and its founder set the pattern of monastic life. The best general study of the life of the Buddha, based on Pali (Theravada) sources, is Michael Carrithers, *The Buddha* (New York: Oxford University Press, 1983). The most valuable introduction to Buddhist monasticism is Heinz Bechert and Richard Gombrich, eds., *The World of Buddhism: Buddhist Monks and Nuns in Society and Culture* (New York: Facts on File Publications, 1984). This pictorial volume provides a series of studies on Buddhist monasticism throughout the ages in various cultures by an outstanding group of scholars. Sukumar Dutt, *Buddhist Monks and Monasteries in India: Their History and Their Contribution to Indian Culture* (London: George Allen & Unwin, 1962), focuses on the growth and development of the Buddhist monastic Order during the first three or four centuries of Buddhism.

Robert C. Lester, *Theravada Buddhism in Southeast Asia* (Ann Arbor: University of Michigan Press, 1973), is a readable and comprehensive treatment of the Theravada tradition. The multifaceted nature of Theravada monastic life is presented in an interpretation of one of northern Thailand's earliest and historically significant monastic centers by Donald K. Swearer, *Wat Haripunjaya: A Study of the Royal Temple of the Buddha's Relic, Lamphun, Thailand* (Missoula, Mont.: Scholars Press, 1976). Holmes Welch, *The Practice of Chinese Buddhism, 1900–1950* (Cambridge, Mass.: Harvard University Press, 1967), based on both documents and oral interviews, introduces Mahayana Buddhist monasticism. An important primary text, *Sayings and Doings of Pai-Chang*, trans. Thomas Cleary (Los Angeles: Center Publications, 1978), tells of Pai-Chang Huai-hai (720–814 C.E.), who established a new monastic code for a Ch'an (Zen) monastic center in Hung-chou, China.

Primary texts and first-hand reports reveal the texture and flavor of monastic life. An engaging and informative autobiographical account of traditional Tibetan (Tantrayana) monastic training is given by Alan Wallace, *The Life and Teachings of Geshe Rabten* (London: George Allen & Unwin, 1980). Jack Kornfield, *Living Buddhist Masters* (Santa Cruz, Calif.: Unity Press, 1977), collects teachings of contemporary Theravada meditation masters in Burma, Thailand, and Laos. Chang Chung-Yuan, *Original Teachings of Ch'an Buddhism* (New York: Vintage Books, 1971), is a set of selections from *The Transmission of the Lamp*, the most famous collection of teachings of Chinese Ch'an (Zen) Buddhist masters. D. T. Suzuki, *The Training of the Zen Buddhist Monk* (New York: University Books, 1965), presents an idealized interpretation of Zen Buddhist monastic life in terms of the categories of humility, labor, service, gratitude, and meditation.

The situation of Buddhist monasticism today is treated in a collection of articles on contemporary developments, Heinrich Dumoulin and John C. Maraldo, eds., *Buddhism in the Modern World* (New York: Collier Books, 1976). For women and Buddhism, see *Spring Wind-Buddhist Cultural Forum* 6/1-3 (1986).

The best introduction to Christian monasticism—its origins, history, types, contemporary forms—is David Knowles, *Christian Monasticism*, World University Library (New York and Toronto: McGraw-Hill Book Company, 1969). Jean Leclercq, *The Love of Learning and the Desire for God: A Study of Monastic Culture*, 3d ed. (New York: Fordham University Press, 1985), treats medieval monastic spirituality. For an engaging treatment of monastic spirituality for laypersons today, see Esther de Waal, *Seeking God: The Way of St. Benedict* (Collegeville, Minn.: The Liturgical Press, 1984).

Rules and teachings and saints' lives are the fundamental stuff of monastic tradition. Timothy Fry, O.S.B., ed., *RB 1980: The Rule of St. Benedict in Latin and English with Notes* (Collegeville, Minn.: The Liturgical Press, 1981), gives an authoritative text enhanced by historical and explanatory essays based on the most recent scholarship. The full volume is available in paperback, as is the Latin and English text without the essays, and the English text by itself. Athanasius, *The Life of Saint Antony*, trans. Robert T. Meyer, Ancient Christian Writers 10 (New York: Newman Press, 1978), became the model for virtually all subsequent Christian monastic biography. The wisdom of early Christian monks is highlighted by Roberta C. Bondi, *To Love as God Loves: Conversations with the Early Church* (Philadelphia: Fortress Press, 1987).

The recent revolution in women's Christian monasticism is vividly documented in Joan Chittister, O.S.B, Stephanie Campbell, O.S.B., Mary Collins, O.S.B., Ernestine Johann, O.S.B., and Johnette Putnam, O.S.B., *Climb along the Cutting Edge: An Analysis of Change in Religious Life* (New York: Paulist Press, 1977). Judith Sutera, O.S.B., *True Daughters: Monastic Identity and American Benedictine Women's History* (Atchison, Kan.: Mount St. Scholastica, 1987), recounts the efforts of American nuns to define their own life.

The process of renewal in monastic communities in the second half of the twentieth century, especially in response to the Second Vatican Council, has generated a wealth of studies, and the venture known as Cistercian Studies Series, with one hundred volumes already in print, has made some of this material (not limited to the Cistercian tradition) available to the public. Of special interest to readers of this book is Stephanie Campbell, O.S.B., ed., *As We Seek God: International Reflections on Contemporary Benedictine Monasticism*, Cistercian Studies Series 70 (Kalamazoo, Mich.: Cistercian Publications, 1983). William Skudlarek, O.S.B., ed., *The Continuing Quest for God: Monastic Spirituality in Tradition and Transition* (Collegeville, Minn.: The Liturgical Press, 1982), is another set of essays inspired, as is the Campbell volume, by the fifteenth centenary of the birth of St. Benedict and his sister St. Scholastica.

Periodically in this book we have circled back to the character of Father Zossima in Fyodor Dostoevsky, *The Brothers Karamazov* (New York: Vintage Books, 1955). The only better way than this novel into the mystery and power of Christian monasticism is to join a monastery.

Finally, we suggest works of the two exemplary monastic figures who are the subject of chapter 1, "The Monastic Vision: Contemplation and Action." Thich Nhat Hanh, *The Miracle of Mindfulness: A Manual on Meditation*, rev. ed. (Boston: Beacon Press, 1988), is an engaging interpretation of Zen mindfulness by a contemporary Vietnamese monk and internationally known exponent of "engaged Buddhism." From the immense Thomas Merton bibliography we single out Brother Patrick Hart, ed., *The Monastic Journey* (Garden City, N.Y.: Image Books, 1978), a selection of Merton's writings on themes of monastic life; Thomas P. McDonnell, ed., *A Thomas Merton Reader*, rev. ed. (Garden City, N.Y.: Image Books, 1974), including examples of autobiography, essays, and poetry; and *Zen and the Birds of Appetite* (New York: New Directions, 1968), a sympathetic interpretation of Zen Buddhism and its monastic traditions by the world's best known Christian monk.

Index

The terms monk, nun, monastery, and monasticism appear so often in the book that their inclusion in the index would be pointless. The terms Buddhist/Buddhism and Christian/Christianity are excluded too, since the organization of the book, indicated in the Table of Contents, makes the distribution of these categories clear enough. Most of the terms in the index are adequately defined in one of their early locations in the text.